KILO 17

KILO 17

Harry Ferguson

First published in Great Britain 2003

Copyright © 2003 by Harry Ferguson

The moral right of the author has been asserted

Bloomsbury Publishing Plc, 38 Soho Square, London W1D 3HB

A CIP catalogue record for this book
is available from the British Library

ISBN 0 7475 6319 5

10 9 8 7 6 5 4 3 2 1

Typeset by Hewer Text Ltd, Edinburgh
Printed in Great Britain by Clays Ltd, St Ives plc

Dedicated to the memories of

Peter Bennett
(Kilo 2)

and my brother-in-law,
John Roberts
(1963–2002)

AUTHOR'S NOTE

Although this is a true story, some names and other details have been changed in order to protect the operational security of HM Customs and Excise.

The Investigation Division (ID) became the National Investigation Service (NIS) in 1996.

ACKNOWLEDGEMENTS

There are many people who have put a great deal of work and thought into this book over the past two years and I would like to thank them all. I am especially grateful to my family for their love, appalling coffee and occasional proofreading.

Most of all I would like to thank the original members of the 'Kilos'. They watched over me for two years with a friendship and good humour which I can never repay. Even as you read this, most of them are still out on the streets hunting drug smugglers. In a team of fifteen officers who are constantly being replaced or reassigned it wasn't possible to mention them all, but the characters of the Widow, Carnaby and the rest are typical of the men and women who make up all the teams of the ID/NIS. They work long hours, often in atrocious conditions and sometimes in danger of their lives. They are the agency most feared by the drug smugglers and yet the agency least known to the general public. They are seldom acknowledged or rewarded. Hopefully this book will bring them some of the recognition that they so richly deserve.

H.F.

February 2003

CONTENTS

1

How to Leave a Secret Society

It wasn't supposed to be like this.

Faced with yet another red traffic light, the Widow wrenched the steering wheel hard to her left and threw our battered old Citroën on to the pavement of Lower Thames Street. She repeatedly punched the horn, blaring a warning to the startled drivers in the queue of traffic as we raced past. They were just blurs and frightened faces to me and I was grateful that there were hardly any pedestrians around at this time of night.

I had a tight grip on the radio handset, ready to give a running commentary to the other cars on our team, and I glanced back through the rear window to see that at least two of them were following close behind.

'Cocksucker!'

I was still looking over my shoulder when the Widow trod on the brakes so hard that I was thrown forward and struck my head against the dashboard. All my carefully arranged maps, pens and the radio handset fell into a disordered heap on the floor. As the cloud of burnt rubber cleared from around our car, I looked up and saw that our front bumper was inches from the legs of some drunken stockbroker who had deliberately stepped in front of us. He had his jacket in one hand and a briefcase in the other. His loosened tie was halfway down his chest. His eyes were wide with alcohol.

'What the fuck do you think you're DOING?' he screamed at us.

He slammed his briefcase on to the bonnet to emphasise the point. 'I'll have the fucking POLICE on you!'

He was a big bastard and I didn't fancy getting out of the car to argue with him. The Widow just stared at him. She slammed the Citroën into reverse to give herself some room and then swung round him. He tried to step forward to block us, but it takes a lot of balls to put yourself in front of half a ton of car apparently driven by a raving madwoman, and he wasn't quite quick enough. The Widow accelerated hard and with a squeal of tyres we swung off the pavement in front of the traffic lights, the car bouncing so hard that the floorpan hit the road with an enormous thump.

I looked back and saw the stockbroker actually drop his briefcase and jacket and start chasing us as we sped away. He was screaming abuse and threw something which bounced off the boot of the car. Then two more of our cars came racing up behind him with their headlights on full beam and their horns blaring, telling him to get the fuck out of the way. They shot past on either side of him, so close they almost took his elbows off. He was left standing there in the middle of the street with his mouth open as we disappeared into the distance.

I pressed a hand against the bruise on my forehead and tried to make out the dial of my watch in the rapidly pulsing glow of the streetlights. We had thirty minutes to make the bottom of the M1 or Van Hohn would have slipped through the net. Dover Unit were with him for now, but they were only just managing to hang on and they were running out of fuel fast. If we didn't get to the handover point in time, the probability was that Van Hohn would escape and all their efforts and those of the Dutch police would have been wasted.

I glanced at my watch to see how much time we had left. It was a Friday night and the roads were really busy. There didn't seem to be any way we could make it.

I looked up and could see that we were heading for the tail-end of another queue of late-night London traffic. Pedestrian barriers lined the road on either side. There would be no mounting the pavement this time.

'GET THE MAPS OFF THE FLOOR, GET YOUR FUCK-ING ACT TOGETHER AND FIND ME A WAY AROUND THIS SHIT!'

The Widow was leaning over me and shouting. Her mouth must have been about one inch from my ear.

And it was then that I was really scared.

Not because the Widow was angry. She was known throughout the Division for her vicious temper. And it wasn't because of her driving. I knew she was one of the best on the team and if it could be done by any power on earth she would get us to the rendezvous in time.

I was scared because as I fumbled around in the dark trying to find the radio and the maps, with the Widow screaming at me and another driver's angry voice in my earpiece demanding that I tell him right now which route to take, I suddenly realised that I couldn't do this job. I was just an analyst, used to spending my days sifting through piles of intelligence reports. I was the officer who had won a promotion for his comprehensive analysis of the complexities of tribal politics in Central Africa. I was supposed to be in a nice quiet office job somewhere in Whitehall, not out here on the streets.

How the hell had I had ended up in this nightmare?

In the first place, I don't think my mistake was in becoming a spy. But once I did become a spy, I should never have come home early from that trip to the Middle East.

It isn't as difficult as you might think to join the British intelligence services, or at least it wasn't in the 1980s. You simply had to attend the right Oxbridge college and sooner or later one tutor or another would ask if you were interested in 'serving your country'. There was no great secret about this, and some students would joke about when the mysterious brown envelope marked

3

HMSO might appear in their pigeonhole. Many of them even claimed to know which of the dons were the secretive 'talent spotters'.

One summer afternoon, a tutor asked if I had ever thought of working for the government 'in a position which might involve sensitive work overseas'. I was so wrapped up in the complexities of Italian fascism or whatever it was we had been discussing that it took a moment to realise what he was talking about. But as realisation slowly dawned, it occurred to me that this might very well be the job I had been looking for.

It would certainly solve two problems. The first was that like most of my friends who were leaving university, I didn't have a clue what I really wanted to do. I had a vague idea that I wanted a job which meant protecting other people and 'doing some good' in the world, but I had no idea what sort of job that would be. I was drifting towards the usual answer of the Army or the Police, but it had never occurred to me that the intelligence services were an option. I just don't come from that sort of background. Now that it was put before me it seemed as if it might be exactly right. I only had the foggiest notion of what the intelligence services actually did, but I thought that if I didn't like it I could always leave.

It would also get me out of my other problem. A few months before, I had met this girl from another college. Her name was Nicky, she was pretty, a talented mathematician, and after knowing her only a few weeks, in a moment of alcohol-induced madness, I had asked her to marry me. She had said yes. Now, while I was still trying to get over the shock, we were preparing for a wedding in the autumn and she was already talking about setting up home and starting a family. So my need for a good job and a regular pay packet was pretty urgent.

Straight away I said I was very interested, but the tutor refused to tell me anything more, only saying mysteriously that I would be contacted soon by the 'proper authorities'.

About a month later I arrived late as usual for a tutorial. 'Scotty' was one of those storybook Oxford dons that you often read about but seldom meet. He shambled about his study in an old tweed jacket with unkempt hair and cake crumbs down his shirt. Rather than teach, he preferred to lie back in his armchair and reminisce about the good old days. This was made worse by the fact that I was supposed to be specialising in twentieth-century history, but he resolutely refused to discuss anything beyond the year 1930 on the grounds that, since he had lived through all of it, this was not history, merely current affairs.

But tutorials were always nice and late in the afternoon, he laid on an excellent tea and really did have some pretty good anecdotes. What I didn't know about him then was that he was a leading talent spotter for MI5. Some years later I tracked down his name in an 'unofficial' history of the Security Service and found that he had been an officer in the Special Operations Executive during the war and was with MI5 for several years afterwards.

That afternoon he was pacing around the room clutching a sheet of paper. He started shaking it at me almost as soon as I got through the door:

'Do you bloody well know what this is, Harry?' he demanded coldly.

Since he was holding the paper upside down, it was hard to tell. I leaned my head to one side trying to read it.

'It looks like a letter.'

'I know it's a bloody letter, boy. Don't you realise who it's from?'

I couldn't work out why he was so angry. I just shrugged.

'It's from the bloody Secret Intelligence Service asking me to recommend you for bloody recruitment!' he shouted. The door was still open and his voice loud enough to carry out into the college quadrangle.

Like a lot of people who don't take a particular interest in these things, I had no idea about the names and differences between the various intelligence services. As Scotty harangued me at some

5

length, it became clear that this was a letter from MI6, the organisation which gathers intelligence overseas.

'That sounds good, sir,' I said hopefully.

'Good? Don't you realise that this college has been sending perfectly good young men to the Security Service for the past fifty years? What the bloody hell do you think you're doing by going behind my back and applying to the bloody opposition?'

Being young and naïve, I was shocked to hear one branch of the intelligence services described as 'the opposition' by another. I hastily told him I'd be happy to work for whichever organisation he recommended, but he thought it was too late: in his opinion the Secret Intelligence Service had 'got its hooks into' me, and after calming down and pouring a cup of tea, he eventually said that he would grudgingly write a letter of approval.

So began a long period of interviews and selection. My performance in these was so bad that I thought I had failed. But despite his grumbles, Scotty must have said some complimentary things about me because at the end of the whole process, MI6 decided that I was best suited to work as a desk officer, and I became a sort of backroom boffin undertaking the research in preparation for overseas operations. Several years passed, during which Nicky and I got married, bought a house and had two wonderful children. I thought that I was set for life.

Far from being a world of gun battles, glamorous blondes and the last-minute defusing of nuclear devices, the vast bulk of espionage is essentially about paperwork: encouraging people to steal it or talk about it, then writing it up again to send around Whitehall where a small proportion of it is read avidly by politicians and civil servants, but most of it is dutifully filed away and quickly forgotten.

I spent long hours sifting through mountains of intelligence reports from stations overseas and from allies such as the CIA, trying to find the handful of them which might be worth issuing. This might sound like a disappointing job, but I loved it. I've always had a good memory for trivia, so I was in my element sorting through the piles of paper, placing pins in maps and drawing up complicated charts trying to pinpoint weaknesses in various terrorist organisations. It felt good to be the expert on a particular region and to be involved in the planning for some often very sensitive operations.

At home I thought things were going well too. Nicky had been raised in a large Roman Catholic family and was adamant that she wanted to stay at home, raise a family and be a traditional mother. Of course that suited me just fine. She began to make curtains and tried to learn how to cook. Sometimes we could even eat the result. Together we started paying off a large mortgage on a small terraced house. Everything seemed to be going perfectly – until the day I came back early from a research trip to the Middle East.

There hadn't been a chance to ring ahead and warn Nicky that I was coming home. I had thought it would be a pleasant surprise. However, as soon as I stepped through the front door I could tell that something was wrong. The house was in a worse mess than our two toddlers could usually produce and although it was well past midday, the children were still in their pyjamas shouting at each other in front of the television. Nicky came out of the kitchen and started to scream at them. She was still in her dressing-gown and the huge fluffy slippers I had bought her for Christmas. She looked pale and worn out. Then she saw me standing at the door and just burst into tears.

While I'd been busy building a career in espionage and patting myself on the back at how well it was all going, Nicky had been going quietly mad. The beautiful baby girl and boy we'd been lucky enough to have produced turned into the usual squealing toddlers. There was no one in the family who was able to give her any help and her days soon became a mind-numbing routine of child-care and housework while she waited for me to get home (often very late) in the evenings. To add to the dreariness of this endless routine, she knew that she had a well-educated brain that she wasn't using

7

for anything more than working out shopping lists. Every day she was just sinking a little deeper into depression.

At that time we were due to be sent on our first overseas posting. It looked like being Eastern Europe and this was in the days just before the fall of the Iron Curtain so it was a strictly 'bring your own loo rolls' type of posting. It would also mark the end of any chance Nicky had of breaking free of the children. She couldn't face it, but she just didn't know how to tell me. My two-week trip to the Middle East had been the final straw. If I had come home on time she would probably have tried to cover everything up and pretended that she had been fine. It was a good thing I hadn't.

All of this came out in a sobbing conversation that afternoon. I took the children to stay with a friend and we sat and talked. Nicky had felt that it was the 'right thing' if she looked after her family as her mother had done. The main question now was: what were we going to do about it?

Nicky had supported me for three years. I felt that now it was my turn. She wanted to train for a job which involved programming computers. She had done a lot of work at university on computer theory and what she needed was some practical skills to add to that. She calculated that it would take two years to get the basic skills so that she would be able to work anywhere in the world.

There only remained one other tricky problem: the children. We talked over all the various child-care options: nannies, au pairs, all-day nurseries. I could see that the one thing holding Nicky back was the guilt of handing the children over to someone we didn't really know. Then, gradually, we began to consider a different idea. Suppose I took a sabbatical and looked after them? Like lots of dads I hated missing out on my children's early years and now there was an opportunity to do something about that. But it was a big step. Even as recently as fifteen years ago, for a man to ask for a break from work for a few years to look after his kids was about as shocking as admitting that he was gay. Most organisations were just not set up to cope with it, and a conservative organisation like MI6 certainly wasn't. But the more Nicky and I talked about the idea, the more it seemed like the right thing to do. It would be good for Nicky, good for the children, and I thought it would be good for me too. After all, what were two years in a career that would probably last another forty?

So I went to see my personnel officer at MI6 and told him what I was planning. To my surprise, he thought it could work, and a date was set. Nicky found a job with a bank in the City of London. We all thought we had achieved the perfect compromise.

But then, with one week to go and Nicky already started at her new job, I was called to see the head of personnel at MI6, known as HPD.

HPD is a powerful man. After a lifetime of climbing the especially slippery career pole in the world of secret intelligence, he has the power of life and death over the career of every officer in the Service. HPD has access to every officer's personnel file listing all their faults and weaknesses. (Even 'C', the head of MI6, isn't allowed to see his own file.) There is an old tradition in MI6, dating from the days of Mansfield Cummings, that only 'C', the Chief of the Service, is permitted to write in green ink. As I headed for the hastily arranged meeting an old friend joked: 'Remember, Harry, "C" may be the only officer allowed to write in green ink, but HPD writes in blood.'

As a sign of his power, HPD had an office on the north side of the tower block which then housed MI6, with a view towards the River Thames. Young officers at the start of their careers or older officers whose careers had not been quite so successful had offices on the south side, overlooking the rundown tenement blocks of North Lambeth.

The man who represented all this power sat at his desk slowly turning the pages of my personnel file while I sat in a threadbare office chair into which I had sunk until my knees were almost level with my chin. He kept me waiting a long time and it seemed to me it was deliberate. I spent the time studying the walls of his office. His

9

whole career was laid out there in framed photographs: in Arab dress on the back of a camel; holding an award in front of Buckingham Palace; a younger version of him wearing combat fatigues.

He slapped the personnel file shut. Then he picked up my sabbatical request which was lying on the desk next to it.

'What the bloody hell is this?' he demanded.

'It looks familiar,' I admitted.

'You know bloody well it's your request to go off and play at babysitting. Who put this bloody stupid idea into your head?'

'Well, I had a personnel meeting two months ago. It was all agreed.'

'Agreed? Agreed by whom?'

'I saw PDO1D over a month ago, sir, if you'd just look at the date at the top of the . . .'

'I don't care what "PDO somebody-or-other" told you over a month ago, the point is I will not have highly trained officers swanning off on mothering duty every time they feel like it!'

'But . . .'

'Do you have any idea how much it costs to train someone like you – explosives, small-arms drills, parachuting, unarmed combat?'

'Well actually, sir, I've never . . .'

'Haven't you ever heard of nannies?'

I tried to explain about feeling a responsibility as a father and not wanting to be posted abroad at this time, about Nicky and her plans and how I was trying to fit all this in, but as Head of Personnel he had other concerns.

After an argument which included a lecture about duty and 'being a man', there was a long pause. Then he decided to try another tactic. He stood up, walked around his desk and sat on the front of it.

'Look . . . er . . .' he glanced down at the top of personnel file '. . . Harry, I don't want you to feel that the Service is being unreasonable. I think you realise that if this sort of thing was to

10

become common it would cause us all kinds of problems in terms of staffing. On the other hand, you don't want to be seen as a troublemaker so early in a promising career, do you? And for our part, we don't really want to cause you difficulties with your family.'

He pursed his lips as he thought about this. Finally, he seemed to reach a decision.

'All right then. How about this? You tender a "technical" resignation. Just a few lines. When you've done your babysitting, in a year or two, you simply resubmit an application to join. We take you back, your children grow up as responsible people, and we don't lose all that time and money invested in your training. Agreed?'

He smiled again.

I asked for time to think it over, but I knew that there was no other way forward: there is no such thing as an industrial employment tribunal for spies. I went home and spoke to Nicky. Like me she was suspicious that returning to the Service would not be as easy as HPD had promised, but she was already wrapped up in the excitement of her new job. We figured we'd sort it out nearer the time.

So, two days later, I wrote a three-line letter of resignation and stuck it in the internal mail. Deep down I suppose I knew I wasn't coming back, but I still hoped that they weren't going to abandon all the money they had invested in my training. What really should have told me that I was finished was Gordon's reaction.

When you're young and you start your very first job, one of the things you hope to find is some older person who will take you under their wing. Someone who will decide that you have potential and teach you the tricks of the trade – someone like Chris in *The Magnificent Seven* or Fast Eddie in *The Color of Money*. For me, that was Gordon. He had been my section head during my most successful year at MI6. He was about fifty, well over six feet tall and painfully thin. He had a terrible temper, a reputation for having no sense of gratitude, and he had worked me harder than a dog. But at the end of it all, he promoted me, far earlier than I had any right to expect.

I bumped into him in a corridor about a week after my meeting with HPD. He was only a few years or so from retirement and I knew he was shortly to go abroad on a prestigious last posting as a reward for all his hard work. He was a deeply thoughtful person who had been in the Service for all his life and cared about it a great deal. I had tremendous respect for him. I started to congratulate him on his posting, but he cut right through it all, hardly deigning even to look at me:

'What's this about you throwing your career away?'

'Oh, come off it, Gordon. It's only a couple of years, I'll be back in time for your retirement party.'

'They won't let you back, you bloody idiot,' he spat and there was real contempt in his eyes as he turned on his heel and strode firmly away down the corridor.

I never saw him again.

Two weeks later HPD was happy and I was stuck at home with the washing-up. For better or worse I had become (and I really hate this term) . . . a house-husband.

Actually, for a while, being a house-husband wasn't too bad. I quickly (and foolishly) decided that being a full-time father was just another job which could be mastered with a little bit of organisation. In a move which would have shocked my mother, I managed to keep the house fairly tidy after discovering that housework is almost bearable if you keep the music turned up really loud. (Remember to pick a fairly light model of vacuum if you want to use it as an air guitar.) I taught the children to read and to count. I even became the only father attending coffee mornings at the local mothers' association and they boldly changed the name of their group from 'Mothers and Toddlers' to 'Parents and Toddlers'. It was a sign of the brave new era.

In the kitchen I had never been able to do much more than make beans on toast, but now I started experimenting with all manner of exotic new recipes and I hoped that Nicky would be suitably impressed. But she tended to come home late and wolf down whatever I had cooked before disappearing to do more paperwork. She was working so hard it was almost as though she was trying to make up for lost time and soon she was promoted to be in charge of a larger team at the bank.

For the first year I would occasionally head in to London for a few drinks with the people I used to work with. I would catch up on all the news and the latest office gossip. It was fun – as though I had merely gone on an extended holiday.

But then, almost imperceptibly, the rot began to set in. Old friends were promoted or moved on to other posts. Whenever I did see those who remained they mentioned officers I had never heard of or laughed at office jokes I no longer understood. Slowly the periods between meetings grew longer and longer.

By the middle of the second year, I was definitely beginning to feel that I couldn't keep this arrangement going for much longer. The educational games for the children had become much less frequent and it was far easier just to leave them in front of the telly. Gradually I began to join them there. I have sat through more episodes of *Teletubbies* than any man who wants to retain his sanity should ever watch.

The ultimate humiliation came from our local vicar. We used to pass each other in the aisles of Sainsbury's and exchange a few words. One day he asked if I fancied a game of squash. Seeing as he was almost fifty, I thought it would be fun to have a gentle game and beat him hollow just to break the monotony. After he had thrashed me in eight straight games he revealed that he had been a half-blue at Cambridge. My self-esteem sank to its lowest point yet.

Meanwhile Nicky was spending a lot of time jetting off to exotic places like New York and Hong Kong. Each night she would return home with news of another triumph, such as a promotion or a presentation which had gone down really well, until the urge to deck her with a frying pan became almost overwhelming.

The only thing that kept me going was the knowledge that I would be re-applying for my old job when the two years were up. I conveniently ignored the fact that I might not be allowed back in.

So two years later, and far more haggard than when they'd last seen me, I was ready to re-apply. It had been a close-run thing. I was desperate to get back to 'real' work before I started talking to the walls. True to her word, Nicky said that she was prepared to settle down to a further stint as a 'real' mother. Secretly I didn't think that giving up her career again would be all that easy for her.

I was called for an interview at an anonymous building in Whitehall. I had hoped that the recruitment officer I saw would be someone I recognised. He wasn't, and the reception I got was polite but rather bemused. We spent five minutes in his office sipping tepid coffee while he said as little as possible. Then at the sound of a buzzer he ushered me into the adjoining interview room.

It was one of the usual Victorian rooms in Whitehall: high ceilings decorated with elaborate plaster mouldings, oil paintings of long-forgotten civil servants spaced evenly around the wooden panelling. A large case clock ticked loudly against one wall. It was a hot July afternoon, but all the windows were closed to dull the noise of the traffic in the Mall outside. Three men sat on one side of a long polished table. I sat in a chair on the other side of the room, so far away that I almost needed a megaphone to speak to them.

It doesn't take long before you know that a job interview is going to go badly. The three of them smiled and nodded, but then the chairman opened the file in front of him and got straight to the point. I still remember his exact words:

'Now, about your commitment problem . . .'

Half an hour later I was out of the room and out of a job. In his office the recruitment officer proffered tea and biscuits and told me not to take it to heart.

I think I was in a state of shock. When I'd spoken to Gordon two years before, I hadn't really thought they'd go through with it. Perhaps I shouldn't have been surprised, but I sat there getting angrier and angrier, not hearing a word the recruiting officer said. Eventually I realised that he was offering me a list of alternative employment.

He placed the list of government departments on the coffee table between us. 'Of course we can't promise anything,' he smiled (and almost winked), 'but we can offer to send you forward with a good recommendation and a high prospect of success.'

When I looked up, I think he could tell by my face that I was thinking of thumping someone – probably him.

'I'll leave you to think about it for a while,' he said, slipping out through the door.

I was still angry and confused as I looked down at the list. But my initial reaction was rapidly being replaced by depression. I hadn't given any thought to what I would do instead of going back to MI6. I hadn't known anything else I'd ever wanted to do.

I ran my eye down the list: Ministry of Agriculture. The Welsh Office. Who the hell ever wanted to work at the Welsh Office?

Then towards the bottom some initials caught my eye: C&EID. Customs and Excise Investigation Division. Suddenly there seemed to be a small ray of hope.

The first time I had heard about the Investigation Division, or the ID as it was more commonly known, was when I had to decide if it should be included in a briefing by MI6. I saw the initials on the list of potential invitees, but had no idea who they were. So I did some digging.

Their job was to investigate large-scale smuggling. For many years this had mainly concerned boring things like watches or nylons. But in the early 1970s the drugs war began in earnest and the ID really took off because the police were overwhelmed. It soon became obvious that the best place actually to stop the drugs was at the point where they were imported into the country. But there was another reason why the ID was a useful weapon in the drugs war. Customs and Excise have extensive powers of search and seizure dating as far back as the reign of Queen Elizabeth I. As a result, the ID played the game against crime without a lot of the modern restraints which hinder the police. Its officers' powers were greater, they could search premises and arrest without a warrant, they had right of audience in the lower courts, they decided whether or not to prosecute without any reference to the Crown Prosecution Service.

All of this power has traditionally been subject to very little official oversight. Even their supposed managers, the ten Commissioners of Customs and Excise, stayed well clear – the Commissioners were career civil servants, most of whom had never come into contact with the ID, and few of them attempted to fathom its particular codes of practice or honour. Since ID officers were unarmed, underfunded and lowly paid, up against an enemy which was well armed, well funded and highly paid, they had a reputation for being unconventional. They worked long hours, often in appalling conditions. But despite all this, they got results and every year seized more illegal drugs and more drugs money than all the UK's police forces put together.

They had good relations with their colleagues in the police forces because what you saw was what you got. They had very few ranks – just a handful of senior managers in the office, whilst the vast majority of officers were out on operational duties. This meant that they didn't have the problems with jealousies and rivalries that dogged other large government organisations.

But above all, they had a reputation for honesty. They had never had an officer charged with corruption. The ID was the nearest thing British law enforcement has ever had to America's 'Untouchables' of the Prohibition era.

The second time I came across them was a more hard-edged form of education into the ways of the ID. In order for their counter-surveillance training to be assessed, MI6 officers are sent on training courses where their skills are tested against Special Branch, A4 (the

16

specialist surveillance section of the MI5) or other agencies. I went on one of these courses when the ID was the 'opposition'.

The exercise was simple: I was supposed to be part of a group organising a drugs importation. I had to go to a meeting at an address in London and then travel by car and train to several points across Kent and Sussex before going to Gatwick airport, where I was to catch a plane to Paris. At some point during the day I would be followed by an ID team. My job was to try to spot them. If at any stage the team felt they had enough evidence, they would arrest me and terminate the exercise. On the other hand, the team wouldn't be told where I was going and if I lost them during the day I would have 'won'.

So I spent the day racing around the South of England trying every ruse I could think of to catch my pursuers out. Even though I hadn't had much official training, I've seen as many spy films as the next guy, so I looked at reflections in shop windows. I got on to trains and then got off again at the last moment to see if anyone was following. When I was on the train I walked the whole length of it, carefully noting as many faces as possible. When I was in a car I tried driving very slowly or very fast as the opportunity arose.

By the time I arrived at Gatwick that evening I was exhausted from the strain of looking out for the surveillance team and waiting for that hand on my shoulder and a voice telling me that I was under arrest. But I also had a pretty long list of ID cars and officers which I had picked out during the day. In fact I was worried that it was rather too long.

I stood looking up at the departures board with a tight knot in my stomach and I found it hard to concentrate on the flight numbers as I glanced around. A fat middle-aged man and his wife were standing next to me trying to find the number of their flight on the board.

'Excuse me, sir.'

Two heavily built thugs dressed in leather jackets, jeans and trainers had appeared on either side of me. One of them waved a suitably impressive warrant card in front of my face. The mouth of the woman next to me dropped open. Oblivious to what was happening, her husband continued staring at the departures board.

I was grabbed firmly by both arms.

'I'm arresting you on suspicion of being involved in the importation of controlled drugs. You do not have to say anything unless you wish to do so.'

One of them took my bag, the other led me away. It was over in a moment and we quickly disappeared into the crowds. I remember looking back and seeing the woman still staring after us, frantically nudging her husband.

The two ID officers dragged me to a suite of rooms behind an unmarked door. It took them less than twenty minutes to rip my carefully rehearsed cover story to shreds, but I did have my revenge. At one point during the day I'd ducked into a shop on a crowded street in order to catch the surveillance team out. The idea was that I should be able to stand in the shop and watch members of the team come past desperately looking for me. But as I stood there no one at all suspicious came by. Meanwhile the Asian shopkeeper wanted to know whether I actually wanted to buy something. With one eye still on the window, I pointed at a large boxed cheese.

The ID officers were looking for a small metal canister which was supposed to contain some drug samples. It was actually hidden in the binding of a book I'd been carrying, but they'd missed it when they had sorted through the rest of my luggage and so they concluded that it must be hidden in the cheese.

With a fine sense of the dramatic, the senior officer placed the cheese on the small table between us in the interview room and said, 'All right, sunshine. What's in this then?'

'It's just a cheese.'

'Oh yeah, I'll bet,' he sneered and he opened the box.

The stench was indescribable. God knows what type of cheese it was, but in the hot and cramped conditions of the tiny interview room it was overpowering. With his eyes watering from the fumes the officer gamely dug his fingers in to search for the cylinder. The

18

more he broke up the cheese, the worse the smell became. Soon everyone's eyes were streaming, partly because we were all desperately trying to hold our breath against the stink and partly because we were all doubled up with laughter.

'You bastard!' gasped his mate through a handkerchief. 'What the fuck is this stuff?'

The interview was terminated abruptly, we dashed out of the room and that was the end of the exercise.

As I sat in the train on the way back home, I thought about the kind of work I had seen during the day. It turned out I had spotted only one car (but had not been able to read the registration), and one female officer (although I had to admit that if she had changed her appearance at all I wouldn't have spotted her again). But I had been expecting them to be there and in fact a team had been with me for most of the day and I hadn't known it. After the debriefing there had been a few drinks so that we could meet our pursuers, and what impressed me most was the camaraderie they all had. In the intelligence world, officers necessarily spend much of their time working alone. In contrast, here was a group of people who worked in small teams and relied on one another completely. There was an understanding and confidence between them that I can only compare to a long-established and successful rugby or football team.

So when the recruitment officer returned, I pointed to the Investigation Division on the list and told him that was where I wanted my name forwarded. He looked surprised, but said that he would see what he could do.

A few weeks later I got a call from the same recruitment officer. They had arranged for me to have an interview. There was a problem because my Civil Service grade was higher than was usual in a new entrant, but the ID had agreed to waive this if I could pass the entrance interview. There was also a condition: in return for MI6 supporting this move, I must never mention that I had worked

19

for them. Only one senior manager at the ID would know my real background. As far as everyone else in the ID was concerned I was just some guy who had transferred from the Foreign Office.

The interview board consisted of two investigation officers and a senior civil servant from somewhere in Customs policy division. I recognised one of the investigators from a BBC documentary series called *The Duty Men*. (I had borrowed some tapes to try to find out more about what I was letting myself in for.) I had heard about the other officer while waiting in the anteroom. Legend had it that during a 'knock' at a remote airfield, a light aircraft laden with drugs had landed and then the pilot, seeing all the car headlights racing towards him across the field and realising that he was about to be arrested, had tried to take off again. This officer had leapt out of his car and thrown himself on to the wing to stop the plane taking off despite the danger of being dropped from several thousand feet. He had clung on until the overloaded plane had been rammed and stopped by other ID vehicles.

As I expected, all the interviewing officers seemed concerned that the Foreign Office hadn't been ideal preparation for life as a Customs investigator. The fat one whom I recognised from the TV series asked which newspaper I read. I gave him the name of some broadsheet, hoping to impress him. He shook his head.

'Jesus Christ. Most of our guys read the *Sun* or the *Sport*,' he said.

'I could work at it,' I replied meekly.

It wasn't that funny, but they all laughed in a friendly way and from that moment I knew they were prepared to give me a chance.

A week later, Jack, the Deputy Chief of the Division overseeing my application, called me: I was in. Jack was supposed to be the only officer in the ID who would ever know about my MI6 background. He congratulated me, but he also wanted to give me a warning.

'Look, you seem determined to go through with this, Harry, and we're desperately short of officers, so if you really want to do it, we won't try and stop you. But you really need to consider one thing very carefully: until now, everyone who has joined the Investigation Division has worked their time as a uniformed officer. Most of them have joined Customs straight from school. They have crawled through ships, searched suitcases, clambered through lorries, visited endless small businesses on dull as dishwater VAT jobs – every boring, dirty job which the management can throw at them. When people who have done that go to the Division, it's a tough move, but at least they get support from the guys around them.

'You're the wrong type of bloke – Oxbridge, Foreign Office and all that. And worse still, you're being allowed to join as a senior officer. You're going to be a marked man and some of these bastards will do everything in their power to make your life miserable.

'If you still want to join, you can start at the beginning of next week. But if you want my opinion, you're mad to try it. I'll give you twenty-four hours to think about it.'

It was a good warning. I probably was mad to take it on. The pay was lousy, the hours were lousy, and the probability was that I wouldn't have any friends from the moment I set foot in the building. As I stared through the window at my kids playing in the garden, I thought about backing away from it all. At least other jobs would be safer. And with less likelihood of failure.

That night I talked it over with Nicky. With our original plan gone, she intended to keep her high-flying job in the City. She had got used to having me at home to look after the children and given the choice she would have preferred to keep things that way. She didn't like the idea of the very long hours which the ID worked and how this might affect the family.

She was also afraid that I was trying to prove something to people at MI6 even though it wouldn't change anything. In a way she was right. I did have something to prove, but not to MI6. I was angry that somebody there thought that a man who wanted to look after his kids couldn't be trusted to do a 'real' job. I would be angry for a long time, but deep down I had accepted that they had their reasons. The person I really needed to prove something to was myself. After two years changing dirty nappies, spooning baby mulch into gaping mouths and sitting bored out of my mind at afternoon playgroups, I still loved my kids but I'd lost any sense of who I was. The Investigation Division was a tough job and I wanted to find out if someone like me could do it.

And there was someone else to prove something to: my father. He had been a copper all his life and he'd never really understood why his only son would want to stay at home and raise the kids. To a man of his generation that was woman's work. I wanted to show him that I could do a job that was every bit as hard as the one he had done.

The following day I made the phone call. I told Jack that I would see him first thing on Monday morning.

2

The Kilos

That first morning as I set off on the train for the ID, I felt sick. It wasn't just the prospect of a potentially dangerous new job. I felt guilty about leaving the children with their new nanny. There was a shortage of trained nannies and despite desperately trying every-where, we had only been able to get a nineteen-year-old girl fresh from the local college where she had completed a course in child-minding. Coupled with that, there seemed to have been a spate of stories in the news recently about nannies beating or molesting small kids in their charge. The girl seemed nice enough, but it's hard to trust your children to someone who is almost a complete stranger, and I started to imagine all sorts of nightmare scenarios. I also began to realise how much I would miss all the little routines I had built up with the children – long breakfasts, trips to the local park, reading favourite picture books. I began to wonder if over the past two years I had become too soft to do this job and as the dreaded day drew nearer I thought more and more about simply calling the whole thing off.

This had caused more than a few harsh words with Nicky that morning. She had no problem about leaving the children with a girl who she thought was perfectly competent and finally she had said this. So we had a row while we waited for the nanny to arrive.

As I stood on the train grinding slowly into London Bridge station, I was thinking about the kids and the row with Nicky as

23

well as feeling sick. What a great start to a first day. I was still trying to drive all these negative feelings out of my mind as I walked up Lower Thames Street.

The ID headquarters is at Customs House on the north bank of the Thames near the Tower of London. It is an impressive four-storey, grey-stone building dating from the reign of Queen Anne, like a little piece of Whitehall dropped amidst the steel and glass offices of London's financial district. From the street it appears very plain, but this is because the building was designed to be seen from the river where a magnificent façade with ornate columns once greeted the merchant vessels that were supposed to dock and declare their cargo.

Due to a last-minute foul-up, I had spent the previous month (which Nicky had taken as parental leave) kicking my heels in Customs Policy Division waiting for my final clearances for the ID to come through. As soon as staff there heard where I was going they had been only too keen to tell me that I wouldn't last five minutes. One secretary told me how a team had broken into her security cabinet and filled it with a consignment of sex toys which they had seized in a raid on a porn warehouse. Another officer told me that a manager had been held out of a second-storey window by his ankles following an argument over a staff report. At first I thought that this was just an attempt to wind me up, but after a while I realised that many of the staff actually believed these stories.

As I approached Customs House I peered to see if there were cars roaring out of the gates and bodies smashing through windows. But the squat, solid building with its walls blackened by the pollution from heavy traffic seemed quiet behind the usual ugly anti-bomb netting which all government offices have. I took a deep breath and strode in through the large double doors and up to the main desk. I mentioned Jack's name. An aged security guard looked impressed and picked up a phone. There was a mumbled conversation and he told me to wait.

I dropped my kitbag on the floor and sat on one of the hard

wooden benches in the entrance foyer. The time passed slowly. It didn't seem as though Jack was in a hurry to come and pick me up. After about fifteen minutes the security guard took pity on me. He wandered over and asked if I fancied a cup of tea. His name turned out to be Bob and we sat and drank the tea while he related what seemed like the entire history of the building – that it was three hundred years old, that half of it had been destroyed by a bomb during the war, even the fact that there had once been a Roman customs house on the site. It was a gentle and friendly introduction to the place and for the rest of my career I always dropped in to see Bob if I was working in London. He seemed to be on first-name terms with everyone in the building and he was one of the real characters in the Division.

Half an hour later, Jack finally appeared and took me into the building. We walked up wide staircases and along seemingly endless corridors. Internally as well as externally, Customs House is an impressive building. The ceilings in the rooms and broad corridors are about fifteen feet high and many of the doors are made of highly polished mahogany. Apparently the senior management of Customs and Excise had long wanted to throw the ID out of this historic building so that they could move in from the concrete tower block they inhabited on the other side of the river.

Eventually Jack ushered me into his sizeable office.

'In a moment I'll take you down to your new Branch. I've decided to put you on a pretty busy Branch 1 team – you'll be working referred cannabis south-east.'

'I hope that doesn't mean I'm going to be chasing a lot of students back from a weekend in Amsterdam with a bit of hash hidden in their rucksacks.'

Jack shook his head.

'The nature of the commodity is just a way of dividing the casework. No gang brings over just one type of drug. They bring whatever will make a profit. The gang bringing in cannabis today could be doing cocaine or heroin next week. And we aren't talking about some spotty herbert bringing back some wacky baccy for his mates – we only target major consignments, hundreds of kilos at a time.

'The Division is divided into five groups: Group A – Drugs, Group B – VAT, Group C – Intelligence, Group D – Customs, Group E – Administration. Group A, where you will be working is further subdivided into four branches: Branch 1 – Cannabis, Branch 2 – Heroin, Branch 3 – Cocaine, and finally Branch 16, a new department which investigates all financial matters related to drug smuggling. Each of the branches is divided into a number of teams – target teams and referred teams. Target teams are dedicated units which spend all their time working against a specific smuggling organisation until they smash it. In contrast, referred teams are like the fire brigade – whenever a port or airport makes a discovery of smuggled drugs, or whenever there is a tip-off, the referred team's job is to get straight down there and trace those behind the importation. It could be a one-off smuggler, it could be a major organisation, they never know until they get there and start work. Every team on the Division is allocated a letter of the alphabet to identify it – yours will be Drugs Team K, the Kilos.

'Each team consists of fifteen officers and is led by an SIO – the Senior Investigation Officer. They are the men who have ultimate power in this organisation. Although there are one or two layers of management above them, these guys make all the operational decisions. I call them the "robber barons" because they do what they like and make the rules up as they go along.

'Within each team there are four or five HEOs – Higher Executive Officers who are like sergeants or corporals – and the rest are EOs – Executive Officers. They are the infantry. Although your grade is HEO you'll be treated like an EO until you've completed your probation. We've never had anyone join the Division as an HEO before, normally someone would have to do about five years here before they earned that grade, so if I were you I would keep it pretty quiet.

'I've chosen the Kilos because they're a really good team, Don is an excellent SIO. He started on the docks at Liverpool and is as easy-going as you could wish. But don't underestimate him, he's been doing this job since literally before you were born. He will be in late this morning, so I am handing you over to the SIO of one of the other referred teams – there are three on the Branch in all. The Branch has some of our best officers, so keep your eyes open and you'll learn a lot. With the supply of drugs the way it is at the moment the Branch has far more work than it can handle, and as a fire brigade team the Kilos get called out first. I hope you told your wife not to expect you for dinner.

'I should also apologise about something. In an ideal world you would be starting with the basic investigators' training course. Unfortunately there is quite a backlog of people waiting to go on it, so it will probably be several months before we can get you on one. In the meantime you will just have to learn as much as you can. Think of it as on-the-job training where no one will forgive you if you make a mistake.' He smiled to show that he was joking – up to a point.

The phone rang, but before he picked it up, Jack said, 'By the way, while you're here I thought you might like to see this.'

He passed a plain brown folder across the desk. I opened it and was amazed to see that it was a summary of my MI6 personnel file. Considering that MI6 officers are never allowed to see their own file this was a unique opportunity. Jack spoke on the phone while I flipped through the few pages. The point which struck me most was how much some of the comments on the file differed from what I had been told during my yearly staff assessments. There was nothing bad, but some of the comments seemed quite different from those I remembered.*

* *In recent intelligence service scandals there have been several accusations that staff reports have been altered, especially in the Tomlinson case. I don't believe anyone has lied, but I am sure the practice of not showing officers what has been written about them produces a tendency in managers to exaggerate any praise and play down criticisms, a problem exacerbated by the fact that written comments can often seem more harsh on the page than a gently expressed verbal summary.*

However, someone in the organisation had decided to put at least one small knife in my back. On top of the file summary was a press cutting showing me holding the two children in my arms. It was not a flattering photograph. I remembered I had done a favour for a friend who was a local journalist. He had begged me to let him write an article about me looking after the children. The paper had sent a photographer who had arrived at some unearthly hour, taken one quick snap and left. As I looked down at the tousled, unshaven man in the photograph, I wondered who at MI6 had been so interested in my progress that they had collected this. I knew the registries wouldn't have picked it up. I also wondered how much this photograph had affected the decision of the interview board. Too late to worry about that now.

When his phone call was over, I handed the file back to Jack.

'Now, remember, your appointment is only probationary. This is a tough job and if you don't make the grade down there I will personally have you kicked out of the Division.'

'And if I do make the grade?'

'Then I'll put you on a front-line target team inside two years. Then you'll really see some action.'

'Sounds good.'

'One last thing: once I drop you off down there, you're on your own. Any problems, sort them out on the team or with Don. That's the way it's done here. Are you clear?'

'Clear.'

'Let's go.'

He led me back out into the corridors and we travelled the length of the building to the north-west corner overlooking Lower Thames Street. He ushered me through an open door and into a long, very narrow room barely wide enough for a government issue desk. Sitting behind this was a stout, dark-haired man with an aggressive face. Although it was only just past nine in the morning he already had his shirt sleeves rolled up and his tie loosened. He looked up from the copy of the *Daily Mail* he was reading. But he didn't stand and he didn't put the paper down.

'This is the young man I rang you about this morning,' said Jack, 'Harry, this is Robert Skinner. SIO of the Juliets. Robert, Harry.'

I stepped forward and stuck out my hand. Skinner ignored it. He gave me a quick glance as if to size me up. Then he returned his attention to Jack.

I let my hand hang in the air for a moment and then stepped back. Jack took no notice of whatever had just happened.

'I'll leave you to introduce him to the team.' Jack turned, smiled, and shook hands with me one last time. 'Good luck.'

And then he was gone.

Skinner sat staring at the empty door until he was sure that Jack was out of earshot. Then he finally lowered his paper. There was a very, very long pause.

'Sit down,' he said finally.

He sat and just stared at me with the same blank expression before he finally asked, 'Where have you come from then?'

'Foreign and Commonwealth Office. CAD.'

'C–A what?' he asked suspiciously

'Central African Department – writing briefing papers for ministers, collating information sent in by embassies, that sort of thing.' There was another long and awkward pause. 'I specialised in Burundi,' I added helpfully.

He spent some time taking this in. Eventually he said, 'You wrote briefing papers?'

'That's right. Mainly about economic development, tribal conflict, that sort of thing.'

'Ever take drugs?' he asked.

'Not while I was writing briefing papers,' I replied in my brightest 'hello sir, I'm keen to impress, let's have a bit of a joke' voice. He ignored it.

'You'll be joining the Kilos – referred cannabis south-east. You won't be the only new man. In fact some soldier from the Special

Air Service joined just last week.' He glanced down at a piece of paper on the desk. 'Robert Pearson.'

My mouth dropped open and I made a sound that was something like 'Gunnurk!'

It was a mistake.

'Did I just say something fucking funny?'

I'd love to give the impression that as an ex-spy I worked with the SAS almost every day and that we were practically on first-name terms. In fact, I had almost never worked with them and 99.9 per cent of them wouldn't have had a clue who I was, but Bob Pearson would. I remembered him well – a tall, craggy-faced, no-nonsense sergeant who looked as if he could break every bone in your body if he wanted to. Bob and I had only had contact in a very minor matter, but for operational reasons I had been using an alias. The meeting might have been two years ago, but there was a good chance he would remember who I was as soon as he saw me. What the hell was he going to think? More to the point, what the hell was he going to do?

My mind was racing. I had been told that I shouldn't mention my MI6 background to anyone and now I was being placed on a team with the only man in an organisation of 2,000 people who would know who I was. This was such an unbelievable coincidence that someone must have arranged it deliberately. Together with the fact that the photograph had been added to my personnel file it seemed that someone at MI6 was very unhappy that an ex-employee was joining a rival organisation. I knew from old friends in the Service that there was already considerable friction over who would take the lead in the drugs war. Following the collapse of the Soviet Union it was the next most tempting intelligence target and whoever didn't get it would find their operational budgets heavily reduced at the very least. But I couldn't believe that my transfer was tied up with something as important as that. How could they see me as a threat?

Finally I realised that Skinner was still staring at me.

'Sorry.'

We began another long silence. He wanted to see if I was taking the piss out of him in some way.

'All right,' he said finally. Then he leant forward as though he was going to impart some great secret.

'I'm going to tell you this in Don's absence, but he'd tell you the same thing and it's only going to be said to you once, so listen carefully. You've got a lot to learn and we don't suffer fools gladly. On the team you keep your mouth shut and do what you're told when you're told. Then you just might get along. Understand?'

I nodded.

'Right, come with me.'

The team room was only a short way down the corridor. It was another big office, but almost every inch of floorspace was taken up by eight desks, a dozen filing cabinets, half a dozen steel security cupboards and a coat rack. There was barely room to pass between the desks and each was overflowing with files, newspapers, half-completed forms, bits of radio kit, dirty clothes, coffee mugs, baseball bats, motorcycle magazines, pictures of kids, half-eaten sandwiches. A transistor radio was blaring out from one corner. Seven men and one woman looked up as we entered.

'Right, listen up!' Skinner shouted above the noise of the radio. 'This is Harry, he's going to be joining the team for a while. Find him a place to sit and try not to hurt him.'

And that was it. He was gone and I was left standing in the doorway looking severely overdressed. Jack had told me to come dressed smartly for a court attendance that day and I was wearing a dark, pin-striped suit. But judging by the range of open-necked shirts, leather and denim jackets I was facing, no one else on the team had heard about it. Perhaps it was some kind of practical joke they played on new officers. But no one was laughing. They were just staring curiously as if a strange sort of alien life form had been dropped into their office.

31

'Better find him a desk,' murmured a big guy with a blond crewcut without looking up.

He was enormous, the muscles of his neck and shoulders bulked up like an amateur body builder's. His biceps were about as round as my thighs. For some reason he was the only one not watching me, his head bowed low over some paperwork.

The only woman in the room sighed loudly and stood up. She was in her late thirties and attractive, slim, with shoulder-length dark hair. In contrast to most of the men in the room she was smartly dressed, wearing a navy-blue trouser suit. She pointed around the room:

'This is Steve, Mac, Vinny, Carl, Dave, Rick and Paul.' Six of them nodded and raised a hand to say hello although I had no idea which was which and promptly forgot all the names anyway. The blond man with the paperwork still didn't look up.

The woman, who hadn't bothered to introduce herself, looked around the room for a moment as if trying to find some space and then said, 'Right. Follow me.'

She led me through a connecting door which had been mostly hidden by the coat rack. I stumbled in her wake, clambering over kitbags, boxes of prisoners' property, and more files. We stepped into an even more crowded room. A radio tuned to a different station was competing for attention with the one next door. Judging by the age of the officers and the amount of floorspace they were allocated, I quickly guessed that most of these were the junior officers on the team. One occupant stood out in particular: in contrast to all the others, he was dressed in a brown three-piece suit and his hair was swept back immaculately with plenty of gel. He was obviously 'king' of the room. He had by far the largest desk which was lined up in front of the huge marble fireplace. Someone had strung a banner across the front of the desk, reading 'Friend of the convicted innocent'. The occupants of the room all stopped chewing gum, drinking coffee or reading their newspapers to stare.

The woman said curtly, 'This is Harry, the new guy we've been

32

hearing about.' I wondered what this meant, but didn't have time to worry as she rattled off another string of names for me to forget. Sitting in the middle of the room with an open file on the desk in front of him was Bob Pearson. As soon as he looked up it was clear that he recognised me. He nodded slightly, then resumed his reading.

The woman looked around the room, clearly wondering where she could squeeze another person in. Then she stepped forward, swept the files off a side table and dumped them on the 'king's' desk with a challenging stare. She grabbed a chair at random and banged it down.

'You work here,' she said. And with that she strode out of the room leaving me to face seven or eight silent officers. The staring continued. Finally the man with the immaculate hair, whose team nickname turned out to be 'Carnaby', decided to break the ice. He smiled and gestured to the chaos around him:

'Welcome to the Black Hole of Lower Thames Street, mate.'

Gum chewing and newspaper reading resumed. I threw my holdall down on to my tiny new desk. It covered it. Carnaby reached out to turn the radio down, then leaned back in his chair and said, 'So come on, tell us all about yourself then. Someone said you've come from the Ministry of Defence or something.'

'Um yes. Hello, everyone. My name's Harry. I'm twenty-six. I have a degree in Modern History from Oxford. From there went to the Foreign Office where my specialist area was sub-Saharan Africa. I once wrote a briefing paper described by an Assistant Under Secretary of State as quote one of the most astute analyses of sub-Saharan power structures written by a junior official in the past twenty years unquote. My hobbies are water-skiing, the music of J.S. Bach and the baroque architecture of middle Europe.'

It was supposed to be a joke. I had in mind an amusing take-off of the sort of statement Miss World contestants make as they stand around in swimsuits. I thought: if they're expecting some public-school twit I'll give them one. I gave them a big grin and waited for the polite laughter. There wasn't any. From the shock on their

33

faces, they clearly thought my little statement was for real. Someone said, 'Jesus Christ!'

'Nah! He doesn't look a bit like Jesus Christ,' said another voice from behind a copy of the *Sun*.

'Well, we've got to call him something,' said a third officer who was wearing a flying cap with large leather ear flaps that made him look like some kind of Labrador.

After a variety of suggestions, some of which were just insulting and some of which were physically improbable, Carnaby said, 'I'll tell you what he sounds like – a right Chumley Warner!'

This met with general approval and a group piled out of the back room into the main office. The main room was dominated by two types of board on the walls: one was the Team Board which had the designations and names of the team members listed down one side. Every officer on a team is given a number and this was recorded on the Team Board. No. 1 was of course the Senior Investigation Officer in charge of the team, No. 2 was usually his deputy and then the other HEOs and EOs down to No. 15 who was the team's administration officer responsible for basic paperwork, running checks and ordering supplies.

There were boxes running across the Team Board representing the days of the week for the next fortnight. Various activities such as court appearances, training courses and surveillance operations were scrawled across it. Wherever you were at any time, it had to be recorded here. It was vital to have one of these boards on a referred team which could be called out at any moment. At a glance an officer taking an emergency call could tell how many officers were available and where they could be contacted.

The other type of board was the Score Board. There was a separate one for each recent year and it recorded every case the team had been involved in – the amount of drugs, the name of the case officer and the result of the trial. I wondered how long it would be before I managed to get my name up there as a successful case officer. It seemed like a very long time away.

'Well, we've christened the bastard!' announced Carnaby, picking up a marker pen which hung on a string by the Team Board. He stared up at the crowded board, trying to find a vacant space.

As a team the Kilos were unusual. Almost ten years earlier they had lost an officer, Peter Bennett, who had been Kilo 2. He was shot dead as he ran towards a suspect to make an arrest – the only ID officer ever killed on active duty (although there have been plenty of other close calls). As a mark of respect, the Division decided that the designation 'Kilo 2' would never be used again and the Kilos were the only team in the Division numbered from 3 to 16.

Strictly speaking, as an HEO, I should have been given a number between 3 and 6, but I certainly hadn't earned that and there wasn't a space free anyway. In fact there wasn't a space anywhere. For a moment this caused Carnaby a problem as he ran his eye down the board. Then he chuckled and drew an extra space on the wall below the board. He scribbled in the number 17 and next to it began to write 'Chumley'.

'Actually,' I said, 'I think you'll find it's spelt C-h-o-l-m-o-n-d-e-l-e-y.'

Carnaby paused to consider this for a moment and then good-naturedly said, 'Fuck off.'

The number provoked a certain amount of discussion. As far as anyone could remember, no one in the history of the ID had ever held a designation as low as 17. It signified that I was less use than the team's administration officer. Out on the streets, every officer who heard that designation on the radio would know exactly who it was. Someone suggested they purchase a team cat and then give me a number below that as well.

In the middle of all this excitement, Don, the Kilos' SIO, arrived. Don was a thin man in his fifties, over six feet tall with greying hair and moustache, dressed in a smart grey suit. He had a ready laugh and a strong Scouse accent. He'd been in the Division for almost twenty years and leading the Kilos was likely to be one of the last of his postings. Although the second officer takes charge of the team out on the streets, the SIO is very much 'the Boss'. He decides which cases will be investigated and how resources will be allocated. Ultimately he shapes the character of the team. I soon learned that Don's long experience and relaxed manner meant that the Kilos were one of the best-led teams on the Division.

After a few welcoming words, Don told the woman that she would be my training officer for the few months. I could tell from the cold stare she gave me that she wasn't happy about it.

As soon as Don had left the office, she took a slow look around the room as if to say, 'Look what I got landed with.' Then she stood up and simply said, 'Well, if I'm going to be mother for the next few months, we'd better go and get some coffee.'

We headed off to the staff canteen. At that hour of the morning there was hardly anyone in there. She chose a quiet table in a corner and pulled a packet of cigarettes from an expensive-looking shoulder bag. She lit one and took a deep drag before blowing out the smoke very slowly. She looked at me through narrowed eyes as if wondering where to start.

'I suppose this means God hates me, doesn't it?' she said.

'Yes, I think it probably does,' I agreed.

She smiled for the first time since I'd met her.

The Kilos were different from almost all other teams on the Division in another respect: the good-looking woman turned out to be Kilo 3, the SIO's deputy. This made her one of the few women in the Division who had ever qualified for the post. The deputy leader is possibly the most important position on the team. The SIO almost never leaves the office, which means that many of the decisions on the ground affecting the operation fall to the deputy. Most teams contained one or two women at the most. There was not a single female team leader in any of the Division's many teams and only one or two other female deputies.

Behind her back, men on the Division simply referred to her as 'the Widow'. You quickly learned three things about her: she was good-looking, she was good at her job and she was also completely untouchable. In a world dominated by male officers where at least 50 per cent of the banter was about shagging, it was recognised that she was not fair game. As far as the team was concerned and despite all appearances to the contrary, she was an honorary bloke. In any case, her temper was legendary and any would-be Lothario who tried it on with her would have probably left with his genitalia in a basket.

She never talked about the death of her husband and no one I knew ever asked. It was the unwritten team rule that the subject was off limits. There were rumours that she was seeing some senior manager in the Customs Policy Division, but I'm not sure anyone ever had the nerve to ask about that either.

Apart from Carnaby and the Widow there were two other HEOs on the Kilos: Patrick and Rick. Rick was a little guy from Liverpool who was the best driver on the team. The story was that he had originally been sent to London from Liverpool after an incident early one morning on Liverpool docks. He was demonstrating a handbrake turn in the senior officer's brand-new car and the car had spun too far and disappeared off the quay into thirty feet of water. They'd saved the vehicle (once it had time to dry out), but the young EO in the car, who was on his first day in the job, had nearly drowned and had been on sick leave with shock for a month. The authorities in Liverpool had decided that there was only one place for a talent like that and sent Rick to the ID.

The Widow explained about the teams on the Branch. There were three referred teams, the Kilos, the Deltas and the Juliets. Kilos and Deltas divided the major south and east coast ports between them, with most work for the Kilos coming from the massive amount of cross-Channel traffic at Dover. The Deltas had to handle jobs as far north as Harwich. The Juliets were dedicated to investigating cannabis smuggling involving yachts and other small craft. They worked closely with Customs Marine Branch which had a number of 'cutters', high-speed boats for intercepting ships at sea.

There were two target teams on the Branch, the Bravos and the Charlies. Because of the demands of constant surveillance on a single target, they usually worked as one large combined team of thirty officers. It was normal practice for new officers to spend a few years on a referred team such as the Kilos before moving to a target team.

I decided to risk asking the Widow about the heavily built officer who was determined not to make eye contact with me back in the office.

'That's Carl. You might have a bit of bother there. Don't get me wrong, he's a good man. Solid as a rock on surveillance, good driver, takes charge of all the radio kit on the team and makes sure it's all working, which is not a popular job, believe me. But I've got to be honest and tell you that he doesn't want to talk to you, doesn't want to work with you and certainly won't get in a car with you.'

'Why? What did I do? I've hardly been here five minutes.'

'Yeah well, you've got to see it from his side. He's been in the Customs since school. He worked the docks up at Sheerness for almost ten years on the rummage crews. He finally managed to get on to the Division and since he's been here he's shown himself to be a top officer, there's not a team on the Division that wouldn't take him. He's only rated EO. Now you come along, never done a day in Customs, with your university degree and your Foreign Office career and straight away you're an HEO plus there's a lot of talk that you've been promised a fast route to senior management.'

'That's not true.'

'Yeah well, it doesn't matter whether it's true or not. Plenty of people round here believe it and Carl's one of 'em. Don't get me wrong, it's no skin off my nose and I don't think Carl is actually going to do anything about it, although he has thumped people for far less. Just tread a bit carefully when you're around him. In fact tread carefully around all of us because it's a touchy subject.'

Then she said more kindly,

'Look, don't worry about it, Harry. You'll get some heavy

ribbing about it, but as long as you can make it through the first couple of weeks without making a complete tit of yourself people will get over it. Hell, I'm over it already.'

I was still digesting this when she dropped the next bombshell. 'Oh, and I'd lay off that stuff about supposedly being in the Foreign Office.'

'What do you mean?' I was immediately thinking of Bob Pearson.

'Oh, come on. This is an organisation of two thousand investigators. We're involved in so much secret work we've got more contacts with the intelligence services than we have with the Old Bill. How long did your lot think it would take us to find out?'

Well, that was one less thing to worry about.

The Widow smiled a little. She stubbed out her cigarette and we headed back to the office. At her desk, she filled my arms with case files until I could barely see over the top of the pile.

'Welcome to the team,' she said. 'Read these. When you've read them, come back and I'll give you some more.'

I spent a lot of that first week reading files, talking to officers about case histories and staying late to go through piles of court exhibits such as address books and till receipts, looking for clues that might have been missed. An ID team always works on several cases at any one time: a target team will only work on one or two because the nature of the work is so intensive, but a referred team can have more than a dozen cases running at once, all at different stages of completion. Some will require days of surveillance to establish patterns of movement by the principal suspects and other cases will be on hold waiting for indications that a particular gang of smugglers is ready to bring the drugs over. There will also be cases which have already been 'knocked', the suspects arrested and waiting to go to court for trial.

All the preparation for court is done by a designated team member known as the 'case officer'. They have the help of the Division's own Solicitor's Office, but since a Customs officer has a right of audience in the lower courts, the case officer will often have to appear in court and conduct proceedings for the Crown in matters such as bail applications. Each officer takes a turn to be in charge of an investigation, with the newer officers supervised by more experienced hands.

I spent a lot of time reading about the Widow's current case: Operation *Kansas*. (To assist in identification, all operation names on the drugs branches have the same initial letter as the team working on the case.) In *Kansas*, three-quarters of a tonne of cannabis had been hidden in a large consignment of machine parts. Unusually for the Kilos, *Kansas* had been a long operation. The smugglers were an off-shoot of a well-known London gang. They had a reputation for violence and ruthlessness which had made the operation especially dangerous for the surveillance team. Following a tip-off, the gang had been kept under surveillance for several weeks by the Kilos as they booked tickets, hired a warehouse and met with the contacts who would distribute the drugs they were bringing in. They had been caught red-handed as they were unpacking the drugs in the warehouse and there had been a violent struggle in which at least one of the smugglers was hospitalised after he was run down by a passing car as he was trying to escape.

The evidence was so overwhelming that the prosecution of the case was expected to be fairly straightforward. In fact it was likely that the suspects would plead guilty at the last moment, a common tactic which allowed the criminals to cause maximum inconvenience and expense whilst still getting time off their sentence for owning up to what they had done.

The weeks of surveillance had created masses of paperwork, all of which had to be processed by the Widow. The pressure of work was such that she had to work on her own most of the time. People always imagine that Customs and Excise has large teams of lawyers working on a case, but it usually comes down to the case officer and just one solicitor, who himself is working on many other cases, to prepare all the paperwork. The Widow had confided to me that she had a bad feeling about the case. The defence lawyers seemed too confident even though the evidence against their clients was so strong. Although we knew the long criminal history of these men, none of that evidence would be given to the jury because it might 'prejudice' the trial. So the trial would come down to the evidence from the operation. We expected the defence lawyers would try their usual tactic of going through the minutiae of the paperwork to get as much evidence as possible excluded on technicalities, but even so there should still be enough to convict. Yet the Widow was worried. She spent many hours, often after a long day's surveillance, desperately trying to find what the Achilles heel in the case might be.

When I wasn't reading files or helping out with *Kansas*, I was trying to scrounge equipment. At that time, the Division's budget for equipment was pretty small and the newest member of any team was always last in line for any decent kit. The worst piece of equipment was my 'funky chicken' radio. Each of our personal radios was a block of metal about ten inches long and two inches thick. It was supposed to be carried in a shoulder holster arrangement which fitted under your right arm to help conceal it. The problem was that it was so bulky that it was about as easy to conceal as a brick. It had to have a heavy rechargeable battery clipped on to the end which made it even more unwieldy. It wasn't too much of a burden when you first put it on, but after a few hours of it trying to bore its way into your armpit, it felt as though it weighed about a ton.

What made matters worse was that the harness had an induction loop incorporated in the shoulder strap which fed the radio transmissions to a tiny, almost undetectable earpiece. The trouble with this was that at times when the signal was poor you tended to lower your ear nearer to your shoulder to improve reception. If you weren't careful, this made you look like Quasimodo.

I could have lived with all of that, but the battery connection on my radio was faulty and when I placed it in the shoulder holster the power would sometimes go altogether. Rather than take the radio out where it might be spotted, I was reduced to squeezing it repeatedly with my arm in a series of funky chicken movements until the connection was jolted back into life. Members of the public who saw me struggling with the radio in shop doorways and side streets when on surveillance must have thought I was something to do with care in the community.

Meantime the Widow was volunteering me for any OP duty that was going. OP stands for observation post, which can be a building, the back of an old van or even a television screen showing pictures relayed from a concealed camera several miles away. OPs may vary in the type of security required and the level of comfort they provide, but they all have one thing in common: boredom. If vehicle surveillance is the most exciting part of the job, OP duty is very definitely the worst. Shifts can last as long as twelve or even eighteen hours, just watching one site and noting any activity in a log book. There would be one other officer to share the duty, but one of you always had to be looking at the screen or through the scope or out of the window. The worst thing was that while you were sitting there developing constipation and backache, you thought about all the better things you could be doing with your time, often while you were watching the drugs smuggler enjoying a luxurious lifestyle which involved driving fast cars and spending his way through large wads of cash. You soon realised why drugs smugglers think that a few years in prison is little more than a calculated business risk.

I used the time to memorise the radio codes and to learn the law relating to Customs work: the Customs and Excise Management Act 1979, the Police and Criminal Evidence Act 1984, the Misuse of Drugs Act 1971 – the list seemed never-ending and an ID officer is expected to know them all. If an officer makes just one error in using his powers you can guarantee that at the trial the defence lawyers will pounce on it. It can lead to a vital piece of evidence being excluded, or even to the collapse of an entire prosecution.

I got back to the office at the end of one of these long OP shifts and looked at the pile of files on my very small desk. It seemed to be getting bigger rather than smaller as people on the team remembered yet another character they thought I ought to know about. I decided that I had time to read a couple more before heading for home. The first file I picked up was headed 'Frank Davies'.

'So who the hell are you?' I thought.

I had no idea how much that name was going to dominate my life over the next two years.

It is impossible to tell the story of my time with the Kilos without also telling the story of Frank Davies, the nearest thing there ever was to a King of the south-coast drug smugglers.

He had started out on the fringes of organised crime in East London, passing on stolen cars by using his connections in the second-hand motor trade, but at some time during the 1970s he became involved in moving stolen luxury cars and electrical goods to Turkey and the Far East. Then he had dropped out of sight as far as Customs files were concerned.

He had re-appeared in the 1980s, moving into an expensive property on the south coast near Southampton. It soon became clear that his main business was bulk smuggling of cannabis, but like all drug smugglers he would bring in whatever his suppliers could get hold of and he was known to do significant amounts of heroin, cocaine and ecstasy. Several officers had taken a look at him over the years, but something else had always come up, the investigation had lapsed and the officer had moved on.

As it happened, I actually saw Davies in the flesh just two days after starting to read his file. The Widow had sent me and Bob Pearson out with Carnaby on a sort of grand tour of criminal activity along the south coast. We drove past the addresses of suspected smugglers, noting any new vehicle numbers. We went to visit haulage yards, lay-bys and back lanes that were often used for the handover of drugs between smugglers and their contacts.

Carnaby showed us good spots to watch from and places where smuggling teams sometimes mounted their own counter-surveillance.

The day finished with a drive down the A27 coast road. Carnaby swung the car off down a small unmarked side road and eventually pulled over where the lane crossed a small rise. There was a good view out over the surrounding farmland, and I could see a big house in the middle distance. Carnaby grabbed a pair of binoculars from the glove compartment and chucked them across. 'This is it boys, the highlight of our tour.'

Bob was looking through the binoculars. 'Bloody hell, look at all them cars.'

He was right, there were a *lot* of cars: top-of-the-range Mercs, BMWs, a couple of Ferraris and a low blue racer that looked like a Lamborghini. All parked randomly around the farmyard like discarded toys.

'This is Frankie Davies' kingdom. You'll get to know it really well. Frankie brings in most of the hash, amphet and ecstasy along the south coast. You name it, Frankie's boys can supply it. They say he's into arcades, road haulage, club security, anything that will help smuggle or sell gear. If someone bought gear within a hundred yards of a nightclub around here in the past three or four years then they've probably done business with good old Frankie.'

Carnaby studied the yard through the binoculars for a while and asked Bob to note down a couple of registration numbers which he thought were new. Then he said, 'Now, this lay-by is okay for the odd drive past to check vehicles and stuff, but if we're working seriously on him, don't use it. We're off the beaten track here and he knows it gives a view over his land, so anyone stopped here is likely to be taking a look at him. He's been known to drive by to see if anyone is using it. And don't be a hero and go too close to the house either. He's got security cameras and some fucking serious guard dogs, and ever since Kenny Noye killed that police officer who was on close sur-

44

veillance, there's always been a chance someone else will have a go. Frankie is just mad enough to try it.'

He looked for a while longer and then said, 'Shit!' He passed the binoculars across to me.

'Take a quick look. That's Frankie himself, getting into the Merc. See him?'

I had just a quick glimpse of a fairly short, stocky, middle-aged man with close-cropped dark hair in a black leather jacket climbing into the car. I passed the binoculars to Bob.

'Time to leave, guys,' said Carnaby. 'It wouldn't do to be caught here.'

We didn't know it then, but it was at about this time, quite possibly that very afternoon, that Frank was involved in a nasty but seemingly unimportant incident which was the start of the chain of events that was to bring him down.

Frank still ran a couple of dealers directly, one of whom worked out of a house on a sprawling estate on the outskirts of South-ampton. There was a joint police and Customs operation attempt-ing to gather evidence against the dealer, but it was the usual problem: everyone on the estate knew the house was used by Frank's dealers but everyone was too scared of reprisals or of being labelled a grass actually to give evidence. The police finally got a break when a young bloke who had just moved on to the estate with his wife and kid offered to help. Apparently he had lost a brother because of drug addiction and was prepared to do anything to stop it. He let the surveillance teams use his house from time to time.

Somehow, the dealer found out and let Frank know.

One afternoon, three of Frank's heavies forced their way into the young bloke's house, tied him and his wife up with baling wire, and hooded and gagged them. Then they dragged them into the kitchen. The kid was carried upstairs and shut in a cupboard. Frank's lieutenant called him on a mobile and told him it was safe to come in.

They took off the husband's hood. Frank turned on the rings on the hob of the electric cooker. He lit a cigarette and waited until the rings were red-hot.

Two of the gang lifted the woman up and held her in front of the stove. As she tried to recoil from the heat Frank pushed her forward, her face getting nearer and nearer the rings. Her hair started to burn. Then Frank asked the guy if he and his family were going to leave the area.

They were gone the next day.

Frank simply moved his dealing operation to another part of the estate and there were no more witnesses. But it's funny how things work out. The head of the Customs team on that operation was Don's best mate. He and Don were out drinking a few nights later when the subject of Frank came up. Don promised that we would go looking for Frank Davies. He was the biggest smuggler on our patch and in a sense it was our responsibility.

At the weekly case meeting a few days later we pulled together what we knew about Davies' operation. Although we had a lot of historical information about his career, we didn't have much on him that was current. But we knew that his activities were centred on the haulage business: to make real money, cannabis has to be smuggled in bulk, hundreds of kilos at a time. It's only really possible to do that by smuggling it in freight consignments. But Frank was always looking for new ways of bringing the stuff in. Like all teams on the Division, we had a dedicated intelligence unit whose job was to collect information about possible targets. Danny, an old officer from the unit in his last post before retirement, was our assigned intelligence officer, and he came to the meeting.

'Well, boys, I've got good news and bad news,' he said. 'The good news is that one of our VAT teams actually managed to nail a case against one of Frankie's gaming arcades recently. He's taken a big financial hit and although he's still got plenty of assets, he's running short of ready cash. That should mean that he's going to have to take a few chances. The bad news is this.'

He passed around some photographs. They showed a large villa, somewhere nice and sunny, probably Spain. It was a big place with a huge swimming pool. I recognised the low blue sports car which was parked at the front of the villa.

'This is Frank's new place in Fuengerola. As you know, Fuengerola is one of the favourite hideaways for ex-pat British criminals on the south coast of Spain. He's also made enquiries about putting the farm in Sussex on the market. It looks like Frank's getting ready to leave for good.'

Don was grim-faced by the end of the meeting.

'All right, we can't devote all our time to this guy – we are still a referred team and that means we have to take whichever job comes along next – but keep your eyes and ears open for any connection to Davies' operation. If we get a choice of two jobs, we go for him. He's on our patch and he thinks he owns it. Let's show him he doesn't.'

It was to be only three days before we got our first opportunity.

It was Friday night at the end of my second week with the team. I was on the train home thinking that this new job wasn't so bad. Nicky had invited some of her friends from the bank to dinner and I had left work early for once so that I could be changed and on my best behaviour by the time they arrived. I knew this evening was important to her.

Just as the train pulled into the station, my pager went off. It said '999', the emergency signal which meant return to London immediately. A train heading the other way had just pulled in to the station. I grabbed my kitbag, raced across to the other platform and leapt aboard just as the train was pulling out. I didn't have a mobile phone and in the frantic dash between platforms I forgot all about calling Nicky to say that I wouldn't be able to get home for dinner. I only remembered as the train had pulled away from the station, but by then it was too late.

I meant to ring from the office, but it took me half an hour to travel back into London and by the time I reached the team room at Customs House, maps were spread out on tables, people were checking out radio equipment or booking out the heavy stuff like dragon lights and boltcutters. The Widow was busy speaking into the phone. She gave me a wave and I began preparing my surveillance kit.

Bob filled me in: the Dutch police had just informed the Division's intelligence section that a well-known Dutch cannabis dealer called Van Hohn was on his way across the Channel and he was involved in something important, possibly a delivery. Van Hohn was a known contact of Frank Davies.

Although he was travelling under an alias, the intelligence team had been able to trace him because he was driving one of several suspect cars which the Dutch police had also recorded. The ferry had already docked at Dover by the time the information was received and uniformed staff at inbound controls at Dover had quickly been informed. Thanks to them, the car had been spotted and the description of the driver fitted that of Van Hohn. He hadn't been stopped for fear of tipping him off that something was wrong, but four cars from the local Dover Investigation Unit had been scrambled and they currently had him under surveillance. The Investigation Units were given similar training to the Division teams, but in those days they were usually only used for local enquiries.

The plan was that since Van Hohn was heading up the A2 towards London, we would take over the surveillance somewhere on the M25 and follow him to the meeting.

The Widow slammed down the phone and gave a shrill whistle which called the room to silence.

'Right, here's the situation: I've just been in touch with Dover on their mobile. This guy's really burning it, doing about a ton the whole way. It's too late for the M2, he's already on the M25 heading for the Dartford Tunnel. Seems like he could be heading for the M1 and going north. Now, there's no way Dover can take him much further. They aren't equipped for this kind of chase, they're low on fuel and most of them were out all last night on another job. We've got to take this off them as soon as possible. We'll head out and if necessary cover the junctions anti-clockwise from the M1. Channel Four Alpha on the radios. Harry, you're with me.'

And that was as much briefing as we got. I had been in court that afternoon and was still wearing my pin-stripe suit. But there was no time to change. We grabbed bags, radios and equipment and raced out to the riverfront car park. The security guards had been warned that there was a job on and they were already pulling open the large wrought-iron gates as we jumped into the vehicles. It was a cold autumn night and already dark. I got into a large Citroën with the Widow. I switched on the car-to-car radio and tested it while she checked the tyres and the lights. I carefully spread my large-scale maps of London across my lap and took the cap off my marker pen. It would be my job to find a route for us out of London that would bring us on to the M25 near the target. At the same time I would be reporting on our progress over the radio to the Operational Control Room and noting the progress of the other cars. I was suffering from a serious case of nerves – this was my first time out with the team on a major job and above all things I didn't want to make a mistake and let them down.

The Widow stabbed at the accelerator and we shot forward into the side road leading to Lower Thames Street.

Now it was just a simple matter of fighting our way through the London evening traffic . . .

3

Van Hohn

As we hurtled towards the queue of traffic which was blocking the road ahead, the Widow didn't wait for me to suggest a route. She suddenly swung our car right across the central reservation and on to the opposite carriageway. Fortunately the traffic on this side of the road was held by a red light at the junction ahead, but we had to get through those lights before they changed and we found ourselves head-on with the oncoming traffic. I held my breath as we raced along on the wrong side of the road, horn blaring and headlights flashing. This seemed to grab the attention of everyone in front of us and the cross traffic ahead braked heavily. Hardly pausing, we quickly wove left and right through the now stationary vehicles and then swerved back on to the right side of the road at the other side of the traffic lights. Leaving chaos behind us, the Widow accelerated away up the now empty carriageway.

Looking back, I think I was in a state of shock for the first few minutes of this journey. Of course I had known that – in theory – surveillance vehicles have to be driven like this, but I had never really thought what it would be like: the near misses, the swerving from side to side through gaps in traffic, the angry reactions by some other drivers who of course didn't have a clue who we were – one of them chased us for about a mile until we cut through the next red traffic light. Thanks to a combination of first-night nerves, the violent movements of the car and the strain of trying to read maps in the semi-darkness, I began to feel really car-sick for the first time in my life.

Fighting to keep my stomach in check, I fumbled in the darkness trying to gather up the maps. Being the second officer in an ID surveillance vehicle isn't just a matter of sitting comfortably and watching the scenery pass by. The second officer is expected to act as navigator, radio operator and – if the target stops – surveillance footman. Modern surveillance is conducted at high speed and this can make it almost impossible for a navigator to find or read street names. To get around this problem, the Division uses a military system for navigation. Maps are marked with red, blue, green, yellow or white dots at every junction (and I mean *every* junction). Every dot is identified by a unique number. So instead of saying that his car is 'heading towards the crossroads at the end of Brixton High Street' the radio operator can simply say 'towards green five seven'. The system is so good that road names become almost redundant for top-line surveillance teams once they have worked in an area for a while. You might ask an officer if he know where such-and-such a road is and he won't have a clue, but ask for something like 'red three five' and he can find it on the map straight away.

And navigation isn't just a matter of following the target. Any drug smuggler can spot a team if they simply stay behind him. Real surveillance means that the navigator is constantly planning – looking for parallel routes, crossovers and oversight positions as well as danger points where counter-surveillance might be waiting. It is a skilled job which takes years to learn properly.

All the maps are covered with plastic so that navigators can plot routes and scribble notes using felt-tipped markers. The maps can then be wiped clean at the end of the day and used again. But the radio operator often has to select a considerable bundle of maps for a forthcoming surveillance and the plastic coverings make them as slippery as eels. Experienced operators soon learn to carry a piece of wire which can be thrust through holes at the side of the maps and bind them together. Even in the dark the wire can be untwisted and the maps re-arranged before using the wire to rebind them again. But this was my first night out on surveillance and I didn't know all this, so I spent a lot of the trip fumbling in the footwell trying to find one out of the thirty or so maps lying there.

Using the radio isn't a simple matter of pressing a button and talking either. The same team of military advisers which had designed the map system a few years before had also recommended changes to the radio communications. Even the lowest level of criminal will use radio scanners to listen for police and customs radio traffic. Smuggling gangs often employ technical experts who are a good deal more professional than that. To combat this, the Division was given radios with a high level of encryption, similar to those used by the SAS. A scanner looking for ID communications would only pick up static. But a skilled operator can detect that the static caused by encoding is different to normal background static and would be able to tell his boss that Customs were working in the area even though he wouldn't know what was being said. That would be enough to cause some of the more professional gangs to abandon that run. To minimise this risk, radio traffic has to be kept to bursts of only a few seconds. The trouble is that during a busy surveillance the average ID team produces more chatter than that famous Polish training squadron in *The Battle of Britain*. Various efforts to cut out all this talk failed until someone had the idea of introducing a simple code. Directions such as 'The target is heading towards' were given a number such as 'seven one'. Places were given simple codewords. The city centre became 'gold', 'home address' became 'burrow', and so on. Instead of saying, 'The target is now heading for the city centre' the radio operator would simply call 'seven one gold'. The code wasn't secret because to hear these words you would have to penetrate military-level encryption, but it did work surprisingly well at cutting down transmissions. However, ID officers then began introducing their own terms and soon radio transmissions became a mixture of official and unofficial language. It was hard enough to remember the official code, but with all the other terms it became like a sort of second language which took new radio operators some time to pick up.

On top of all this, the second officer has to be an extra pair of eyes for his driver, constantly watching out for vehicles or pedestrians who might pose a hazard and calling a warning if he feels the driver hasn't seen them. The whole job requires well-rehearsed teamwork and once you find someone you work well with you tend to work together wherever possible. Some officers can never adapt to these intense pressures and are never picked for front-line surveillance teams.

While I was trying to deal with all these problems, I could hear 'Control' in my earpiece steadily and calmly relaying the target's position and speed from the transmissions of the Dover team. Control is an office at Customs House manned twenty-four hours a day and it provides radio communications links for all major operations. They also have access to all major databases such a CEDRIC, the Customs and Excise computer, and the various criminal databases of the police so that they can provide information on known suspects almost instantly (well, that's the theory – sometimes it works).

The news from the Dover team (call sign 'Dingoes') wasn't good.

'Control, Kilo 3.'

'Kilo 3,' I responded.

'Relay, Dingo 7, target vehicle now Junction Three, M25, sierra nine zero, burning, burning.'

I knew 'sierra' meant speed and 'burning' meant that the target was accelerating. Where were the traffic police when you needed them? Despite the worry that Van Hohn was getting too far ahead of us, even I knew that his extreme speed was a good sign: according to the Dutch police, this man was a major player in a powerful syndicate and driving illegally fast was a classic way of trying to throw off a surveillance team. After all, the only thing which would dare to stay with you would have to be either police or Customs. Something big must be going down. We had to hope that Dover could hang on and that we could get to them in time.

Looking over my shoulder, I saw that the other cars were no longer with us. As I was thrown from side to side and the plastic-covered maps slid off my lap for the umpteenth time, I managed to ask where they'd gone.

'Other routes,' growled the Widow, brushing her hair out of her eyes and thumping the horn yet again. 'That way we don't all get stuck in the same jam. Now, where the fuck are we?'

I know now that the only thing which saved us that night was that the Widow knew London well enough to find a route out despite my garbled instructions. By the time we finally swept down the slip road at the start of the M1, Control was telling us that the Dutchman was already some way ahead of us and still going flat out.

Hurtling through the darkness, I marvelled that the cars could take this kind of punishment regularly. Despite their often battered and nondescript appearance, all the Division's operational cars are kept tuned for high-speed driving and the standing instructions were that after driving one, it had to be left in the team parking bay with a full tank of petrol, and water and tyres checked ready for a quick departure. I was beginning to understand why.

As we picked up speed on the M1, it soon became clear that of our five cars, we had made it out of London fastest. But we had still been too slow. Van Hohn was well ahead of us on the M1, with the Dover team struggling to stay with him. Two of their vehicles had been forced to drop out and only three were left. As for the Kilos, I could hear Carl screaming blasphemies over the radio about some minicab driver who had almost hit him on the Pentonville Road, but his voice and those of the rest of the team faded quickly as our car accelerated out of radio range. As we picked up speed on the comparatively open motorway, the needle on the speedometer often touched 120 miles an hour.

Hurtling up behind other vehicles in the outside lane, the Widow relied on continually flashing the headlights. It was our only means of warning other vehicles.

Most cars moved out of our way. Whenever we were blocked by some moron who refused to move over, or if the traffic ahead was just too heavy, the Widow would take us past it on the inside, using the hard shoulder of the motorway when there was no other choice. Our major problem was the kind of idiot who would be cruising idly in the middle lane, see us coming up fast behind him and suddenly swerve out in front of us as if he were personally enforcing the speed limit. This only happened twice, but it was so dangerous that twice was quite enough. Such moments severely tested our brakes, my nerves and the Widow's vocabulary.

We were rapidly approaching the junction of the M1 and the M6 when the radio suddenly sprang into life with the excited chatter of Dover Unit still in close pursuit of Van Hohn. They must be somewhere in the dark just ahead of us. The Widow grabbed the radio handset from me and gave our position.

'Nice of you to join us, Your Majesty!'

'Very funny,' muttered the Widow. 'Hit red twice.'

One of the sets of tail-lights up ahead of us brightened twice as the last Dover car in the convoy touched his brakes.

'Red seen,' barked the Widow and passed the handset back to me.

We began to overtake Dover vehicles in the tail. We were still doing well over a hundred miles an hour. Then just as we thought that we were getting into the game, blue lights appeared in the rear-view mirror. Looking over my shoulder, I could see a glaringly striped police Jaguar bearing down on us. The Widow spat expletives, not so much because we were being stopped, but because this could attract Van Hohn's attention to what was happening behind him. She eased our car over towards the hard shoulder and our speed quickly fell away. Cars from the Dover team began to overtake us again. The police Jaguar pulled alongside us to guide us on to the hard shoulder.

'Get out of there, Kilo 3!' barked the voice of one of the Dover cars. 'I'll take him! I'm practically out of petrol anyway.'

I barely had time to gasp before a dark Ford Sierra cut viciously across our nose and that of the Jaguar. As the Jaguar rolled to a halt on the hard shoulder, the Sierra pulled up diagonally across it, blocking it in. Our car had almost come to a stop, but the Widow changed down, punched the accelerator and threw the wheel hard to the right. We swerved back out into the line of traffic, leaving the Jaguar baulked behind us. My last sight was of the Dover officer leaping out of his vehicle, waving his warrant card over his head and trying to stop a full-scale police alert going out.

Now we closed rapidly on the target vehicle. Luckily for all of us, his speed was dropping well below a hundred. Either he was satisfied that he had thrown off any tailing vehicles or he was approaching his destination. The radio came alive with the call signs of other Kilo vehicles checking in as they joined the tail.

We passed the last Dover car.

'There he is, Kilo 3, four sets of lights up on you now. He's all yours.' Then, as a parting shot, he snarled, 'Don't drop the ball, you fuckers!'

It was only after I'd been on the Division for some time that I understood his anger: Dover Unit and the Kilos were at war with each other. To understand why, you need to know a little about how Customs and Excise is organised. The country is split into a number of administrative areas known as Collections. Each one is managed by an officer known as the Collector for that region. In those days, each unit had an Investigation Unit to deal with small-scale smuggling and similar excise-related crimes. All other work was supposed to be passed to Divisional teams based in London and one or two of the larger northern cities such as Liverpool and Manchester. The Kilos were the Divisional team which took all large cannabis jobs which came through Dover – we rarely touched anything less than a hundred kilos. The problem was that this was particularly galling for the Investigation Unit at Dover. Hundreds of jobs came their way because Dover is the busiest port in the country. They were always first on the scene and frequently had to do the first (and hardest) part of the investigation or surveillance.

You can imagine how they felt when, every time they got a really interesting job, the Kilos swanned down from London and took it from them. There was nothing any of us could do about it, but the tension between the two teams was always high.

On top of all this, the handover of a target between two surveillance teams is the most dangerous time. New eyes aren't yet accustomed to the vehicle's shape or tell-tale driving habits. It is during handover that most targets are lost by the team following them. The worst case I ever heard of was when one team misunderstood the instructions of another at a handover and managed to lose a thirty-foot articulated lorry completely (they were never allowed to forget it).

These guys from Dover had done an almost superhuman job tailing Van Hohn this far at ridiculous speeds without killing themselves or anyone else. Now they were being forced to hand it over and if we made a mistake they would never let us forget it either.

I put my head down over the map with the torch closely covered by my hand to keep the light from distracting the Widow. I was trying to find out what options Van Hohn might have on the road ahead. The trouble was, I had to find out where we were first. I'd got as far as the last junction when: 'Fuck me!'

The Widow hurled the Citroën sharply to the left and I was almost thrown into her lap. The Dutchman had come off at the slip road for motorway services, but the Widow's concentration had slipped for a moment and she had only realised where he had gone just as we were about to overshoot the turning. We missed the crash barrier by inches. It was just this sort of thing that Dover were afraid of, that momentary loss of concentration just as you think you have the whole thing under control.

I suddenly realised that it was my job to make sure the other vehicles didn't miss the turning. Almost panicking, I hit the transmit button and shouted, 'It's an off, off, off at blue one seven.'

'It's a radio, not a fucking megaphone,' growled the Widow as she eased off the accelerator. Ahead of us, the Dutchman had turned slowly into the lorry park. We couldn't simply follow him, that would be too obvious – especially after our last manoeuvre. We drove round the bend towards the services building and out of the Dutchman's line of sight. The Widow stopped the car.

'Out,' she said.

'What?' I couldn't believe she was serious. I was the new guy. I wasn't ready for this.

'Out now and fucking obs the bastard! I'll cover the exit.'

Acting automatically, I grabbed my radio from the dashboard and opened the door. I quickly circled our position on the map as I had been taught and then I was out, slamming the door behind me. Immediately the Widow accelerated away into the darkness.

I was left in the middle of the darkened slip road clutching my radio. The whole job was now resting on my shoulders. I suddenly wished I'd been on that training course. For the moment I was hidden from the lorry park by part of a low hedge that ran around the perimeter. But I couldn't see anything from where I was. I had to get closer. My first thought was that I would just walk openly across. But what was my excuse for that supposed to be? Where was I supposed to be walking to? My next thought was to crawl in through the bushes and get into a position from where I could see Van Hohn. But what happened if I was seen? That would really give the whole game away and a major drugs job would be down the drain!

A Kilo car cruised past me towards the services car park. It looked like Carnaby and one of the EOs called Ozzy. I realised that I had to do something, right now, even if it was wrong. Standing around like a complete twit doing nothing would be the most unforgivable of the various sins I might commit. Tucking my radio into the holster under my jacket, I tried to walk unobtrusively across the lorry park. I was barely halfway across before the radio started to slip out of its holster and I had to stoop slightly to rest it on my hip as I walked. To make matters worse, I was still in my pin-striped suit.

To any of the lorry drivers who caught sight of me, I must have looked like some sort of hunchbacked accountant.

I could see Van Hohn's car parked near the hedge to one side. I was close enough to hear the engine ticking as it cooled in the night air. But it was empty. Where was Van Hohn? Still walking, I glanced around as casually as possible, but I couldn't see any sign of him. There were two rows of heavy-goods lorries parked up for the night. I changed my course so that I could walk between them. All the cabs appeared to be empty, except for one or two where drawn curtains and chinks of light showed that the driver was bedding down.

Then I saw him standing between two of the vehicles. He was just a few feet away from me, looking up and talking to one of the drivers who was sitting in the cab. They were so intent on their conversation that neither of them even glanced at me. I knew that I couldn't afford to pause, but I managed to memorise the registration number of the lorry without staring or breaking step. With my heart thudding, I continued to walk along the line of vehicles towards the services building. This was my big moment. The meet had happened and I'd seen it!

Slightly dizzy with excitement, I reached under my jacket and pressed the transmit button on my radio. I called the Widow.

Nothing.

I called again.

Still nothing.

Running out of lorries to walk past, I prayed that no one was watching me and did my funky chicken act with my arm, banging the radio to try to improve the contact. Still nothing. I could hear the Widow calling me, so the set was receiving okay, but clearly it wasn't transmitting. I could hear one of the other Kilo vehicles asking who had been sent to keep an eye on Van Hohn. I was desperate. I had to let someone know about the lorry, but at the same time I had to keep an eye on both Van Hohn's car and the lorry in case either of them moved off again.

I had now come to the end of the line of HGVs and had run out of any sort of excuse for being there. Just to make my evening complete, it started to rain. Standing there in the middle of a lorry park in a sodden pin-striped suit with my damp hair plastered across my forehead, I was beginning to make the one-legged man in the arse-kicking contest look like Nijinsky.

I had to do something.

I decided that the most important thing was to let someone know about the lorry. I set off towards the car park, hoping to see the Citroën. If I couldn't get in touch by radio, I would have to find the Widow. But as I was walking back across the lorry park, I was plagued by doubts and I hesitated. Shouldn't I be watching Van Hohn and the driver? Suppose something was handed over? Was I supposed to be close enough to hear what they were saying? I had no idea how you get that close without being seen and if they did see me, how would I explain what I was doing there?

Standing there in the dark and rain not knowing what to do was just about the worst moment I had in the Division. It was my first live job with my new team and it felt like every decision I was making was the wrong one. Any moment now I was likely to blow the whole job.

Just then my radio spluttered into life again. It was Carnaby.

'Kilo 3, Kilo 6. Zulu 1 in contact with Dutch HGV. Driver, IC1, about forty, dark hair, six feet tall, fat, wearing a red and white checked lumberjack style shirt. Zulu 1 has just handed over a small package. HGV is a grey with red markings on the side. Blue cab. Registration number follows . . .'

I couldn't believe it. I looked around. Where the hell was he? I couldn't see him, but wherever he was he had made my role pretty redundant. The best thing I could do was get out of there. Feeling pretty hopeless, I trudged across the car park towards the main services building. I had to get back to my vehicle because Van Hohn or the lorry could be on the move again at any moment. I wandered round and round the car park, but in the rain and the dark, I couldn't find the Citroën anywhere. Eventually, I saw one of the Dover vehicles waiting in the filling station, probably preparing to make the long journey home. I asked if they could track down Kilo 3 for me. They looked at me like I was a pretty poor specimen and told me she was parked by the barrier at the illegal exit from the services.

When I got there I saw that she had chosen this spot because it was raised ground where the road led up to a bridge over the motorway. Normally this road was closed to all but police vehicles and motorway services traffic. Not only did this position give her an overall view of the car park, it improved the radio communications for everyone else as our car could act as a base station.

I climbed in. She was studying the local maps with a torch.

'Radio's dead,' I muttered, waiting for a stream of curses in my direction, but she just shrugged. I sat in the dark listening to the radio transmissions from various members of the team out on the ground and mentally calling myself all the names I thought the Widow was secretly calling me. Carnaby's voice crackled on the radio: 'Kilo 3, Zulu 2 appears to be locking up the HGV. Zulu 2 and Zulu 1 are heading for the car.'

'Looks like they're packing up for the night,' muttered the Widow. She took the handset from me.

'Kilo 5, go with the X-Ray 1, find out where they're bedding down. If it looks like another meet call for backup. All others hold your position. Kilo 3 has the eyeball.'

I listened to the commentary as the car with the Dutchman and the lorry left the services. Then the Widow started up the car and we headed out into the car park. She pulled into one of the ranks of cars from where we could clearly see the darkened cab of the HGV.

'Shouldn't we be keeping an eye on Van Hohn?' I asked

She didn't even look at me.

'According to the intelligence, Van Hohn's been organising a big cannabis deal. He never deals in anything under half a tonne, so my guess is that it must be on the lorry and now our priority is to stay with that lorry. If we lose Van Hohn, it's bad, but it doesn't matter too much. He'll be back on another day, another job. The main thing at this stage is not to lose the drugs. So we stay with the lorry. Just because those two have gone doesn't mean that someone else isn't going to turn up with some keys and drive it away, does it?'

I nodded.

'Right,' she said, 'you're the new boy, you get first watch for the night. If anything happens you don't understand, wake me,' And with that she got out of the car and climbed into the back. Within a few minutes, she was snoring gently.

She stirred briefly when her pager warbled. 'They're at a motel about five miles away,' she yawned. 'Pass the message.'

I did. At least I got that right. I heard the other mobiles close down for the night. I looked at my watch, it was about 1.30 a.m. I sat listening to a light drizzle pattering on to the roof of the car and the Widow's steady breathing behind me. I occasionally ran the engine to keep the windows from steaming up. I could have switched on the car radio for the comfort of a bit of late-night music – I would still have heard the car-to-car radio if anything had happened – but I didn't want anything to distract me. Keeping watch for the team while they slept was something I was determined not to muck up. Anyway, I couldn't have slept. There was enough adrenalin coursing through my system to keep me awake for a week.

The night wore on very, very slowly. Places like motorway service stations have a life-cycle all their own. I watched several cars full of late-nightclubbers turn up in a convoy, the bass beats of their stereos audible right across the car park. I'd forgotten it was the beginning of the weekend. I wondered idly what sort of drugs they had taken and whether the stuff we were intercepting would mean that they would go short next weekend. A fight broke out between the clubbers and some yobs wearing baseball hats who had arrived in another car. The police came, but by the time they arrived the fight was over and the people involved were long gone. I watched

62

the night staff at the services interviewed in the foyer and then saw them clean up the debris that was left behind.

At about five in the morning, one of the other cars took over from me. I got what sleep I could, hunched in the front passenger seat, but it was pretty fitful, and when I finally woke the pains in my back made me wish I hadn't bothered. However, the drug smugglers must have slept well. It was ten o'clock in the morning before the radios crackled into life with the surveillance team returning from the motel. I picked up my maps and pens from the dashboard and saw the Widow come running back from the services building where she'd been grabbing some breakfast.

The now familiar Dutch car came and pulled up in front of the lorry. The driver got out and swung straight up into his cab. This time I got a good look at him. The car roared off, the lorry followed. It swept past the petrol station at the exit where the Widow and I were parked at a pump and we followed it down the slip road on to the motorway. At suitable intervals, the rest of the Kilo vehicles fell in behind.

For several hours, we headed north. The HGV was slow, and strange as it may seem, this made it difficult to follow: people tend to notice if a string of cars are pottering along in the inside lane at a steady sixty miles an hour. It was completely different from the night before. We were forced to follow at a considerable distance, just keeping the HGV in view. One car would be sent far ahead out of sight of both the HGV and Van Hohn. If the tailing cars lost sight of the target, the car in front would ease back to confirm that it was still there.

However, the snail's pace of our progress did give us time to prepare. The Widow was now convinced that something big was going down. We were heading towards Manchester. It was possible we were going further, but the city's appetite for drugs is so huge that it was the most likely place. She phoned ahead to get help from the Division's office there and to see if they had any local intelligence about an importation. Manchester officers would be fresh and they would know the ground and the local operators far better than us.

As the morning wound on towards early afternoon and we entered the suburbs, five Manchester vehicles joined the convoy. Now we were in heavily built-up areas and the surveillance became far more tricky. We had to follow much more closely as the traffic thickened and that meant more frequent changes of the tailing car (known as the 'eyeball').

Finally, the HGV swung off a busy High Street and into a narrow side road. This led to an immense yard surrounded by warehouses and other derelict buildings. The Customs vehicles quickly split up to try to find all the exits. We soon discovered that there were at least five or six exits for vehicles, as well as several small alleys where someone could come or go on foot. It was as well we'd called for more help.

Once again the Widow told me to get out and try to get a sight of the activity in the main yard. This time I was better prepared. I'd used the time at the service station to change into scruffier clothes, and I found a corner of a building from which I was pretty well covered but could still see the lorry together with Van Hohn's car in the middle of the yard. Three men were standing by the lorry, deep in conversation. Two of them were Van Hohn and the lorry driver, but the other was new. The yard was busy but no one seemed to be paying them any particular attention.

Just as I was about to call in a description of the newcomer, one of the Manchester boys radioed a description from where he was. I'd done better than the night before, but I hadn't been fast enough. It quickly became clear that this officer must actually have been in the yard as he could hear what the smugglers were saying. Then I saw him standing by the corner of the HGV just out of sight of the three men. There was a fourth man on the far side of the yard, leaning against a wall and smoking. He was staring all about him and was almost certainly some sort of lookout. I radioed a warning to the Manchester officer who acknowledged it and took care to stay out of the lookout's line of vision. I admired his nerve for going that close. One sighting of him listening to the conversation and the whole job could have been over. The Widow called me back to the car and we found a spot in a nearby side road covering what seemed to be an exit from the yard. Now we had to wait and see if the drugs were going to be transferred here or whether this was just a temporary stop before the real destination.

The Manchester officer radioed that Van Hohn and the new-comer, who seemed to be local, were leaving to deal with the money. Van Hohn's car soon left the area at high speed. The Widow sent three of the Manchester vehicles after it. That left us a little short-handed to cover all the exits from the yard, but as far as we knew the drugs were still in the lorry and we had a good view of that.

Soon work started on the lorry. The rear doors were opened and fork-lifts removed most of the load which was then stacked nearby. Several youths clambered into the back of the lorry and when the Manchester officer next radioed in we could hear the sounds of hammering carrying over his radio. Now reports came from officers at other posts of one, two, then three transit vans coming into the yard and parking near the HGV. Word had obviously gone out that the gear had arrived.

The Widow had to think quickly. Once the drugs started coming out of the back of the lorry, the vans would leave as soon as they had their share. We had to get to the drugs before anyone left and preferably while it was all in one place. But if we struck too early, before the drugs were removed from their hiding place, we would leave the couriers with the defence that they thought they were collecting something other than drugs, such as tobacco. It was a defence that had been run time and again and a little patience now could save a lot of wasted effort in court later. On the other hand, we needed to move in and make the arrests quickly before the organisers returned. There was a considerable danger that on the journey back they would see one of the Customs vehicles and make a run for it: at best there could be an untidy high-speed pursuit across Manchester; at worst they might get clean away.

The Widow listened to commentary from the Manchester cars which were shadowing Van Hohn. They were at a house about half a mile away. She decided she could count on them being away for at least ten to fifteen minutes if we acted now. It was a small window of opportunity, but she decided it was enough.

The Manchester officer in the yard reported that packages were starting to come out of the back of the lorry. She took the radio handset from me: 'Kilo 3 to all mobiles, knock, knock, knock!'

It was the first time I had heard those famous code words spoken. We accelerated towards the exit we'd been covering. We had been parked just off the main High Street and I remember watching all the Saturday afternoon shoppers as we cut across the traffic, causing several cars to screech to a stop.

I remember seeing all the pedestrians' heads turning towards us in those few seconds as we raced towards the yard. I was thinking that a few weeks ago that would have been me, completely unaware of what was happening only a few yards away. Here we were charging in to arrest a group of drug smugglers who could be armed with anything – in a few moments there could be shooting or a chase through the shopping precinct, yet these people knew nothing about it. For a moment I felt strangely detached from normal activities like going shopping on a Saturday, as though I had become a character in some novel rather than part of the real world.

Then the Widow was cursing loudly yet again. What we had thought to be an entrance to the warehouse complex in fact ended in a brick wall six feet high at the back of the High Street shops. I jumped out and the Widow reversed at speed to find another entrance. Gallons of adrenalin gave me the power to haul myself to the top of the wall and I quickly looked round to get my bearings. I seemed to be at the back of a row of HGVs. I could see the target lorry in the centre of the yard and a variety of men, none of whom I recognised, running about. I couldn't tell who was Customs and who wasn't.

I dropped to the ground between the lorries and turned to see a tall man in a denim jacket running away from the yard. I was blocked in by an HGV on both the left and the right and he was coming right for me. I knew that it was my job to arrest him, but he was considerably taller and heavier than me and I couldn't see if he was armed. I caught sight of a pile of bricks and other rubble just behind me. There was a short length of metal railing poking out of the pile. I decided that if things got desperate that metal bar was going to be the first thing I'd reach for.

I held up my warrant card. I had no idea what I was supposed to say, but I had seen plenty of films, so I shouted, 'Customs and Excise! Stand where you are!'

'Oh fuck!' he replied in a broad Mancunian accent.

He hoisted his jacket far enough to show me the Customs ID hanging from his belt and then charged back to the yard. I raced after him. There hadn't been any shooting yet, but then for a cannabis load you wouldn't expect any. If this had been heroin or cocaine, however, it might have been different – the penalty for knowingly importing these drugs can be life, the same as it is for murder and then anything goes.

Looking quickly around the yard, I didn't see anyone who seemed in need of help. Most arrests had been made over by the lorry where a small crowd of officers including some of the Kilos was standing behind a line of five or six men who were spread-eagled against the side of the HGV.

In the centre of the yard, however, there was a small brick building. No one seemed to have been there yet and I followed the tall Manchester officer who was heading in that direction. To my complete surprise, it appeared to be some sort of café. All hell had broken loose outside and a number of men were sitting around with a variety of lunchtime fry-ups in front of them. Some of them hardly bothered to look up from their newspapers, but others stared at us defiantly as if they knew who we were. It was possible that any one of the gang could have ducked in here in the confusion. There were two of us to arrest about twenty of them. I wouldn't have known where to start. The cook stared at us over the griddle with a cigarette hanging out of the corner of his mouth. Fortunately the Manchester officer knew just what he was doing.

'All right, lads, Customs and Excise. You're all under arrest for the moment. Just sit quiet while we check out who everyone is.'

I waited for someone to make a run for it, but they mostly just sat back in surprise. Someone murmured 'Fucking hell', but otherwise there was just the hiss of the cooking and the sound of pop music from a radio. We went from one man to another asking why they were there and checking their documents. Three of them were clearly foreign truck drivers who weren't anything to do with our job. We 'un-arrested' them. But two of the others were just 'hanging around waiting for work'. This was too vague for safety and we sat them at a separate table where we could keep an eye on them. The cook kept protesting that no one had come running in during the last five minutes, but we didn't take his word for it.

The Widow walked in. After some fighting outside everything was under control except that the driver of the Dutch lorry had somehow got away in the confusion. All the buildings had been searched, but he seemed to have disappeared from the face of the planet.

The tall Mancunian I had been following was the senior officer with the local ID team. He and the Widow decided that we had to clear the yard for the return of the organisers. Those who had been arrested were piled into cars and taken away to custody offices at police stations that had been put on standby earlier. About a dozen of us remained in the café watching the lorry.

Sure enough, just ten minutes later, the target car came sweeping into the yard. Two men got out. For a moment they stood there looking around as if wondering where everyone had gone. We waited until they were clear of their car and heading towards the lorry, then four officers went out and walked up to them. There was no fuss, no cavalry charge as there had been earlier. In general, charges encourage suspects to make a run for it – at the time of a drugs delivery, members of a gang fear a rip-off by a rival gang almost as much as they fear the chance of arrest. With a calm, deliberate approach, suspects are often under arrest before they know what has happened.

Van Hohn spoke pretty good English. He kept insisting that he was a businessman and knew nothing about what was going on here. If only he'd known that we'd followed him the whole way. He had that surprise to come. The drugs were concealed beneath the floor of the trailer – almost a tonne of cannabis resin in small brown plastic-wrapped packages. They had been sealed under the floor with a layer of resin which explained all the hammering we had heard earlier. It was also one reason why the drugs dogs hadn't picked up the scent during inspections at Dover. The knock had been almost perfectly timed. According to the guys who got to the back of the lorry first, the men in the trailer had just broken into the concealment and were handing out the first of the drugs packages as they were arrested.

There was only one black spot in the afternoon. The lorry driver. We couldn't believe that he had got away and we all felt pretty bad about it. We arranged for the last of the suspects to be taken away for interview and one of the officers who was a trained HGV driver climbed up into the cab to drive the lorry away to a secure yard where the rest of the drugs could be removed.

As he climbed into the cab he heard snoring. He looked behind him and there in the bunk behind the driver's seat was the Dutch lorry driver, fast asleep! In all the excitement, no one had thought to check the back of the cab. It was a silly mistake, but when you have two teams from opposite ends of the country and a knock in a totally unknown place, these things happen.

The driver awoke to see about four grinning Customs officers staring down at him from the front of the cab.

'Bonjour, sunshine, vous êtes nicked,' Carl told him. I think he got the message.

The arrests didn't mark the end of the job. Even though we were all exhausted from the nervous strain of the surveillance and having been on duty almost continuously for about thirty hours, there was plenty of work to do. All the vehicles involved had to be taken to a secure compound. The lorry had to be taken to the nearest Queen's Warehouse so that the rest of the concealment could be opened and the large consignment of cannabis locked in a vault. Within a few days almost all of this would be destroyed in specially filtered furnaces at a secret location. Only a small amount would be retained as physical evidence for the courts.

All the suspects had to be taken to nearby police stations to be charged and interviewed. (At this time the ID didn't have custody facilities of its own and always had to rely on the police – heaven help you if you made a big arrest on a Friday or Saturday night as you could expect to be hanging around for several hours while a queue of arrested drunks and other assorted yobs were processed ahead of you.) Before the suspects could be interviewed and while we were waiting for their lawyers to arrive, it was necessary to choose interview teams and go through any property which had been in their possession so that they could be questioned about it. All this was in addition to the mountain of paperwork a large job like this generated.

I was chosen to assist with interviewing one of the men who had helped to cut open the floor of the lorry and unpack the drugs. The police computer had already revealed that he had a long criminal record of petty violence and vandalism, peppered with drugs offences. Since this was my first ever interview I wanted to get it right and spent some time going over the suspect's property. In particular there was a scrap of paper with some scribbled notes which appeared to be about the delivery and where it was to be taken to next. As this suspect had been caught red-handed, I was looking forward to hearing what he had to say about it all.

It was to be my first taste of how the criminal justice system really works in Britain. The man had been with his lawyer for about an hour, but as we impatiently paced up and down the corridor outside, it felt like longer. Every minute we waited made it more likely that others connected to the job would get away. The lawyer asked if some mugs of tea and some biscuits could be sent in and we waited another half-hour. He finally announced that his client was refreshed and ready to be interviewed.

His answer to all questions except a request for his name was a sneering 'No comment'. For evidential purposes, it was important to put every question to him and ask about every suspicious piece of paper found on him, even though he mechanically repeated 'No comment' to everything.

Despite the fact that I had been warned what to expect by some of the other Kilos, I was a little shocked. The fact that someone caught at the scene of the crime could simply refuse to say anything at all seemed completely wrong. It meant that there was almost no chance of catching the others involved in the importation. Even if we found out from other sources it would be far too late. And I was soon to learn that these were only the first steps in a system which allows the criminal to find out about the whole case against him whilst giving nothing away himself, so that he can either concoct a defence which has the best chance of clearing him or plead guilty at the last moment when there is no chance of escape – knowing that he has at least wasted as much time as possible. In later years, I would get so used to this charade that I never wasted too much effort on it and was surprised if a suspect ever said anything at all.

But what I found especially irritating was the lawyer's attitude. He sat there smugly through the whole thing with a half-smile on his face which seemed to say, 'I'm getting paid about five times what you guys get for risking your lives and all for telling this guy to say nothing – just to make your job as difficult as possible.' Even though I tried to tell myself he was just someone doing a job, it was hard not to hate him for it.

As we left the interview room the news arrived that the Kilos could head back for London: the job was being handed over to Manchester. It made perfect sense as the knock was on their patch and they would be best placed for all the court appearances and follow-up investigations. Even so, for once we knew a little bit of what Dover must have felt every time we 'nicked' one of their jobs.

As we trudged across the car park at the Customs offices to begin the long drive back to London, the Widow said, 'Sorry about that, Harry, I was going to make you case officer, but once Manchester asked for it, Don didn't really have a leg to stand on.'

So, despite my poor performance the night before, she was still prepared to give me a chance. I began to feel a lot better. Carl, who was walking just behind us, quickly cut me down to size again. 'Then thank fuck they gave it to Manchester,' he muttered just loud enough for me to hear.

The Manchester office did a good job. Some of the minor players got off on the grounds that they 'hadn't known drugs were involved' when they were told to turn up at the yard, but most of them were convicted at the trial about a year later, including Van Hohn and his contact, who got six years each. That sounds good, but with remission (which cuts the sentence in half) and time allowed for the period they had spent on remand, they were out again almost straight away. Intelligence later confirmed that Davies had been the main money man behind the importation, but there was never enough evidence from a cash deal like this to arrest him for it. At least we had the satisfaction of knowing that we had hurt him financially.

It was only a small consolation. According to the intelligence Danny was getting, his smuggling activities showed no signs of slowing down. And that was always the problem with Davies: his organisation was so large, how could we ever hope to stop him?

4

Case Officer

Back at home someone else wasn't going to forgive me in a hurry. For three years Nicky had been used to her career coming first. She didn't easily accept that working on the Division, especially on a referred team, meant that you couldn't reserve time off. If a job came up, you had to go out and cover it. I think she accepted this in theory, but the practice was something else.

The dinner party hadn't gone well. The children had got over-excited and played hell. There had been long, awkward silences as Nicky had repeatedly to dash off and deal with them or the dinner – hardly the powerful executive businesswoman image she was hoping to project.

She described the evening as a disaster and my feeble protests that people were used to this sort of thing happening fell on deaf ears – apparently none of the couples at the dinner had kids. We didn't have a major row, but this was the first sign that there might be trouble ahead.

Back in the office, it was one thing to declare Frank Davies a target, but it was going to be quite another to actually get evidence against him. When it came down to it, the best we could hope for was to chip away at Davies until a target team could take over or we got a lucky break which implicated Davies himself. As far as I was concerned at that time, all this was someone else's problem. Davies was an important target who required the attentions of an officer who knew about the cannabis business. I was quite busy enough just trying to survive on the team from day to day without making too many mistakes.

So it was quite a shock when the Widow came out of her weekly meeting with Don and threw an empty case folder at my desk.

'Don thinks it would be a useful exercise for you to work up the investigation on Davies,' she said matter-of-factly.

'But I don't know anything about him.'

'Look, you used to be an analyst, so bloody well analyse. You won't be short of material on a target like Davies. Besides, there's no one else – all the real officers are buried under existing casework.'

I looked across the office at the 'real' officers: Patrick was deep in his copy of the *Sun*. Carnaby and Ozzy were trying to organise a game of indoor cricket.

I looked at her helplessly.

'See these little boxes. Fill them in. Then in six months' time, come and bother me again.'

Her worries over *Kansas* were making her grumpier by the day. I looked down at the file in front of me. Official HMSO stamp. Drugs Case Control Folder. It looked as if the design hadn't changed since the 1920s.

I carefully filled in the name on the front of the folder in my best printing: 'Frank Davies'. So far, so good. I ran my eye down the rest of the page. Some of the boxes were straightforward: date of birth, middle names. But there were others I didn't understand. What the heck was a D111 check?

There was one box in the lower left-hand section of the cover framed with a heavy black line. It asked a simple question: 'Flagged at NCIS?' NCIS was the National Criminal Intelligence Service. This was a joint police and Customs organisation set up to pool intelligence, but also to register interest in major criminal targets in order to stop the two organisations tripping over each other as they have done on occasions in the past. Registering Davies would mean that he was my target. It would give me six months to come up with something before the flagging lapsed and anyone else could claim him. The chances of catching Davies were very slim, but I decided to go for broke and applied for the flagging.

Over the next three weeks, the checks began to trickle back. Electoral roll, electricity bills, company directorships, bank transactions, a list of the phones being called from his home address. Of course they were innocuous. What did I expect? Drugs cash would be filtered through off-shore accounts to which we didn't have access. All the money spent to support Davies' luxurious lifestyle would be in cash so there would be no trace of it in any UK bank account. As for running the organisation, he'd be using mobile phones, pagers, call-boxes and face-to-face meetings.

But he wasn't perfect. There would have been times when there had been an emergency or he had been too lazy to use his normal precautions. Somewhere in here would be the clues to his organisation, but it was going to take a lot of sifting to find them.

Days drifted into weeks, the weeks turned into a month, and although the files got thicker I wasn't making any substantive progress. I had more than enough other work. Slowly Davies began to slip further and further down my list of priorities.

Then on a rest day following a very dull all-night surveillance, I watched an old episode of *Dragnet* on afternoon television. Lantern-jawed men in immaculately pressed suits moved smartly from one clue to another, gradually closing in on the criminal mastermind. The clues were clear, their logic was sharp. This was how people always imagined criminal investigations should be. I decided to go back into the office the following day and give Davies one last thorough analysis. If nothing happened, then at least I could let the case lapse with a clear conscience.

The basic checks had yielded an avalanche of paper, much of which came from CEDRIC, the ID's central computer system. The sheer volume of small bits of seemingly disconnected information was bewildering. Davies owned property here, had been seen associating with a known criminal there, he had been spotted driving a car registered to someone else on such-and-such a date. There was even a report from Spanish police who had seen him at a hotel in Barcelona in the company of a known smuggler.

I took a large sheet of paper and put Frank's name at the middle of it. Then I began dividing the intelligence into different types: people, places, money. Slowly over the next few days I began to get an idea of the extent of his influence. Some names kept recurring. Frank clearly had a trusted lieutenant called Charlie Johnson, who ran an arcade near Hastings. Johnson also provided door security at some dodgy nightclubs. He had a string of convictions for violence and the photographs on file showed a big, shaven-headed bull of a man. Johnson had connections to half a dozen other characters who had records for burglary and violence. According to informant records, he could have a team of heavies ready to go with just a couple of phone calls.

Davies also used an electronics expert called Carpenter because he was paranoid about premises being bugged. Carpenter was an ex-telecoms engineer who hired himself out to various criminal gangs who wanted protection against electronic surveillance, and he was regularly called in to sweep Frank's house for electronic bugs. I added Carpenter's name together with his associated addresses and phones to the diagram.

Freight haulage clearly played a large part in Frank's organisation. Once or twice lorries carrying drugs had been stopped which had connections to companies Frank was involved with. But the drivers always took the blame and it was impossible to connect the smuggling with the directors. Frank made a lot of use of off-shore registration in the Isle of Man and Jersey and used proxy directors. His own name was never mentioned. It was always a mystery to me why the islands never clamped down on this abuse.

Although Frank's base was in the south-east, he seemed to have contacts all over the country, including Liverpool and Manchester. The problem was trying to isolate which people were one-time deals and which were his regular contacts. If you spent long enough tracing names and their associations on the computer, it began to seem like every criminal in Britain knew every other one. In a way I had almost too much information.

Danny, our dedicated intelligence branch officer, helped out and frequently came up with good suggestions about where we might try to break into the circle of Davies' contacts. But he was also mildly amused at the idea that I was trying to form a case against an experienced villain like Davies.

In films, the cop always cracks the case by going and sitting outside the chief suspect's house, following him and learning some vital piece of information. In desperation I even tried this. I didn't expect any great breakthrough, but at the very least I thought I might get a feel for Frank, the way he acted, the places he went. So on a couple of my off-duty nights I actually drove over there and parked up in the lay-by which Carnaby had showed me. I didn't tell anyone because strictly speaking it wasn't allowed – too dangerous without backup. But it was a quiet country lane and hardly anything drove past. With the binoculars I had a good view of the house and the yard. I wasn't going to be stupid enough to follow Frank, but I did hope that I might get the registration number of someone attending a meeting at the house.

I was able to add a few more car numbers to my ever-growing list and I saw more of other members of the Davies family, Frank's wife and his overweight, double-chinned son who on our target list was officially known as 'Zulu 4', but whom the team promptly christened 'Lard Boy'. Apart from uncomfortable evenings slumped in a car and more late returns home which annoyed Nicky, I added nothing of real value to the case. As other work crowded in, Davies began to drift down the list again.

But even though I wasn't making much visible progress with Davies, it was during this period that I experienced the first inkling of how it felt when a job goes right, and the first glimmerings of acceptance by the rest of the team.

The Bravo and Charlie target teams were running a case which had implicated a well-known criminal. Intelligence indicated that he was going to make an important new contact that day and it was absolutely vital that the team went with him, but they were having trouble fielding enough bodies and so had asked the Kilos to supply a car and two officers. The Kilos were equally hard pressed, but target team work always took priority wherever possible, so an EO called Jimmy and I were teamed together for the first time. He would drive, I would be his navigator.

Like all target teams, the 'Bs and Cs' were a pretty close-knit bunch. They were out on surveillance almost every day. They had got used to each other's style of working. They knew which members of their team were the best drivers and best footmen. They counted on each other and they didn't take easily to strangers. Each day that they followed one of their targets raised the stakes for failure a little higher – it was another day of work which would be all for nothing if they 'showed out'. So, when we were detailed to assist them for a day or two, the job for Jimmy and myself was simple. We were just there to make up the numbers. We were to stay at the back of the 'caravan' and only move up when we were told to do so – which would probably be never.

For me, the good thing about Jimmy was that he was just about the most relaxed member of the team. He was a young Irish officer who already had several years' experience of the job and was an outstanding footman. He would later go on to become one of the Division's leading intelligence officers. But his real strength was that he was one of those people who get along with almost everyone. There was no chip on his shoulder about where I'd come from – at least if there was he masked it well. That morning he acted as though we'd been working together for years, didn't question my calls and even asked for my advice. By the time we'd been on surveillance for the first few hours, my confidence was sky-high.

The target was a small-time boxing promoter who was known to be heavily into drugs as a sideline. His boxing connections gave him access to a ready supply of minders. He always used a chauffeur and often took precautions against being followed – not because he expected Customs, it could just have easily been police, Inland Revenue or worse still, some of his 'competitors'.

The tail had gone routinely for several hours as the target made several calls around town. Every time he stopped we would 'ground' him (a technical term meaning that one officer covers the target while the other vehicles cover all the possible exits), then sit and wait. When he moved off we picked him up again. Simple. But he still hadn't made the new contact the 'Bs and Cs' really wanted and there was a lot of pressure to stay with him.

We were in North London. There were roadworks in a busy High Street. It seemed as though the traffic was snarled up for miles in all directions. Either as a result of lack of attention or just plain bad luck, the surveillance team had got strung out behind the target with no one on a parallel route as a safeguard, which would have been our normal practice. Jimmy and I were at the back of the 'caravan', with me studiously plotting our progress on the laminated maps.

The radio crackled into life. 'Charlie 5, Charlie 5, X-Ray 12 through lights at Green two seven. Charlie 5 is baulked. Any mobile on an alternative?'

'Bravo 10, no, no.'

'Charlie 7, no, no.'

'Charlie 2, no, no.'

I was staring at the map. X-Ray 12 was the code word for the target vehicle. I could clearly see the green dot marked 27. Looking at the map, I could see where the target was heading. The other vehicles were caught in the queue with heavy traffic both ways so they couldn't force their way into side streets. We had just entered the High Street but were adjacent to a side road which led into a maze of other little streets on an estate. I'd worked on a job in the same area for another team only the previous week and although on the map it looked as though there was no way out of the estate, I knew that it was possible to drive over some derelict land to get out

79

the other side. I quickly ran my pen through the maze to the point where the target must come out.

'I think we can do it.'

Jimmy, who had been fiddling with the cassette player, glanced at me and then down at the map. 'Are you sure?'

'I think we've got a good chance – he's got to be making for this dual carriageway.'

Jimmy slammed the car into gear and gunned the engine. 'Good enough for me. Call it!'

I grabbed the handset and braced myself against the door as we swerved sideways into a side road. Jimmy leant on the car horn to scatter pedestrians. Someone banged on the roof of the car and shouted as we pushed our way through.

'Kilo 14. Attempting nine nine.'

For the first time, despite the adrenalin, I actually managed to sound calm.

Driving through a heavily built-up area at speed requires really close co-operation. Both driver and navigator have to be looking for possible hazards. It only takes one kid to step out from behind a parked car for the whole thing to end in tragedy. When driving at high speeds, the driver only has time to glance, and at every junction the navigator's job is to check traffic coming from the left and call 'Clear' if he thinks it's safe.

We swung left and right a dozen times through the little side streets. The tyres screeched and the engine roared. We hardly left second gear during the whole trip, but it was ninety-degree turn after ninety-degree turn and we couldn't let up.

Then I missed a turn and we swung into a dead end.

A few weeks earlier, I would have panicked, but not this time. 'Missed one. Back her up,' I said.

The car screeched to a halt and Jimmy swung round in his seat as he reversed the car at high speed. He hit the horn as he swung backwards to warn an oncoming car and then we were off again with only a few seconds lost.

Every officer of any law enforcement service who has been in a car chase or on high-speed surveillance will know what we were feeling. Some civilians call it 'red mist', a single-minded determination to get the target at any cost. But it's not that. The exhilaration comes from working so hard and at such speed, but still getting it right. It is like scoring a winning goal or hitting a six. We had all been on surveillance so many times when it went wrong, but there are also certain days when you can feel that you are getting it right. You see everything clearly, almost in slow motion. No waffle, no wasted energy, everything just sharp, sharp, sharp.

We burst out on to the dual carriageway about two hundred metres from traffic lights at a junction. The lights were just changing, but I caught sight of a flash of white which I knew was the rear end of the target car as it turned right.

'Kilo 14, White five two, X-Ray 12 turning two three at lights.'

The target car disappeared round the bend. We were blocked by the traffic queue ahead, which was slowing down and stopping as the lights changed.

'Kilo 14, no longer nine nine.'

And I thought that was it.

'Stay with him, Kilos, this is Charlie 2 making ground.'

That command was effectively our clearance to try anything we could. Jimmy glanced over at me. The target was out of sight, we could take the risk. I knew what was on his mind.

'Do it.'

Barely slowing, Jimmy swung the car across the kerb of the central reservation. If we'd been any closer to the lights, steel barriers would have stopped us. There was a huge bang as we crashed over the kerb and then we were racing down the carriageway on the wrong side of the road. Jimmy was concentrating on making the turn ahead without rolling the car or losing it in a skid. I was concentrating on the cross traffic. We both knew the lights must be changing to green.

81

'Still clear.'

'Still clear.'

'Here they come!'

Jimmy could have chickened out right there. He could have simply pulled off the road and given up. It might have left us on the wrong side of the road looking like a couple of prats, but at least we would have been safe. Instead he went for it. He swerved across the junction just as the cross traffic moved off and we hurtled off on to the road the target had taken.

'Yes, yes, yes!' Jimmy was thumping the steering wheel with the sheer exhilaration of having made it. It was a fantastic piece of driving.

'Kilo 14, *nine nine*,' I radioed, emphasising those crucial code numbers which meant the whole day hadn't been wasted.

That was the point about surveillance driving: much of the time it was fairly routine – you drove fast, but you didn't take unnecessary risks. This was one of those few occasions when we had decided to gamble. It was a decision only the guys in the car could make. There was no management to advise you (although they would certainly have taken an interest if we had got it wrong). When a decision worked, there was almost no better feeling in the world.

Within a minute we caught sight of the target car rounding a bend ahead of us and we eased off. We were stuck with the tail for the next ten minutes as the rest of the team tried to make ground through the heavy traffic. That was the trouble with London – once you got detached from a surveillance, you were really detached.

The target led us far out into the countryside. Car surveillance in rural areas is a completely different game from surveillance in town. There the heavy traffic helps to act as camouflage and the tail has to stay pretty close because of the danger of losing the target. Out in the country, there are fewer chances for the target to lose the tail, but it is easier for the surveillance vehicles to 'show out' and they have to stay further back. Parallel routes are also harder to find than in urban areas. The technique for following in a rural area is known as 'peeping', which means just being able to see the tail of the target vehicle as it goes around bends ahead, but not so close that the target can see you in the rear-view mirror. It requires complete concentration and a very fine judgement of distance, but that afternoon we could do no wrong.

The rest of the team had almost caught up with us when the target turned into what appeared to be a new housing development – so recent that it wasn't on our maps. Jimmy turned into the estate and we actually passed the target vehicle a few moments later. Our man was still in it making a call on his mobile phone. Jimmy dropped me round the corner and I walked back to keep watch. I was in luck because there was a bus shelter just across the road. I was able to stand there and cover the target while the rest of the team moved into position.

Finally our man climbed out of the back of the car, crossed the road past me, walked up to a very expensive detached house with a double garage, and went inside. It looked as though we had found the new contact.

The surveillance commander called us out and once again we were reduced to being 'tail-end charlies'. But we didn't care. The main thing was that we hadn't dropped the ball when it mattered. The target team was pretty generous and sent a note to Don thanking us for a good job. It was the first time I stood down from a surveillance feeling that I'd done a proper day's work rather than just being a passenger. Perhaps I really was becoming part of the Kilos.

But it wasn't all glory.

The following week we were asked to work with one of the Regional Crime Squads (RCS). They had received a tip-off from one of their informants about a load of cannabis coming through Dover in a French-registered lorry. Since it was an importation, strictly speaking it was a Customs job, but because it was police information, it was agreed to run the surveillance jointly and the police would carry out the actual knock.

Of course, this wasn't just altruism. There were several advantages for the local RCS in sharing the job with the Kilos: in the first place, the drugs were coming through Dover and no one knew the ferry port as well as us. We worked it all the time, we knew the best places to watch from, and inside the port we had access to all the security cameras. We also knew the places where any counter-surveillance by the smugglers might be taking place. Another consideration was that if the RCS lost the tail and therefore the drugs, there would have been some very serious questions asked, possibly at a ministerial level. Sharing the job not only made a loss less likely by providing extra experienced troops, it also covered everyone's back if there was a disaster.

Co-operation between Customs and the police wasn't always this good. The RCS which covered our area was number 9. They were a good bunch of officers and we had a good relationship with them. Because of the autonomy enjoyed by regional police forces elsewhere in the country this wasn't always the case, and relations could often become strained when police discovered a massive consignment of drugs after a 'routine traffic stop' when the drugs had clearly just been smuggled into the country and the police had known about it all the time. The problem was that the police had the best street-level informants, but it was Customs who had the responsibility for intercepting the drugs as they came into the country.

That particular evening, we picked the lorry up coming off the ferry and followed it through the Customs checks. A uniformed officer at inbound control gave us a description of the driver. The lorry went straight through the port without the driver making any contact. Elsewhere members of the joint team were sweeping the likely lookout points for anyone who was parked up watching for surveillance.

I was with a female RCS detective constable. On one of these sweeps we spotted a suspicious vehicle parked in a lay-by at the top of Jubilee Way, the road which leads down over the flyover directly into the ferry terminal. There was nothing obviously wrong with the car, but we both agreed that something was not quite right. The constable went out on foot, choosing a route which meant that she could approach the car from behind. I drove around to the far side of the lay-by to pick her up.

'He's got a radio scanner on the seat next to him,' she said, climbing into the car. 'He's not even trying to hide it.'

She had memorised the number plate and I dropped her off at a call-box so that she could check it on the police database. It didn't trace as suspicious but that was no real surprise; the gang wouldn't take the risk of using a known or stolen car on a job like this. We warned the rest of the team that someone was monitoring airwaves.

We kept an eye on our friend with the scanner, but after half an hour he appeared to be satisfied and left the area. In the dark there was no hope of getting any photographs of him as evidence and we just didn't have enough vehicles to risk following him as well as the lorry. So, reluctantly, we had to let him go and hope that we could trace the car later.

The surveillance of the lorry itself was actually very dull. He plodded up the A2 and on to the M25 at a steady sixty miles an hour, with us strung out behind him. By the time we were on the M25, my vehicle was eyeball. At about midnight it began to rain and soon it was tipping down like a monsoon and we were forced to drive ever closer to the target lorry to keep it in sight.

On surveillance in the dark all you are really doing is following a set of tail-lights. This is how even a target as big as a lorry can get lost if you stay too far back. Visibility becomes poor, you mistake one set of tail-lights for a moment, and then ten minutes later find out that you have been following the wrong vehicle.

I also knew from my limited experience that these conditions were difficult for vehicles at the rear of the tail. In the rain and the dark, it's hard to estimate how far you are from the target unless you have constant updates. Radio transmissions are not always reliable at a distance and it is very easy to lose all contact with the eyeball vehicle if the target suddenly leaves the motorway.

Since we had the RCS with us, I wanted to turn in a good performance as the commentator. Every few minutes I radioed: 'Kilo 17, nine nine. X-Ray 1 sierra sixty. Junction Two [or whatever] now three miles.'

I thought that this was pretty good and that everyone would know exactly what their spacing was and where the target was.

We came off the M25 and down the A13. The lorry went to a warehouse facility and parked in a large car park. A car came and picked up the driver. The team vehicles went to ready positions and waited. Eventually a call came through to say that the RCS team for the knock was in position and we could stand down.

We left the RCS behind and the Kilos all met up in front of an all-night burger stand well away from the scene. I was feeling pretty pleased with myself. Everything had gone well even though I had been paired with an unfamiliar driver, and after the previous week's success with Jimmy I felt that I was beginning to get the hang of surveillance. Carl gestured to me and I followed him over to one of the vehicles. By chance, we had none of the HEOs out with us and he was the senior officer on the ground that night. He turned round suddenly and put his face close to mine:

'What the fuck was all that noise about?' he hissed angrily.

'Noise?'

'Radio calls every ten seconds about every bloody thing you could think of!'

'Reassurance calls,' I explained, mentioning the conditions and the speed of the tail.

'Listen to me,' he said menacingly, waving a finger under my nose, 'we don't need "reassurance calls". Some of us do this for a fucking living. You showed us up in front of another team and what's worse, a team that isn't even ID. In future, keep your fucking mouth shut unless or until something happens.'

As he strode back to the burger van, I could see that several of the team were watching, and from their faces they clearly agreed with Carl.

I don't know if it was tiredness (I'd been out three nights in a row) or whether it was just the shock of coming from a high to a sudden low, but I felt devastated. I think if I'd been given the chance to quit right there and then I would have taken it. The drive home was very long and lonely that night.

However, the Widow had the last word on the subject.

Late one evening about a week later when there was no one else in the office, Ozzy came and sat on the edge of my desk. I got on all right with Ozzy. Like Jimmy, he was easy-going, one of those people every team needs to make sure some of the less forgiving characters can work together.

'I hear you really fucked up the other night,' he grinned.

'Thanks a lot,' I replied.

'Carl had a go at you, did he?'

I shrugged.

'He can be a right wanker sometimes.'

I liked Ozzy better and better. We sat in silence for a while.

'Anyway, you haven't heard the best bit. Someone must have told the Widow what happened in the morning meeting today because she came straight out of it, walks right up to his desk and tells him in front of the whole office that the only person who tells you when you've fucked up is her and if he goes over her head again she'll hand him his balls on a tea tray.'

He was still chuckling as he wandered back to his desk.

I felt better that the Widow had stuck up for me, but I knew deep down that Carl had been right.

This was about my lowest point. Despite one or two small successes and the friendship of some good people, I still didn't feel part of the team. First there was the fact that the case against Davies was going nowhere. Then there was the conflict with Carl.

And there was the constant friction at home. Nicky thought I wasn't supporting her enough with the children: I was never there to collect them from the nanny, never there to look after them if they were sick, never there to cover when she had to go on a trip abroad. She thought that I had lost interest in them.

In fact the opposite was the case. I had looked after them for almost three years. I missed them very much. No one else on the team seemed to have the same problem. Almost all of them were either divorced or single.

The first real crisis came one Saturday evening. Nicky had arranged a surprise birthday party for her father at an expensive restaurant in a fairly central location for all the relations who were attending but a long way from where we lived.

Late on Friday evening Ozzy, who was one of the on-call officers that weekend, begged me to swap duties with him, and in the end, I agreed. I knew it was stupid, but I had plenty of good reasons: in the first place, Ozzy was a good friend. He was one of the few people who hadn't given me a lot of grief since joining the team and I wanted to help him out. In the second place, I thought I could swap the duty with someone else before leaving that evening and even if I couldn't, things had been so quiet that there was very little chance we would be called out.

But of course I couldn't swap the duty and as we were driving to the restaurant, my pager went off.

'What the hell is that?' demanded Nicky as it warbled away.

I pulled the car over to the side and rang the Widow. There was no way out. She needed every available body following the discovery of almost a tonne of cannabis hidden in a refuse lorry.

I quickly explained to Nicky that it was an emergency, but she was quite rightly furious. We were only a mile or so from the restaurant, but she would have to get a lift home. Only the fact that the kids were in the back of the car stopped a full-scale shouting match there and then. But it had been brewing for some time and the next morning we had a major row.

Whilst parked in a car on surveillance a few nights later, I told Ozzy all about it. He apologised for causing the trouble, but I quickly told him it wasn't his fault – it was definitely mine.

'She doesn't seem to understand that I can't just make room for her and the family every time I feel like it. I was in the wrong this time, but there have been plenty of other occasions when it wasn't my fault. She just doesn't understand the job.'

'Yeah, I know exactly what you mean,' said Ozzy sympathetically as he tilted back his seat in preparation for another snooze. 'That's just the way it was before my divorce.'

That worried me. I sat in the dark for the rest of the evening and tried to work out how serious things were getting. I decided I was going to have to make more time for Nicky. It might mean losing brownie points on the team, but I didn't want our marriage to end up as another statistic.

All these things might not have been so bad if I could at least have made some progress against Davies.

One night, the Widow and I were stuck in an empty flat keeping watch on a premises for a Branch 2 target team. A gang had spent some weeks in an industrial unit, building a drugs concealment into a freight container. It wasn't due to be collected for several days, but it was important that it was watched day and night in case the container was collected early and disappeared. Our job was simply to call the target team out if there was any sign that the container was about to move.

For once, despite the cold and the boredom of the OP, the Widow seemed to be in a good mood, and we talked about the Davies case. I told her that I felt I should be doing better.

'It's my first job. Rick said it the other day – you couldn't ask for an easier target than Davies. Everyone knows what he's up to. I can't understand why we can't stop him.'

'Don't knock yourself out about it. You'll be okay.' The flat was in darkness, but I could just about make her out. She had her seat tilted right back and her feet propped up on the window ledge. She was sipping coffee.

'Don't kid yourself that he's easy, Harry. Ever wondered why a target team hasn't taken him on yet? Target teams do one of the hardest jobs in the world. Surveillance practically twenty-four/ seven. Bugging devices, telephone taps, the whole show. And how many jobs can a target team take on in a year? Three, maybe four. Now look at the number of major criminals in the country. You think it's bad down here? Wait till you start working in Manchester, Leeds, Liverpool. Davies is the big fish on our patch, but he's almost too big. If the Bravos and Charlies get a lead they'll take him, but otherwise it could tie down all their resources for at least a year before they're able to pin him to anything. That sort of thing doesn't look good on the annual performance figures.

'Each year, the management raise the targets to show govern-ment how good we are – the amount of drugs seized, the number of criminal organisations broken up, the amount of drugs prevented – the figures always rise. So it stands to reason you can't spend all of a team's resources on one target. You need nice middle-sized gangs to keep the hit rate ticking over. As for the big criminals, you wait. Eventually you get a good informant or a nice piece of intelligence and then you take them down.

'The reason we're looking at Frank Davies is precisely because he is such a tough nut to crack. All you can do is wait, Harry. Something will happen sooner or later. Then we'll have him.'

She was almost prophetic. Just three weeks later the break finally came. And it all happened thanks to a couple of stupid mules.

5

The Chancers

Mules come in many shapes and sizes. To a Customs officer a mule is any one of the low-level smugglers involved in transporting drugs for one of the big gangs, from stuffers and swallowers who actually carry the drugs in their bodies to the haulage drivers who bring a few extra boxes over in their lorries on the cross-Channel ferries.

They get paid a pittance – a few thousand pounds, if they're lucky, more often a few hundred. Some do it for a tiny share of the drugs in order to feed their own habit. They take all the risks. But the profits for the organisers are huge (in 1999 it was estimated that illegal importation of drugs accounted for a turnover of more than £20 *billion* per year). Many of them are caught, but the organisers aren't bothered as long as the mule keeps his or her mouth shut. They persuade the unfortunate mule to do this by a combination of threats if they talk, promises to look after their families if they don't, and the old criminal's code of not being a 'grass'. The gangs are assisted in this, knowingly or unknowingly, by defence lawyers who often prevent Customs and police from developing the case by advising the mules to say nothing during interviews.

Many of the mules are addicts, but even those that aren't are, for whatever reason, often desperately in need of money. The two mules who were to give us our first real break against Davies were neither, but they were young and greedy and that was enough to drag them in.

Bob Pearson (the ex-SAS sergeant) and I had just returned from six weeks on what was probably the strangest BITs (Basic Investigation Techniques) course that the ID had ever conducted. I had now been with the Kilos for eight months and in the short time since I had joined, the Division had been conducting an experiment to widen their recruitment range. They had attracted a number of people from industry, including some with banking or accounting experience. This was in part because an increasing amount of the work in tracking down a smuggling gang meant tracing the drugs money and the front companies used to launder it, rather than the old tactic of keeping the gang under surveillance until it finally made an importation. A number of armed forces personnel had also been recruited following the success of Bob Pearson's transfer from the SAS. I was still the only direct-entrant HEO, but at least I didn't feel quite so unusual any more.

Bob and I had got along well once I had managed to explain to him that there was no secret MI6 plot against Customs and that he could stop trying to break my arm. He had explained that his recruitment by the ID was part of a new policy for the SAS. Finding work for soldiers leaving the Regiment was an ever-increasing problem. Most were only in their forties and had a range of specialist skills such as close surveillance, which could be very useful in the right job. The ID and the war against drugs seemed like the perfect opportunity and so, as an experiment, six soldiers due for retirement were to join the Division. Bob was the first to arrive.

Bob was as concerned as I was that we had ended up on the same team and we both carried out enquiries through old friends to find out why. At the end of the day it just appeared to be an enormous cock-up. Jack hadn't been told that Bob was on the team when he placed me there and the personnel department of MI6 wasn't even aware that the SAS were sending men to the Division. As for the photograph of me with the kids, I finally found out that an old friend of mine had sent it to personnel to be added to my file because he thought he was doing me a favour. God save us from our friends.

Much of the training on a BITs course is based on role-playing – arrest and search incidents are played out as if for real, often on the streets of towns along the south coast. Bob's presence, together with that of other ex-soldiers, had made the course a surprising experience for several role-players who are often told to 'resist arrest'. As you may have heard, the SAS do not muck about and the experience of making a civilian arrest was something new and strange to them. One role-player 'resisting arrest' outside Dover railway station found himself thrown ten feet through the air on to the roof of a nearby taxi. After X-rays it was discovered that his arm wasn't broken but it was a close-run thing. On a later exercise, another role-player tried to escape from a knock by running away through woodland. He clearly didn't hear the heavy feet running close behind him as Bob overtook him, placed a hand in the small of his back and ran him into a tree. When he recovered consciousness about ten minutes later he still didn't know what had happened.

The biggest shock was for the role-player who pulled a gun on a team during a house-search exercise. He had played this trick on the same exercise every year and he was used to trainees nervously backing away and letting him make his escape. This time he found himself suddenly pounded into the ground by representatives of the SAS, the Royal Green Jackets and the Parachute Regiment. The course leaders heard him scream from two streets away.

It wasn't all fun and physical violence on the course. Although the ex-military types excelled at the physical exercises, tests requiring accounting or legal skills were often more problematic. I still remember three burly ex-soldiers sitting around a table late into the night arguing about how to work out a VAT bill. For me, the biggest problem was surveillance. A surveillance team following a target on foot can be almost any size depending on the awareness level of the target, but the basic system for any size of surveillance is based upon a team of three officers usually designated as A, B and C – the 'eyeball', backup to the eyeball and the 'floater'. As the target moves around, the three officers constantly change positions within the system. It sounds almost too simple, but it has proved its worth through real surveillance over decades and I have seen it used by all organisations including the Security Service and the FBI. It requires really close co-operation between the three officers, and teams which have worked together for a long time develop an anticipation of one another's moves which is almost psychic.

Like surveillance driving, foot surveillance is an essential skill which all officers must learn to a high degree or they might as well quit the Division. But after years of training in how to detect surveillance I found it almost impossible to follow someone without the fear that I was 'showing out'. As a consequence I was always too far from the target, managing to miss almost every encounter and failing to gel with the rest of my three-person team. At other times I would be so anxious to make up for earlier mistakes that I would get too close to the target and I was spotted time after time. It was getting to be a serious problem and I began to worry that I was going to fail the course when I met my salvation in the form of Pete, a five-foot six-inch, eighteen-stone bundle of fun who was one of the cocaine target team's top surveillance officers. He had once managed to sit right next to a cocaine cartel meeting in a hotel despite them being on the lookout for Customs surveillance. He was so good that even at their trial they were still refusing to believe that he had been there.

One night at the bar I poured out my troubles to him.

'Look,' he said, 'it's simple. Everyone has a natural distance at which they look for surveillance. They rule out everything that's too far away, but they also filter out everything that's too close.' He moved about ten feet away. 'You see, at this distance you're quite happy to clock me, yeah? But,' he moved up to stand next to me, almost peering up my right nostril, 'what about now?' He raised his eyebrows suggestively until I cracked up. He was absolutely right and although it took me a while to learn, that one-minute lecture probably saved my career as a surveillance officer.

He also told me not to worry about the constant ribbing and hostility I was getting from some officers.

'So what? You think you've got it bad? When I joined I had years of it. Guess what it is was with me?'

'Your hairstyle?' I ventured

He put me into an arm-lock.

'Your weight, your weight!' I yelped.

'Exactly. I'll tell you the sort of thing they did. You know what I hate? Spiders. Can't stand the bastards. So one day, we have to search this freighter carrying bananas up from South America. They often hide packets of cocaine in the refrigeration system and some poor bastard has to crawl through the air ducts to search them. They gave me the job knowing what I was likely to find. Sure enough, I was squeezing through these ventilation ducts with a torch held between my teeth because there was no room to move my arms, when I came to a corner and there, not three inches from my face, was the biggest fucking tarantula you've seen in your life. Of course it was dead, but I didn't know that. So I started yelling and wriggling to get back out of there, but my bouncing around in the duct is just bouncing this bloody thing closer to me. So I start panicking, and do you know what those bastards did? They screwed the cover back on to the opening of the shaft so that I couldn't get out. In the end I had to kick my way out and I was fined £600 for damage to the coolant system of the ship.'

After hearing that I didn't feel so bad, and somehow managed to squeeze through the rest of the surveillance section of the course. But it was clear that if I wanted to pass my probationary period successfully I was going to have to work harder. All thought of working for a target team in the near future went right out of the window.

Bob and I had just returned from the course and we were getting ready to go out and assist another team when Don called me in to his office.

'Tony Graves on the Intel team down at Newhaven says he's got a rhib you might be interested in. It's linked with a car which is down to you on CEDRIC or something. It doesn't sound too promising, but check it out when you get a moment.'

A 'rhib' is a rigid hulled inflatable boat – a high-powered motorboat with a solid hull and an inflatable rubber tube around the sides to aid buoyancy. You often see the commandos and special forces roaring around in them in films.

They are also very popular with a certain breed of smuggler. With two big outboard motors on the back they can reach tremendous speeds, making them almost impossible to catch unless you can ambush them as they are dropping the drugs off. They have a very low profile which makes them difficult to pick up on radar. They are highly mobile because you can simply load them on to a trailer behind a car and launch them from almost anywhere.

Their heyday was the 1970s when importation of drugs first became a serious problem. The short distance across the Channel meant they were perfect for running small to medium-size loads into secluded beaches and inlets. Some smugglers ran them as far up the coast as Holland. Don himself had spent several years as a junior officer trying to catch a rhib pilot known as 'the Dutchman'. The fact that the boat could be launched from almost anywhere made him almost impossible to catch. Eventually, greed put an end to the Dutchman's run of luck. He tried one run in fog and was believed either to have hit or been hit by something in mid-Channel. His body was found some weeks later.

But gradually Customs learnt how to counter the small boats. Customs cutters and coastguard stations received improved radar which could detect them more easily. On land a 'Rhib Watch' scheme was set up whereby any movement of these boats by land was logged by Customs, police or coastguard and the registration number of the vehicles towing them logged and checked. If the checks raised suspicions, an investigation could be launched. These days rhibs were mainly used to collect drugs from yachts which could lie off-shore or from buoys where the yacht had left the drugs for later collection, a process known as 'coopering' since the days when smugglers used wooden barrels as floats for smuggled goods left in the water by their French contacts.

It certainly wasn't Davies' style. Like most of the big importers, he had learnt that his best chance was in getting big loads through a major port using the busy freight or passenger traffic. Besides that, Newhaven was a quiet little ferry port with only some minor tourist trade to Dieppe. Although it was on Davies' patch, it hardly supplied the weight of traffic which he normally needed, as at Dover, Sheerness or Harwich.

So it was without much enthusiasm that I picked up the phone a few days later to ring Graves. I still thought my best chance was an Intel team at one of the major ports. Newhaven was the Customs equivalent of Sleepy Hollow. I looked them up in the organisation book. The intelligence team consisted of just two men. It didn't sound like the sort of group who could crack the Davies operation.

But Tony Graves had a very interesting story to tell. About a month before, two youths had gone into a local boat yard. They said they wanted to buy a rhib but didn't appear to know anything about them. They had also wanted the fastest one in the yard. That wasn't so strange. There are plenty of youths who come into a bit of money, either legally or illegally, and who want to splash out on a fast car or a boat. The boat yard was quite happy to take their money. It was when they paid the full amount in cash that alarm bells started ringing.

Suspicions increased when the pair asked if the red and green navigation lights could be removed before they collected it. It was pointed out that the lights were there for safety and without them, they risked being in collision with another vessel, but the pair simply said it wouldn't be a problem. It now seemed to the manager of the yard that one of the pair wasn't saying very much, so he deliberately asked him a few questions. When the second youth answered in a thick Irish accent it was all the manager could do to stop himself dashing into the back of the shop and calling the police there and then.

As soon as they drove away, he carefully wrote down the registration number of their car and phoned the local police. Once he mentioned the Irish accent, his information was quickly passed on to Special Branch.

But after a short investigation, Special Branch decided there was no IRA connection. At this point the information was very nearly lost completely, but one of the Special Branch officers who had worked with Customs before thought that there might be a drugs connection and passed the information to Newhaven Intelligence Team. They had run checks on the youths which came back no trace. But the vehicle they had been driving was listed on CEDRIC as one which had been seen at Frank Davies' farm.

It still didn't sound like Davies' style. My first thought was that one of the youths might be Lard Boy, but they were both described as 'slim', and even in a dark workshop there was no way you would describe him as that. Still, it was a possible lead, and the following week I drove down to Newhaven to check it out.

The Customs offices at Newhaven are housed in a modern block near the railway station and the intelligence team worked from one tiny room. As soon as Tony and his partner started talking it was clear that they were enthusiasts – guys who knew the area, knew the local villains and took an active interest in looking for leads. They knew Davies well. He was the big name on their patch and although there was no sign that he had ever had a direct interest in Newhaven before, that hadn't stopped them from keeping an eye on his activities.

Tony drove me into town to have a look at the boat yard. The manager had seen the pair again. He chuckled as he related how only days after taking delivery of the rhib, they had returned rather white-faced. Apparently some cruiser had almost run them down in the dark and they'd decided that navigation lights were a good idea after all. A few weeks after that they were back again. This time they had brought the rhib back for repairs.

'They'd completely sheared the propellers and almost torn through the hull in three places. That can mean only one thing.'

The manager and Tony nodded sagely at each other.

'High-speed landings,' Tony explained. 'They've been running the rhib straight on to the beach with the engines full on. The Royal Marines do it when they want to get troops on shore as quickly as possible. Smugglers do it so they can quickly get the loads off the boat and into a vehicle. You have to lift the outboards at just the right time or else you can shear the blades off the propeller as they obviously did.'

'I can't see them making it across the Channel, they clearly don't know one end of the boat from another,' muttered the manager, shaking his head.

'It gets even better than that,' said Tony as we walked away from the yard. 'I've been asking around in case anyone has seen these jokers. This section of the south coast is a popular retirement area. Quite a lot of the bungalows and flats along the seafront are owned by pensioners. A lot of them have good views out over the sea and others are out all hours walking their dogs along the shore, that sort of thing. Quite a few of them are signed up in the local "Coast Watch" scheme. It works on the same basis as a Neighbourhood Watch. We give them a twenty-four-hour access number and they report anything suspicious they see. They love it. And you'd be amazed at the bits of information they pick up. Anyway, one of our regulars called up and said that he'd seen this rhib for the past week or so, zooming up and down the coast. He thought it was just a couple of local lads. Didn't think a lot about it. But then the other morning he found them running the boat up the beach just near Rottingdean. He sat on the cliffs and watched them. Says they were at it for over an hour. Running out to sea and then running back in. He reckons they were trying to fix the landmarks so they'd be able to find it again. There's a nice little car park not a hundred metres away. There was a blue Range Rover there and as far as he could see the guys in the boat went and spoke to the guy in the car, but he was too far away to get the number or a description. On the plus side it looks like we could have a possible landing site.'

'So what's the Davies connection?' I asked

'Oh, that's the best bit,' Tony grinned. 'I was just taking a walk round the harbour yesterday very early in the morning, clocking what was in, what was out. It was just after dawn and what should I see chugging up the Channel but the rhib. Complete with our two boys. They'd clearly been out in the dark. I managed to dash back to the office and get a camera. I watched them winch the rhib up the slipway on to a trailer. Then a blue Range Rover pulls up and guess who gets out?'

He passed me a photograph – it was a bit grainy, but there was no doubt it was Lard Boy.

'Two gets you ten that the blue four-by-four our Coast Watch guy saw was the same car. Davies' son took the rhib away, but the other two got into some battered old Ford Escort. I've checked the registration. It comes out to some address in Edenbridge.'

'They were a long way from home.'

'Looks good, doesn't it?'

'It looks bloody good!'

We went back to the office, opened some beers and spent the next few hours studying maps of the coastline and intelligence reports, working out when the best time for a run would be according to the tides and the moon. We looked at the route from the car park near Rottingdean, trying to judge where road-blocks might be placed and where the best points to watch from might be. Their shift had actually finished hours ago but Tony and his partner didn't complain. They were as enthusiastic as if they were planning their own smuggling run.

And their enthusiasm was infectious. For the first time I felt as if I was getting somewhere. We still didn't know if the smugglers were planning to go all the way across the Channel or were meeting another larger boat somewhere off the coast. But it didn't really matter, because wherever they collected the drugs, we would be waiting for them on the beach when they got back. And this was all thanks to a couple of officers who, even though they were stuck in a port which was considered to be a bit of a backwater, had the experience and energy to make an operation out of the slimmest of leads. It only remained for me to go back to the office, brief Don and work out how we were going to tackle the job.

On the way back to London I took a detour to Edenbridge. It's a sleepy little Kentish commuter town. Because it is not on the direct rail line to London, it isn't as busy as some other Kent towns such as Ashford or Tunbridge Wells and it's still possible to see the village it once was. I passed the address on a small modern housing estate on the edge of town where the Escort was registered and sure enough there it was, parked outside. I wrote down the numbers of other cars in the cul-de-sac so that I could check them later.

I now had to take a calculated risk. We could easily find out who was registered at that address from our own checks, but the local police might well have some useful information which wouldn't be on our systems. They would often keep a card index of information which was too minor to enter on the central computer system and many of them had worked in an area for a long time and had a wealth of local knowledge, if you took the time to talk to them.

The risk is that once you've decided that you're placing a local villain under surveillance everyone in the area becomes a possible security leak. Not that we were worried about the risk of a corrupt officer, but on operations like this, the 'need to know' principle always applied. We were another agency and the intelligence officer might feel the need to keep his Chief Inspector informed, or he might mention it to a close friend. Just by turning up at the front desk it was likely that there would soon be gossip at the station that Customs were nosing around. Still, I decided it was worth the risk because I needed to confirm the link with Davies if I was going to convince Don that this case was worth investigating.

The officer on the desk had to look twice at my Customs badge as he'd clearly never seen one before. Eventually I was shown into an office where I met the local beat officer. He turned out to be a jolly bloke, close to retirement, who was halfway through a steaming mug of tea.

He was quite happy for me to look at his records, but he had nothing for the address.

'It wouldn't surprise me though on that estate, you've got several bad ones up there. Got a description?'

I gave him what I had.

'Could be one of the Williams lads. This wouldn't be something to do with Frank Davies, would it?'

I was stunned.

'You know Frank Davies?'

He burst into laughter. 'Know him? Bloody hell, I must have been the first person to nick him! About seventeen he was, caught him trying to break into the village hall. This is where he grew up.'

'Strewth, a quiet little place like this?'

'Hah, not that quiet. You go and do some research and you'll find we're quite popular with a certain brand of villain. I could name you a dozen fairly heavy characters who've started round here.'

'What's so popular about this place?'

'It was the war. By the end of the Blitz, most of the East End was rubble. A lot of families were rehoused on new housing estates around here just after the war. The trouble was that with a load of East End families you also brought down a load of East End criminals. Some of the families came down, saw what a nice quiet area it was and simply took up where they left off in London.'

'So what's the connection with Williams?'

'Couldn't say exactly. I think I know the chap you mean. Bit of a local nuisance when he was younger, but he's not been caught doing anything serious. It's just that when you mentioned that address I remembered that I saw Frank getting out of a car there just a couple of weeks ago. He's often seen around the village, but he's generally over the other side at his mum's.'

102

It hadn't occurred to me until that moment that Davies had a mother. You rarely think of targets as people with families, let alone as kids.

'My brother was at the local primary school with him. Mind you, that was a few years ago now. But this'll make you laugh. They had a nativity play and guess who was Joseph? Frank Davies! God, I wish I could have taken a picture.'

'Have you got a card on Frank?'

'Nah, he's moved on and up long ago. I keep an eye out for him when he's in the area, just in case like, but he wouldn't do anything round here – you know the rule, don't shit on your own doorstep.'

He was going off duty and offered to show me round the town, which sounded as though it might be useful if the Kilos were going to be doing surveillance there. So for the next hour or so I drove him round and he pointed out where Frank had lived as a kid, where his mother lived now, the pub in the High Street which Frank sometimes used 'if he was about', although he also warned me that it was the sort of local where they very quickly spotted strangers, so it was best to keep the team out of there. He also told me the quickest routes in and out of the town using the country lanes.

By the time I returned to London I had a wealth of information, including the identity of at least one guy who was working for Davies (or rather for Lard Boy), the probable landing site and a number of possible dates when they might do the run. Now, after all those weeks of waiting, I felt we had the information that would enable us to move against Davies.

So I was stunned when at a meeting with Don and the HEOs, Don's reaction to all this intelligence was barely lukewarm. There were a number of court cases coming up and we had several other jobs on the go. He just didn't think we had the manpower. 'Don't get me wrong, Harry. You've done well, it's a real feather in your cap. But we've got to be realistic. They will probably unload from a yacht or something just off-shore. Now, if it's a boat job it's down to the Juliets and I know that they haven't got much on at the moment. If these guys are doing a run straight across to France or Holland, chances are they aren't going to bring in a big enough quantity for us and it becomes a job for one of the local units. But I don't think they're doing that. You said yourself that Newhaven think they don't know one end of a boat from the other. I can't see them chancing a night run all the way across the Channel.' He waited for one of the HEOs to disagree with him. No one did.

'I'm sorry, Harry. I can see it's a nice little job and as you know, I'd love to have at a crack at Davies, but it's not for us. Pass the papers to the Juliets and see what they make of it. There'll be another time.'

I turned and looked despairingly at the Widow who was sitting quietly in the corner. She pursed her lips as she thought for a moment. The meeting began to break up.

'What about Brighton?'

Don looked at the Widow and waved a hand dismissively. 'The fucking Crazy Gang? The last thing I want is to get them involved.'

The Widow shrugged. 'They could babysit it for us. You know what these jobs are like. These chancers could go for it next week, but it will more likely be months before they get themselves organised. By then we might want to take it. If it happens quick, the Juliets or Brighton can have it anyway. We don't lose anything.'

Don sighed. He looked at her, then at the other HEOs. None of them raised an objection.

'Okay, Harry. We'll give it a try. Patrick, you've got some good contacts on the Unit in Brighton, see if you can get them on side. Tell them if it's under eighty kilos they can take it. Let them know who's behind it. Davies is on their patch too. It might persuade them that it's worth a look.'

Brighton Unit took it. Patrick had a good mate, Mickey, who was a senior HEO there. They had worked on rummage teams at Heathrow airport and Mickey had been in the Division for a few years. Patrick drove me down to Brighton to explain the job to them.

'Don called them the Crazy Gang.'

We were hurtling along the M23. Patrick always drove fast whether we were on surveillance or not and he only ever seemed to have one hand on the wheel. It used to scare the life out of me.

'Yeah. It's nothing like Dover. Most of these guys are ex-Division, but they've opted for the quiet life on the Unit. They don't get the same money, but the advantage is that they get to work in the same area all the time. They know all the local villains. They know all the favourite meeting places, they know the street maps like the back of their hands. With us, we're never in the same place twice. Sure we go down to Dover a lot, but most of our surveillance is done in towns we've never seen before. More to the point, they haven't got a big-time controller staring over their shoulders like in Dover. They do pretty much what they want to do. As long as they meet their annual targets everyone's happy. It's a bit like being on the Division, only better. Don thinks they are a bit out of control, but I'd go and work there tomorrow if I could afford it.'

Patrick laughed as he swerved and overtook yet another vehicle on the inside.

'Don't worry – you'll see what I mean.'

The Brighton Unit office is in a two-storey brick building just behind Shoreham harbour to the west of Brighton. The whole coastline is so crowded with buildings that you can't tell where Brighton ends and Shoreham begins. The area is rundown and shabby. The modern brick building housing the Unit could have contained any old set of offices and the car park round the back is a sea of cracked concrete and rubble. There is no outward sign that a Customs investigation team is based here.

There was no one in the reception area downstairs, but Patrick knew the number code for the security door. He punched it in and we walked up the stairs. Loud music was coming from above us.

The office ran the whole length of the rear of the building with views out over the harbour. There were papers everywhere, dismembered radio kits, head office circulars covered by obscene holiday postcards or press cuttings announcing their latest triumph. Members of the Unit were sitting around reading the paper, chatting, smoking or head down in case files. It really was the ID by the sea.

'Paddy!'

It must have been Mickey sitting on a desk in the middle of all this chaos. He was dressed fairly smartly in a jacket and tie. He was in his early forties, just starting to grey at the temples. He had a cigarette hanging out of the corner of his mouth and the knot of his tie was halfway down his shirt. If I had seen him in the street I would have taken him for a second-hand car salesman. When we came into the office he was rhythmically nodding his head to the beat of the music throbbing out of a ghetto blaster on a nearby desk. He extended a hand, but when Patrick went to shake it, he suddenly jerked it back and winked. I could see why Patrick got on with him. They had the same schoolboy sense of humour.

'This is Chumley,' said Patrick, 'the one I told you about.'

As I was wondering what that meant, Mickey looked me up and down slowly. Then he nodded and said, 'Okay. Welcome, Chumley. What have you got for us?'

I quickly described the information we had so far. When I'd finished, Patrick asked Mickey what he thought. Mickey said it sounded good, but that we had to go and see 'the Boss'.

The door of the SEO's office was open. Behind a desk was a man in his fifties wearing an expensive suit, who was in the middle of studying several thick folders of court papers. In contrast to the team room this office was scrupulously tidy. The SEO had strikingly clear blue eyes and a grim face. He listened to me carefully as I told the whole story again, and asked several questions. For a moment I didn't think he would go for it, but since Davies was involved and knowing that it would leave the Kilos owing him a favour, he finally agreed to a joint investigation. After some quick negotiation the case name was agreed: Operation *Krossfire* was born.

Afterwards, Mickey took me for a pint on Brighton seafront. As we were standing on the promenade overlooking the beach, Mickey pointed out the number of clubs.

'You can see why Davies is doing so well. All these nightclubs represent a massive demand and the town keeps giving licences for more. Even if the clubs run proper security, the clubbers just take the stuff before they go in, so there's no way of stopping it. I've been living here for ten years and every year I see more of it. The street price of the drugs drops almost every year – even the hard stuff – which means that more and more of it is getting in. We're not even holding the line any more. If I could think of something else to do that pays as well I would have packed the job in years ago.'

I said that I thought it must be great working in the same area all the time. One of the things I'd found hardest with the Kilos was that we were always working somewhere different. The Brighton Unit knew the area, knew the players, knew which houses and streets were commonly used for dealing. It must be great.

'Well, it's pluses and minuses. You know some of the local players, but at the same time, they get to know you. Take last month: I was walking on the Palace Pier with the wife and all of a sudden I felt this tap on my shoulder. I span round and there was this big geezer whom I'd helped to put away on a thirty-kilo job two years earlier. He got four years, but was out in no time of course. I tell you, he was a really fucking huge bastard and he hadn't got any smaller while he was away. He clearly knew who I was and I thought, "Fuck me, it's all over." And he said, "You're one of those bastard Cuzzies what done me, aren't you?" and all I could do was nod and think about where I wanted to be buried. Then all he does is give this big grin and say, "I bet I scared the fucking life out of you," laughs and walks off. Might not be so funny next time.'

As we were walking up a side street to where the car was parked,

Mickey stopped to light a cigarette and said, 'See that guy up ahead in the dark baseball cap – watch what happens.'

Sure enough, there was a kid in a baseball cap slouching along about twenty yards ahead of us. He didn't look more than fifteen. An older youth in an expensive bomber jacket was coming the other way. Probably a student. The two stopped, their hands touched for a moment, and then they both turned and walked back the way they had come. I was careful not to make eye contact with the youth in the baseball cap, but glanced at him as he passed us. I had been right, he was no older than sixteen, possibly younger, with a mass of acne. He disappeared round the corner.

'That's how simple it is,' said Mickey. 'They agree the deal elsewhere, agree to meet in a side street about ten minutes later, the dealer goes to whoever is holding the stash, gets one wrap, they meet, quick swap of gear and money and it's all over. That way, if the dealer gets grabbed he's only got a personal-use amount on him.'

'Did you catch sight of his mate on the other side of the road?' I hadn't.

'A minder, just in case someone tries to rip off the first guy. Or, if there is an arrest, the minder can also simply tell everyone that Old Bill is in the area and they can simply close down until the coast is clear.

'They've got loads of different ways of doing it. Some of them work out of flats or squats. Some use the parks. Others use cars. They just stop at a pre-arranged point. Pick up the customer, drive about fifty yards as they do the deal, then stop and drop the customer off again. It means the handover is never seen even if they're under surveillance and they never carry more in the car than is needed for a couple of deals. Local Old Bill does their best, but they just haven't got the manpower. You know, I've sometimes wondered how many of those deals go on in Brighton on a Friday night. Hundreds, easily. Possibly a couple of thousand. Over the country as a whole? God knows. Makes you wonder why we bother.'

So Brighton took over watching the Newhaven job and whenever we could, we would send down a team to help them out. The problem was that we didn't know where the boat was being stored.

In the meantime, having had our first break against Davies after months of silence, we now had a second lead within a week. Davies' name was flagged to me at NCIS. Just a few days after we began regular surveillance of Williams and his friend, I received a phone call from a detective constable in the Kent Police. He had an informant who had come up with some news about Davies and a possible drugs run in a small boat. He asked if I might be interested. I told him that I would be there that afternoon.

The informant turned out to be a petty burglar and shoplifter with a drugs habit who didn't know Davies or Lard Boy, but he did know Williams. The detective constable played me an audio tape from his last meeting with the informant. The story was that Williams and a friend called Shannon were both mates of Lard Boy. Williams and Shannon were a couple of wannabe hoodlums who would have a go at anything provided it didn't involve hard work, and they had jumped at the chance to pilot the rhib when Lard Boy had proposed it. Neither of them had much experience with boats, but Davies had agreed to fund them while they worked out how to use it, in preparation for a run across the Channel. The informant described Williams as a 'head case' who was ready for anything and warned us that he drove like a maniac even though he didn't have a licence.

Williams and Shannon had done a lot of work, finding a landing point and practising navigation using satellite navigation devices. But now, without warning, Davies had suddenly told them to forget Newhaven and find a landing site further down the coast near Southampton. Apparently, Davies had organised a team to meet them who were based near Southampton and the rhib had been taken down there. Recently Lard Boy had been going out in the rhib as though he might be on the run across the Channel as well. The informant didn't know where the rhib was or exactly when the run was going to happen, but he thought that it would be soon.

Don decided that this was good enough information for us to invest some work in the operation. He cancelled other commitments and scheduled three days of surveillance for Operation *Krossfire*.

But the first day turned out to be a disaster.

Perhaps we were getting over-confident. On a new target (unless there is firm intelligence that a target will be moving at a particular time), surveillance days always start early. The team will 'plot up' at about five o'clock or even earlier. Often this early rising is wasted effort as drug smugglers tend to spend a lot of their mornings in bed, but it is important to establish everything about a target's pattern of behaviour. Williams was no exception to the usual rule and didn't get up before midday. By the time he slouched into his car and set off down the country lanes, most of the Kilos had already been on duty for eight hours – eight hours sitting in a car and waiting . . .

The informant had said that Williams liked to drive fast and he wasn't wrong. Williams also liked to cut through red lights and straight across blind junctions. The team's positions were too widely spaced and before the surveillance had been going very long we were playing catch-up.

We had only been going for fifteen minutes when: 'Kilo 4 to all mobiles we've had a slight RTA. No problem but we're out of the tail.'

RTA was short for road traffic accident and Kilo 4 was Rick, supposedly our best driver. The Widow and I were at the back of the tail and I was just waiting for her to call off the chase when a very weak signal was picked up by our car-to-car radio: 'Kilo 6, we've had a pretty bad smash. Immediate assistance at red seven four.'

We raced to the scene. Carnaby was just pulling Ozzy from a

wreck, most of which was under the rear of an articulated lorry. Ozzy's face was white and he was shaking as Carnaby lowered him to the ground, but I couldn't see any blood. The Widow was on her mobile calling for an ambulance when Ozzy weakly told her to forget it.

He wasn't badly hurt, although he was suffering from shock. Carnaby's Rover saloon was a write-off, although the HGV was hardly scratched. Apparently, Carnaby and Ozzy had been moving up to take over the eyeball position in the surveillance when they heard about Rick's RTA. Distracted for a moment by the news, Carnaby had started to move out to overtake the lorry when a car had pulled out of a side road right in front of it. The lorry had slammed on its brakes and before there was time to react Carnaby's car had smashed into the back of it. Fortunately the T-bar at the back of the lorry had prevented the Rover from going completely under the lorry which would probably have killed both men, but it had opened up the nearside of the Rover like a can opener and stopped just short of the passenger seat. Another foot or so and it would have ripped Ozzy's head off.

Rick turned up a few minutes later. One side of his car was badly dented and scratched, but it was drivable. He had been the eyeball car behind Williams and was concentrating on staying just far enough back so that Williams didn't see him, when the car suddenly skidded in some loose gravel on a bend. On the narrow country lane there wasn't much room to do anything, but Rick had been able to kill most of the speed before he slid sideways into a stone wall bordering the road. The only thing badly damaged was his pride.

I think we all were in a state of shock for a little while. In all the surveillance I have done with the ID over the years, teams I have been working with have been involved in only three accidents and two of them were that afternoon. Oddly enough, despite all the high-speed driving in the Division, the accident rate is far lower than for normal road traffic and certainly lower than for the police who have the advantage of blue lights and sirens. This might seem odd, but there are probably two reasons: the first is that all ID surveillance drivers are trained to a very high standard and they have to attend regular refresher courses in both driving and surveillance. Police drivers can vary in training from the superb Class 1 drivers down to those who have only been on the Standard Driving Course. The other reason is probably that blue lights and sirens, whilst very useful in some situations, can actually give a false sense of security – officers expect people to get out of the way. ID drivers know that their cars look no different from any other vehicle and they can't count on anyone giving them room.

This wasn't the first tail the Kilos had lost – it just happens sometimes and you put it down to experience – but it was the first time we'd lost the tail due to an accident and the team was pretty upset about it. Rick, who prided himself on never being outdriven, was particularly incensed. As we watched the tow truck take the remains of the Rover away, he turned to me and said, 'Tomorrow, I'm going to nail that bastard.'

So the following day we were much better prepared. We made sure that our positions surrounding the target were tighter and we borrowed a couple of GTi hatchbacks from one of the target teams which had better mid-range acceleration than our usual cars. Williams obliged us by coming out to play earlier than the day before.

We had just settled down into our standby positions. I was teamed with Ozzy, who had shown considerable courage by coming straight back out on surveillance and insisting that no one but him was going to drive any car he was in.

He had just bought himself coffee and a bacon sandwich. Wherever we were, he always liked to set things up so he had home comforts as close to hand as possible, so it wasn't surprising that we had the position nearest to the local café. Then suddenly the Widow's voice crackled through our earpieces. 'Stand by, stand by. Zulu 1 from Hotel Alpha, complete X-Ray 1.'

'Ah, shit.' Ozzy gave me a look which seemed to say, 'That's bloody typical,' then he stuffed most of the sandwich into his mouth and poured the coffee out of the window as he started the engine.

Williams set off at his usual high speed and this time took a different route out of town. But Rick was right behind him the whole way, this time, backed up closely by Carnaby. They both felt they had something to prove.

Some time later, on the outskirts of Crowborough, Williams pulled up outside a new semi-detached property and went inside.

We plotted up once more and sat there, slowly broiling on what was a surprisingly hot September day. Every car tried to find a patch of shade and used the covert microphones in the cars rather than open handsets so that they could keep the windows wound down, but it didn't help much.

The Widow and Carl had the eyeball. It doesn't pay to have everyone close in, you need to have some backstops, and Ozzy and I were some way from the target premises in a position from where we could quickly cover any one of three junctions if the need arose. At that distance we could afford to be fairly relaxed. Time passed very slowly.

I spent about an hour trying to explain to Ozzy how to complete the cryptic crossword in my copy of the *Telegraph*. Then we did the crossword in Ozzy's copy of the *Sun* – which took all of five minutes. Then we played I-Spy. Then we gambled on how long it would take the cigarette lighter in the car to heat up. Then we played rock, scissors, paper. Finally we just dozed.

We had been parked in the shade for four hours when through half-closed eyes I watched a police patrol car roll slowly up the street. I could guess what was coming. The patrol car pulled up level with us and a uniformed officer nodded to me. I showed him my warrant card.

'Ah right, I thought it must be something like that. It was just that the lady who lives in number thirty-two across the road is about seventy years old and she lives alone. She saw you'd been here a while and she was a bit nervous. Thought you might be burglars. I thought something was going on. I've spotted one of your other cars about three roads over. I'll let her know everything's okay.'

We went back to dozing. Well, I did. Ozzy seemed to be snoring his head off.

Ten minutes later, there was a sudden rap on the windscreen. With a huge snort like an exploding pig Ozzy woke up and grabbed the steering wheel. A little old lady was standing next to the car.

'I'm sorry to bother you,' she said, 'but my son was in the Special Branch for many years. I thought you might appreciate a cup of tea.'

She lifted her arms and there on a tray were two steaming cups of tea in what appeared to be her best bone china. There was also a milk jug, sugar bowl and a plate of biscuits. We were both so gobsmacked that we just stared at her. This had to be some sort of massive wind-up.

'I could make some cheese sandwiches too,' she added hesitantly.

Perhaps it was nerves, but I just burst out laughing.

'Jesus Christ,' muttered Ozzy and then, seeing her look of horror, added, 'No, sorry, thanks, this is really great.'

She handed the tray in through the open window and Ozzy sat there with it on his lap still unable to believe what was happening.

'Just put the tray in the porch of number thirty-two when you've finished,' she said and disappeared through a gate in the hedge.

Ozzy stared down at the tray in silence for quite some time.

'Chummers, I've been chased off plot by a couple of IC3s armed with baseball bats. I've even been in an obs van that was overturned by a group of fucking cyclists because we were blocking a cycle track. But I have never, ever heard of anything like this.'

And it was good tea. Like schoolboys on their best behaviour we even wrote her a thank-you note and left it in the porch with the tray.

Finally, at two in the afternoon, Williams and Shannon emerged and we set off in pursuit once again. It was soon clear that they were heading south and our hopes rose higher when it was clear that they were aiming for Southampton. They collected the rhib and then headed for the coast.

Eventually they turned off the main road and took a long winding lane which led to the shore.

'All mobiles, hold back,' said the Widow.

Most of us had anticipated her and were already plotted up covering the various exit roads from the area. We waited for her to organise things.

'All mobiles, Kilo 3. Kilo 5 [that was Patrick] is on foot and has eyeball on the targets who are on the beach. Kilo 17, plot up on the fork at the top of the lane. You can call it as they pass you on the way back and give a heads-up to the other two. Kilo 11, take the north road, Kilo 6, take the west. Sit tight, everyone. Kilo 5 will give us a heads up.'

Ozzy and I drove the short distance to the crossroads. This was clearly an expensive area. Seven or eight large houses with wide gravel drives were dotted around the junction. We could cover the junction from a cul-de-sac which formed one of the arms of the crossroads. But there was no sense sitting there waiting to be seen, it could be hours before Williams and Shannon returned from the beach. Ozzy pulled up on to one of the drives. A high hedge gave us pretty good cover from passing vehicles. I climbed out and went and knocked on the door – we didn't want nervous house owners calling the police. No one was in.

So once more we sat in the car, glad to be in the shade and prepared to doze off again.

'Kilo 11 to all mobiles. I've got a dark blue four-by-four just passed me at the top of the lane. I didn't get a good look, but it could be Zulu 1.'

Zulu 1 was Davies. That made us sit up and take notice.

He must have been travelling at speed, because hardly had Ozzy and I heard the radio message than his Range Rover passed the bottom of the drive, heading towards the shore. As it swung round the bend I couldn't see the driver, but I caught enough of the number plate for a positive identification.

'Kilo 17, that's a confirmation on X-Ray 1 past my position. Driver not seen.'

This was getting interesting. It got more so when the Widow relayed a message that it was definitely Davies who was climbing out of the car in the small car park at the end of the lane. He spent about ten minutes talking to Williams and Shannon and then left as quickly as he had arrived. We stayed put.

A short time later, Patrick reported that Williams and Shannon had launched the rhib and were racing about in it not far from the shore. They hadn't set off further out to sea.

About an hour later I noticed two cyclists, a man and a woman, coming slowly towards the junction from the north. I nudged Ozzy. The thing that caught my attention was that all their equipment, including the bikes, was so new and shiny. They were dressed in shorts and T-shirts so white that they could have been advertising washing powder. My first thought was that they had to be tourists because they were cycling so slowly, but this place was so far off the beaten track that it seemed a bit odd.

I looked questioningly at Ozzy. Counter-surveillance is something a team always has to be aware of. Ozzy read my unspoken thoughts.

'Nah! Cyclists? Have you ever known any self-respecting villain ride a fucking bicycle?'

He slumped back in his seat, but I still kept an eye on them. They cycled very slowly round and round in the centre of the junction five or six times. But it wasn't as though they were lost, to me it looked more as though they were studying the houses. I thought they must be tourists, but it still wasn't right.

When they cycled off past the end of our drive the woman looked to her left and saw us. A moment later they cycled back again and then engaged in a long pantomime of him getting off his bike and supposedly checking the chain while actually checking us out. I could practically read his lips as he memorised the number plate. Ozzy was watching him too. 'What a pillock,' he muttered.

'I've had enough of this,' I replied and opened the door to go and have a word with them. But they didn't wait, they were cycling off, and by the time I got to the end of the drive they were nowhere in sight.

'Fuck 'em,' I thought and returned to the car.

I was just in time. The Widow relayed that our boys were hitching the rhib back on to their car.

'Kilo 3 to Kilo 17, when we get this lift-off I'm going to be detached while I pick up Kilo 5. Whichever route out they take, one of the other mobiles will be detached too. So once you've called the direction, get after him quick.'

'Roger that.'

Ten minutes later the Widow radioed again.

'And that's a lift-off, seven one you, Kilo 17.'

I got out and walked across the road to the cul-de-sac. I would be able to see which way Shannon and Williams went without their catching sight of the car. As I crossed the road I noticed that the male cyclist had returned and was once again riding in small circles about a hundred metres further up the road. Clearly something was up. Perhaps the woman had gone to a call-box to dial 999, but there was no time to go chasing after him now.

Barely had I got into the cul-de-sac, when the car with the rhib went roaring past. As usual Williams was driving at rally speed. They went west.

'That's a four four, four four, seven one you, Kilo 6,' I shouted into my radio as I raced back towards the house.

Ozzy's car shot out of the drive in a shower of gravel. He screeched to a halt next to me and I leapt in. We started to pull away when the brakes were almost immediately slammed on again.

'What the fuck is this?' roared Ozzy.

I looked up to see that the suspicious cyclist had pedalled furiously down the road and pulled his bike up right across the front of the car. I swung the door open and standing on the door sill waved my warrant card over my head: 'Customs and Excise! Move that fucking bike or I'll nick you for obstruction NOW!'

117

I must have got the voice of command just right because he instantly pulled his bike out of our path. Ozzy hit the gas and I was pulled back into the car by the sheer force of the acceleration.

As we sped past the cyclist he shouted something which I barely heard over the roar of the engine. I thought it was: 'Oh, so you're a policeman!'

Yeah, too right, matey, now piss off, I thought.

We raced through the twisting lanes. As soon as Ozzy estimated that he was close enough to take the eyeball if necessary, he simply said to me, 'Got it.'

'That's Kilo 17 now five five.'

It was then that Ozzy burst into fits of laughter even though we were still travelling at speed through the lanes. For a moment I thought he'd gone mad.

'What the hell is up?'

'It was the way you screamed at the poor bastard on the bike. He must have leapt nearly ten feet in the air. Jesus Christ, Chumley, I never knew you had it in you. What have we done to you? Whatever happened to "I say, old boy, would you mind just stepping aside for a moment"?'

The route Williams was taking was new to us and I hoped we didn't meet anything coming the other way. Kilo 6 was ahead and had successfully got into position behind the car with the trailer.

After a couple of miles we emerged on to a main road. There were sirens in the distance.

Up ahead there was a roundabout. Williams and Shannon were now trapped in a slow-moving queue of holiday traffic, so we patiently took our place in the queue a few cars behind Kilo 6. The sirens were getting ominously louder. Williams and Shannon got across the roundabout with Kilo 6 close behind. We were moving slowly forward in the queue and I was searching through the map for a parallel route when: 'Oh fuck.'

Ozzy nodded to one of the other exits where a police patrol car with flashing blue lights had emerged, travelled halfway round the roundabout and then stopped. The driver was looking straight at us and was clearly waiting for us to reach the threshold of the roundabout so he could pull in front of us. In the wing mirrors we could see at least two more patrol cars roaring up behind us on the wrong side of the road, blue lights flashing and sirens blaring. A horrible truth began to dawn.

We couldn't afford to drag all this any closer to Williams as it would simply alert him, so there was no point in going any further. We pulled over and both climbed out of the car with our hands up and our warrant cards held high.

The police cars disgorged six officers who came racing towards us. We were quickly surrounded, but as soon as they caught sight of the warrant cards there were groans of disappointment.

'Sorry, guys,' said Ozzy, 'better luck next time.'

Several of the officers turned and headed back to their vehicles, but a heavily built sergeant pushed his way between them and came striding up to me.

'Oh no,' he said, pointing a finger, 'you're not getting away with this. You're under arrest for assaulting a police officer.'

'You've got to be joking,' I said. 'What police officer?'

'On a bicycle, a robbery squad officer. You assaulted him.'

'Oh, come on, that pillock on the bike? How was I supposed to know he was a police officer?'

The Widow and Carl pulled up alongside.

'What's going on, Harry?' she demanded.

'It seems I've assaulted a police officer,' I said.

'Get it sorted,' she said bluntly and the car roared off across the roundabout. Moments later another Kilo car roared past on the wrong side of the road, horn blaring and headlights flashing, to clear oncoming traffic out of the way. The sergeant stared at it as if he didn't believe what he was seeing.

'We're on a live surveillance aimed at preventing a large importation of drugs,' I explained.

'That doesn't change anything as far as I'm concerned,' said the sergeant.

Ozzy shook his head in disbelief. 'There's always one,' he muttered.

He lay on the bonnet of the car and put on his sunglasses. The sergeant shot him a look.

'Don't get too cocky, sonny, you're in this up to your neck as well.'

But Ozzy was right. Whenever there was a foul-up like this, nine out of ten police officers you dealt with were fine – they checked who you were and what you were doing and you were on your way. But this jobsworth had clearly decided that since he'd been disturbed from wherever he had been snoozing someone was going to suffer.

He carefully copied the details from our warrant cards into his notebook and then reluctantly handed them back.

'Your boss will be hearing from my Superintendent about this,' he said threateningly.

And that really pissed me off.

'I should bloody well hope so,' I said, pulling out my own official notebook from a back pocket. 'You have obstructed a Customs officer in the execution of his duty thereby endangering a major drugs investigation and may face prosecution under the provisions of the Customs and Excise Management Act 1979. I'm taking your shoulder flash number and the registration of your vehicle and believe me, your Superintendent will be hearing from my boss.'

That was it for the day anyway. By the time we caught up with the team, Williams and Shannon had dropped the rhib off at an address connected to Davies on a housing estate on the outskirts of Southampton. Then they had headed off in the direction of Edenbridge. We decided not to follow them any further. We'd discovered where the new landing site was and we had the bonus of linking Davies to the job.

Back at the office, we contacted Danny on the Branch 1

intelligence team and asked him to work out likely times when the moon and tides would be right for a run across the Channel and also to trawl once more through the yacht intelligence to see if there was any lead on a boat connected to Davies which the rhib might be going to meet.

The problem was that it didn't matter about the phases of the moon, tides or other boats. The key to the importation was the rhib. We knew where it was and we had to stay with it. We contacted Brighton and arranged a rota by which a two-man team could keep watch. Other vehicles and officers would be on standby to be called out as soon as it looked as though the run was on. Everything seemed to be going perfectly – too perfectly.

Two days later, Don got a call from Brighton. They had been responsible for following the rhib that day. At about midday, Williams had turned up without Shannon, hitched up the trailer and set off. The Unit had followed. Williams didn't make for the coast, but instead headed east along the A27. He was not travelling at his usual breakneck pace and was easy to follow.

At first they thought he was heading back towards Newhaven. But soon he turned north and drove inland, so the team's next assumption was that he was making for Edenbridge. But he didn't stop there either. That was when the Unit rang Don.

We were at a loss. There didn't seem to be any danger of losing the rhib so it was just a matter of sitting and waiting to see where it ended up. We sat for an hour trying to think what was happening. Perhaps the boat was going to be modified in some way? Perhaps Williams was stealing it? None of the explanations we came up with made much sense.

Finally, Brighton rang again. Williams had taken the rhib to a pub somewhere near the village of Hadlow in Kent. He had backed the trailer into a large shed behind the pub and unhitched it. The shed, which was empty, had been left open as though he was expected, but he had a problem because the rhib was slightly too long for the shed and the doors couldn't be fully closed. Eventually Williams left the doors ajar and went into the pub. He emerged later with a chain which he wrapped around the door handles and padlocked. According to the Brighton officer who had sat in the pub watching, the nose of the rhib could be clearly seen poking through the gap between the doors. Williams had then visited the barman, handed over some cash and left. It looked as though the boat had been put into storage.

This was a setback, but not necessarily fatal to the operation. We simply changed the rota and monitored the rhib at the pub rather than in Southampton. After a week, however, no one had been near it. We tried to find out what was happening from the police informant. The news was devastating. According to Williams, the run was off for good. He didn't say why and the informant didn't ask because he thought that Williams had become suspicious.

Something must have spooked them. It had happened just after the encounter with the police at the beach, so some of the team thought that was where the leak was. All it took was someone to mention it in the canteen or in the pub after hours. It was more than likely that Davies had contacts. But in truth, it could have been anything. Davies or one of his team might have seen something while they were on the beach. They might have had counter-surveillance out which we just didn't spot. It might even have been some problem with Davies' gang. To this day, we don't know exactly what it was that caused them to call the job off.

Don tried to be phlegmatic. We hadn't invested too much time on the case and at least had received some surveillance practice. In the meantime, a standing notice was put out stating that anyone on the Branch driving down to that part of Kent should drive past the pub and see if the rhib was still there. The shed was quite visible from the road.

I even asked my father, who was retired and lived in the area, to drive past whenever he could and see if the boat had moved. He went one step further and practically became a regular at the pub. When he finally thought it was safe to ask about the boat, the barman would only say that someone had rented the place and that he didn't know anything else about it.

It looked as though the job was over and Davies had escaped the net again. That was so typical of so many operations. They could start with the slimmest of information, quickly escalate into a major operation and then just as suddenly die again for no apparent reason. You could spend months on surveillance on a promising job which eventually went nowhere, whereas some of the biggest operations could be over and done with within twenty-four hours.

Once again, we were forced to wait.

6

The Chancers Return

It was a bad time for the Kilos.

We had come so close to getting Davies and then had lost him. Meanwhile, just as she had feared, the Widow had lost Operation *Kansas*. The presentation in court seemed to have gone as well as she could have hoped. The weeks of surveillance, the account of the arrests and how the criminals were caught red-handed were laid out for the jury. The only defence the suspects could raise was that they had been 'fitted up'. It seemed as though they hadn't a hope.

But the Widow was still worried. The defendants were just too cocky. Naturally she was concerned that they would try to get at the jury somehow. She had asked for protection for the jurors, but without evidence of attempted coercion or bribery, she couldn't get it. The police and court officers just don't have the resources. She organised ID officers to keep an eye on things as well as she could, but this had to be discreet in case the defence lawyers found out and alleged that Customs were trying to create the fear of a plot by the defendants in order to influence the jury.

The jury were out for less than an hour. This seemed fine considering that it was an open-and-shut case. I was in court when the foreman of the jury stood up and said, 'Not guilty.' There were gasps all round the courtroom, then silence. Even counsel for the defence had the decency to hang his head in embarrassment.

The judge was so disgusted with the jury that he actually said to the usher, 'Get them out of my sight!'

As they filed out of the courtroom, one member of the jury actually turned and winked to the men in the dock. We all saw it. The jury had been got at.

The management of the ID was outraged and called for an immediate investigation. But it was all too late. Unlike the defendants, we had no right of appeal. The Deputy Chief himself came down to the office to commiserate with the Widow. Jack told her that they understood she had done everything within her power and that it wasn't her fault.

It was a big blow to the team's morale. If you added up all the man-hours spent on the operation, it was over a year's work straight down the toilet. What made it worse was that this wasn't an uncommon occurrence. It didn't even rate a mention in the national press.

The following month it happened again. This time the case was Carl's, an officer you would have bet your mortgage on to secure a conviction. A lorry driver found with a quarter of a tonne of cannabis hidden in a secret compartment in his lorry told the interviewing officers that 'a man he had met in a pub' had explained to him how the concealment could be built and he had built it because he thought it might be useful for storing tools. He then claimed that a gang of smugglers must have found out about the compartment and secretly slipped the cannabis into it while he was in Holland.

This story was so preposterous that we thought the driver was bound to plead guilty on the opening day of the trial. Even so, Carl was an experienced officer and he didn't take any risks. He prepared the case as carefully as if the driver had given us a rock-solid excuse. But the driver didn't plead guilty. Instead, the whole of the prosecution case was presented and then on the third day the defence opened by putting the driver in the witness box. Defence counsel said, 'Tell us what really happened.'

The driver then proceeded to claim that he had been forced to build the compartment and smuggle the cannabis by an evil gang who had threatened his family and that he had been too scared to mention this before.

And the jury fell for it.

Carl was incandescent with rage. If he could have got across the courtroom to the defence lawyers, I think he might have happily strangled them.

Following so quickly after the *Kansas* débâcle, this hit team morale really hard. We were used to perverse verdicts, it was all part of the job. But now it seemed that we couldn't put these bastards away even if we caught them red-handed.

In the meantime, I had finally managed to get a place on a surveillance driving course. I had been dreading it. I had learnt to drive at eighteen, but hadn't then owned a car, so I actually had the driving skills of a small wombat. Once, on a training course for MI6, I was supposed to practise debriefing an agent while driving a counter-surveillance route. This involved memorising a complicated route through narrow back streets, picking up the 'agent' and then driving the carefully designated route while trying to spot any surveillance.

On the night of the exercise, it was dark and raining and I hadn't actually driven for about six months. I was desperately trying to remember the route, peering through the windscreen trying to find a street name I recognised. The role-player acting as the agent was supposed to make it as difficult as possible for me to extract information from him. About two minutes into the interview he suddenly exclaimed, 'Jesus Christ!'

'What?'

'Why did you just drive through that red light?'

'What red light?'

His next words were spoken very slowly and deliberately: 'Pull over right now. I will tell you everything I know.'

I was the only person who scored full marks on that exercise.

So it was a tall order for the police instructors. But they almost managed to get me through it.

The surveillance driving course is a little odd: it is not really designed to prepare officers to drive on surveillance at all. The police instructors are excellent and they teach the 'System', a method of high-speed driving which the police have used success-fully for many years now. The 'System' is perfect if you have a nice open stretch of road or blue lights and sirens on top of your car to clear traffic out of the way.

But for reasons of policy, police instructors are not allowed to teach the skills which surveillance drivers really need. For instance, they are not permitted to exceed the speed limits during training except on motorways and de-restricted roads. ID drivers spend most of their time in urban areas in heavy traffic following men for whom the speed limit isn't even a consideration. Also, the police could hardly instruct us in driving on the wrong side of the road, on pavements or the wrong way up one-way streets. Finally, they can't re-create the pressures of driving with a navigator who is barking instructions at you while trying to co-ordinate four or five other vehicles.

The course was far from a waste of time. Restricted as they were, the police instructors still managed to convey a great deal about high-speed driving. But the only way to really learn how to drive on surveillance is actually to be out on the streets doing it. It always seemed to us that the primary reason for the course was so that if there was a serious accident involving a driver the management at Customs could say, 'Well, these officers are trained by the police.'

Despite the heroic efforts of the instructors, when the results of the final test came through I had failed to pass by a couple of marks. I was gutted. An officer who can't drive on surveillance is no use on the Division, and I was still on my probationary period. Now it looked as though I might not have a job there at all.

When I got back from the course, Nicky was sympathetic, but

not entirely displeased. Just before I had left for the course, she had been offered a job by a bank in Germany and she was keen to take it. It was a lot more money and would be a big step forward in her career. More than that, we could both see that it would be good for the children: they were still young enough not to mind being uprooted from their friends and they would benefit from being brought up with a second language and all the experiences of living in another country. Although Nicky tried to hide it, I could tell that she was hoping that this latest problem had weakened my enthusiasm for the Division.

But it hadn't. Things were just beginning to get easier for me in the job. The team was beginning to accept me and I was starting to pull my weight out on the ground. I felt that if I could just stay with the Kilos for a little longer I could make it. So I spent the night after the course sweating about what Don would say when I gave him the bad news. I went in early so that I could see him in his office before having to face the rest of the team.

When I told him the result of the course, he raised his eyes to the ceiling, shook his head and swore.

'Did you fail by much?' he asked.

'Three marks.'

He thought for a while, then scribbled a brief note which he handed to me. 'Take that to the training department. Get yourself put on the next available course and God help you if you fail this time.'

I thanked him and stood up to go. When I got as far as the door he called out, 'Hey!'

I turned and he said, 'Don't tell anyone on the team, but fifteen years ago I failed my first driving course.'

I smiled and nodded in thanks.

'Just make sure you bloody well pass this time because I didn't fail twice, all right?'

A few weeks later I made my second attempt and this time things went much better. It helped that the atmosphere at the new test centre was much more relaxed and that my partner on the course was a grizzled veteran from a target team who gave me plenty of useful advice. Greg was old enough to be an SIO, but either he didn't have the ambition or he hadn't had the luck. 'All these guys want to know is that you are not going to go back to London and prang some civvie first time you're out on the road,' he said. 'Drive safe, not fast. Fast can come later.'

The course also showed that it wasn't only Customs and police who have moments of friction: the training cars are unmarked except for a tiny magnetic strip on the boot which reads: 'Caution: Police driver under instruction'. It is so small that you have to be about three feet away to read it and most people never even notice it. It was certainly no use when I was stopped on the M1 having been clocked doing 137 mph.

The officer who had stopped us was from one county whereas the officer instructing was from another. As we were parked on the hard shoulder, the two of them seemed to be having a quiet discussion at the back of the car. But their voices became louder and louder until those of us who were rolling around with laughter in the car heard: 'I don't care what you do in your bloody county, you broke the limit and he'll be booked.'

'Don't be a prat. Our Chief Constable will just write the bloody thing off!'

'I don't think my Chief Constable will sodding well allow that!'

'Well, you can stuff your Chief Constable up your arse!'

When the day came for my final assessment drive on the course, it was Greg's advice which saved me. The drive had gone well, but somewhere out in the twisting back lanes of Wiltshire I got stuck behind some old pensioner driving painfully slowly in a little hatchback car. Most of the time there was barely room for two cars to pass and every time I got a clear view for an overtake it seemed another vehicle would appear around a bend ahead and I was forced back. There was a brown Labrador dog in the back of the pensioner's car which stared back at us as we followed him for what seemed like forever, and all the time I could sense the examiner sitting next to me becoming more and more impatient. We were probably only held up for forty-five seconds or a minute, but on a surveillance driving test that feels like a very long time. I was sure that I had failed. But on the other hand it is an automatic fail to make any move which the examiner considers dangerous and I kept hearing Greg's voice telling me to play it safe and not risk blowing the whole test on one dodgy manoeuvre.

When we arrived back at the test centre, the police inspector who was acting as my examiner wrote on the results sheet for a very long time. Then he put down his pen and said, 'I got sick and tired of staring at that bloody dog for hours. What the hell was all that about?'

I took a deep breath. 'Sorry. I just couldn't find a safe place to get past him.'

The examiner thought for a moment and then said, 'Right answer. Stick with that and you'll be all right. You have passed.'

Of course I was elated. A future on the Division was possible again. But then I had to go back to Nicky. We talked a lot and it was clear that there was nothing I could do in Germany and that I would eventually resent her for dragging me out there, so in the end, very reluctantly, she dropped the whole idea. There was no bitterness about it from either of us, however. We really were trying to do the best for each other. But it was another bit of trouble stored up for the future and sooner or later we were going to have to face it.

When I returned to the team I found that I wasn't the newest officer any more. As part of the ID management's new recruitment strategy the latest member of the team was an ex-inspector in the Canadian Police. He was in his late forties, with a wealth of experience in just about every area of police work. The team promptly dubbed him 'Granville'.

One of the first things I did when I got back into the office was ring around and check on Davies. The boat still hadn't moved. But

Davies was busy on other fronts. The farm had been taken off the market, but according to Danny, Davies was spending a lot of time out at his new villa in Spain. No one knew what he was up to. Intelligence checks on phone calls, businesses and bank accounts yielded nothing.

However, there was one bit of good news. The Tangos had taken down a large consignment of cocaine at Southampton and the word was that a good slice of the financial backing for the importation was down to Davies. They couldn't connect him evidentially, but it should have hurt his cash flow again. I wondered how many of these hits his organisation could take. There was still hope that we would get another chance.

Christmas came and went with lots of routine investigation work, and was only notable for a near massacre in a nightclub during our Christmas party. The social life of the ID is marked by two special events. The first is the annual dinner – almost one thousand officers all crammed into one huge venue in London. The atmosphere is incredible and the Division is very careful that only those who are truly considered its friends are invited. In the international law enforcement community it is considered quite an honour to be included on the guest list. The dinner is also renowned for its comedy show which mercilessly lampoons senior managers, stupid regulations and anyone who is deemed to have 'fucked up' badly during the year. The management tolerate this because it is one of the most reliable ways of gauging the feelings of the staff.

The other event is the team's Christmas party. Because of the dangers of being called out the following day if they were in London, teams usually book themselves into a remote hotel for a couple of days, and once news leaks out about a particularly good venue several teams often congregate at the same hotel. This year the Kilos had gone to a hotel in the West Country. The dinner went well and then everyone headed for a club in the basement of the hotel. Everything was fine until a yob standing at the bar started to smoke a joint while standing next to Carl. Carl quickly recognised the distinctive aroma. After what had happened in court recently, he did not feel too kindly towards cannabis smugglers or anyone who supported them and promptly knocked the joint out of the yob's mouth. The yob must have been too far gone to realise how big Carl was and swung a punch. This was stupid because Carl promptly lifted him off his feet and over the bar. The yob's three mates then stepped forward to have a go at Carl, which was a mistake as they suddenly realised that he was with a crowd of other people – the Kilos . . . and the Juliets and the Sierras and the Bravos and the Charlies. For a moment it looked as though the yobs were going to be leaving feet first but Don, probably realising these guys could get seriously hurt, stepped in to save them. I still remember how one shout from him stopped twenty guys in their tracks.

When it was all over the Sierras' number two came over to have a beer and find out what had started it all. He wasn't too pleased when he found out.

'You mean that all this was over a spliff? Jesus! We thought World War Three had broken out. If we'd known it was only a fucking spliff we wouldn't have bothered.'

But the Widow was on Carl's side. 'He did the right thing. You don't stop enforcing the law just because it's the end of your shift. It's about time someone woke these morons up. We see the type of bastards who get richer every day from this crap.'

'Yeah, well, that may be true but you don't see off-duty traffic cops chasing speeding cars down the motorway either. Your guy needs to chill out a bit if you're going to take him out in public.'

And that pretty much summed up how people on the Division felt – they were just like a broad cross-section of society. For some of us it was a personal crusade. We could see every ten or twenty pound note handed to a street dealer as if it was placed on a little conveyor belt which wound its way through many levels of dealers until it reached the major suppliers – men who dealt in terrorism, child labour and enforced prostitution. Drugs money sponsors all these things and as far as we were concerned the job was worth doing every moment of every day. But for others it was just a matter of enforcing a law like any other. One day, as with Prohibition in America, that law might change. In the meantime you did your job as well as you could and at the end of the day you went home and got on with the rest of your life.

I may not have always agreed with him, but I invariably admired Carl's courage. For him it was a point of principle, unfashionable or not, and he would have stepped in that night even if there had been twenty of them.

The strangest thing about the incident for me though was the first yob's obvious shock that anyone would object to him smoking a cannabis joint in a public bar. He didn't think he was doing anything particularly daring. I had been so intent on enforcing the law over the past year that I had started to forget how regularly you see it broken in pubs and clubs. The incident brought home to me that if the drugs war was being lost it wasn't because the police or the ID weren't trying hard, it was because there is such a huge market for drugs in the UK. We were being overrun by the sheer scale of the problem. No amount of government initiatives or crackdowns stands a chance in the face of that sort of demand.

It was only a few weeks after this that the one small incident which would eventually lead to the downfall of Frank Davies finally occurred.

Just before New Year's Eve, the phone rang. It was Tony Graves from Newhaven.

'You'll never guess what, Harry – your boat has gone.'

'Really?'

'Really.'

'Shit.'

'Last time Eddie or I saw it was a week ago. We've let Brighton know and they're out now looking for it. They're trying the beach first, just in case there's an empty trailer sitting there. Then they're going to try the home addresses and a couple of other likely spots after that. If that fails, we're stuffed.'

A week gave plenty of opportunity to do a run across the Channel. Had we missed it? On the off-chance that we could narrow down how long it had been gone for, I rang my father.

'You remember that boat in the shed behind the pub?'

'I thought that was over and done with.'

'It's not. Have you seen it recently?'

'Well, like I said, I thought you'd pretty much forgotten about it, but as it happens you're in luck. I actually drove past yesterday evening about eleven. It was still there then.'

'It's gone now.'

'Really?'

'Really.'

'Looks like you're stuffed then,' he said jovially.

They could have done a run. The Christmas period is a favourite for many smugglers who figure that staffing levels will be low at ports and airports and that any staff who are on duty will have their minds on other things. We would just have to see. The question was, where was the rhib now?

Fortunately Brighton Unit came up trumps again. They found it back on the estate in Southampton. There was no sign it had been to sea yet and there was no sign of Williams or Shannon either. We had no idea what this meant. Was the job still on? Was the run going to be done by another team?

Finding the boat only solved part of the problem. Brighton Unit couldn't sit on it forever and neither could we. The last thing we needed was another long static surveillance. But we had a further slice of luck. Within an hour, Danny appeared with a new piece of intelligence. The police informant had resurfaced and Williams had made it clear that the job was on again. Patrick and I drove down as fast as we could to the Brighton Unit office at Shoreham.

A short while later Patrick, Mickey and I were examining a map of the estate. 'If it moves there's really only two ways off the estate,' said Mickey. 'We've got one mobile covering each exit with a couple of backups at the local police station who can join either tail at a few minutes' notice.'

'Any chance of getting an OP?' asked Paul

'We checked with the Old Bill. They did have the addresses of a couple of places on the estate where the natives were friendly, but none with a view on the address we wanted. Other than that it's not the sort of place to go asking.'

'That really only leaves us one choice then. We'll have to lump it.'

'Lump' was the word for any one of several alarm or tracking devices which could be fitted to a vehicle or trailer. If the trailer was fitted with the right device we wouldn't have to watch the estate at all.

Patrick rang Don to tell him what the situation was. Don agreed to the proposal.

'He's sending Carnaby and Ozzy down with a tracking device.'

'Rather you than me,' said Mickey. 'I've seen where it's parked. Right on the fucking drive. And I don't think these guys are just going to ring for the local Old Bill if they see someone tampering with their property, know what I mean?'

Normally we didn't bother with tracking devices, although you might think that they would have been the answer to our prayers. In a James Bond movie, the hero simply sticks something about the size of a matchbox underneath the bumper of the car he is following and a detailed map on his dashboard shows him exactly where the villain is going.

In reality, the devices we had to use were more like a jumbo pack of Cuban cigars than a matchbox – no wonder they were known as 'lumps'. They had a tendency to stop transmitting just when you needed them most. When they did work they were wildly un-reliable, affected by almost anything from mobile phone masts to passing badgers. The most you could do was use them as a backup on a really important job such as a live delivery. Then you would still use your normal surveillance team and resort to the device only if you lost sight of the target.

135

But in this case it didn't matter so much. Mickey and Patrick only wanted to know whether the boat was still in the same place. If you had enough time and you could get them in just the right place on a car, they were practically undetectable. But neither of them had ever lumped a boat trailer before.

For some targets the operation was straightforward: they had their car parked on the street or on their drive and an officer simply had to come along at the best time of night or day, slide under the car and place the lump – an operation which only took a couple of minutes. At the other end of the scale, I heard of one team working in Leeds who had a target who was very wary and kept losing his surveillance team. To keep tabs on him they had to use a complicated tracking device that took an hour to install. The vehicle would actually have to be taken away while technicians fitted it.

The target was always checking the street from his window at odd hours. The team decided it was too risky to move the vehicle from where he could see it. So they used about twenty vehicles to block all the parking spaces in the road in the hour or so before he got home. When his surveillance team announced that he was on his way, they left a space for him just around the corner. He duly parked in the only available space and the car was removed and fitted with the device without his knowledge. All this just for one lumping operation, but then you always have to adjust your resources to the difficulty of the target.

The only problem with lumping a vehicle parked in the street was if someone saw you doing it. We all had our own plans for what to do if that happened. In 99 per cent of cases the plan was simple: run like hell. This was a rough old estate – it was here that Frank had held the woman's head to the hotplate – and neither Patrick nor Mickey relished the thought of being caught.

The right time to lump the vehicle depends on the target and the location. With late-risers the best time to bug the car is the middle of the morning, which is also a time when members of the public are less suspicious. In other cases the graveyard hours of three or four in the morning are safer. It's harder to explain what you're doing, but less likely you'll be spotted. Patrick and Mickey decided to get the job done that night.

In the early hours of the following morning they parked their car a couple of streets away and walked towards the house. All seemed quiet. They stood in the shadow of a tree across the road from where they could see the rhib parked up on the drive. Still nothing stirred. Tossing his cigarette into the gutter, Patrick wandered across the road and on to the drive and then ducked under the boat.

A few minutes passed, then a few minutes more. If all goes well a lump can usually be attached in about two minutes. After five, Mickey began to worry. He knew that Patrick had never lumped a boat trailer before, but it shouldn't have taken this long. He called Patrick up on the radio and was relieved to hear two beeps in his earpiece which indicated that he was okay.

Then things took a turn for the worse.

The lights at the front of a house about two doors away came on, the front door opened and a old man stepped out. Mickey wondered if this was because Patrick had been seen. Worse still, the man was accompanied by a dog. As the two of them walked slowly down the drive, the old man talking to the dog all the way, Mickey prayed that they would go the other way down the street. But God wasn't listening and they turned straight towards the target house.

'Kilo 5, stay still, one civilian and a dog approaching,' Mike whispered into his radio. Hopefully they would walk right on past.

The dog, an arthritic black Labrador so fat that it could barely walk, had sensed that something was wrong and started to waddle up the drive towards the rhib. It found one of Patrick's feet and began to snuffle round his trainers. Patrick pulled his legs up as far as possible, but there wasn't much space under the boat.

'Come away from there,' called the old man and started to walk up the drive.

'Get ready to leg it,' whispered Mickey.

There was an extra loud beep in his earpiece which meant that Patrick knew full well what was happening.

Then to their relief the Labrador cocked its leg, pissed over Patrick's leg and wandered unsteadily back towards its owner.

As soon as they turned the corner, Patrick came sprinting back across the road. 'Done it,' he muttered.

As they walked away, Mickey realised that Patrick stank of dog's urine and whisky. It turned out that, unlike the rest of us, Patrick's plan had never been to do a runner if he was spotted. Instead he carried a half-bottle of whisky. The idea was that he would pour half of it over himself and then emerge waving the bottle, singing at the top of his voice and pretending to be blind drunk. God knows if it would have ever worked, but as soon as Patrick felt the dog sniffing round his ankles, he had drenched himself.

Still, the boat was lumped which meant it could be covered by one vehicle with a tracker sitting some way off. The only thing to do now was wait.

This is always the problem with anti-smuggling operations. The biggest advantage the smuggler has is that the authorities don't know when and where he will strike. Often we would know who the major players were, and even how they intended to accomplish the job. But that information is useless unless you know when the importation will happen.

I have sat in OPs for weeks watching a lorry and waiting for the criminals to get their act together. This is not an efficient use of resources and the worst thing is that the longer a vehicle or site is watched, the worse a show-out becomes because even more valuable time has been wasted.

Nothing changes. I once read an account by an eighteenth-century Customs officer who faced the same problems. He often knew which local fishermen were planning a run across the Channel, but he didn't know when. If he was seen showing too much interest in a particular boat, the run would be cancelled until he had left the area. This was the dilemma we found ourselves in with the rhib.

Fortunately we didn't have long to wait. Two days after the rhib had moved down to Southampton, it was collected by Williams and Shannon. The informant had been able to let us know that the run was imminent and the Kilos were scrambled from the local police station where we had been based. We quickly moved into position for the surveillance. As we drove through the night it soon became clear that the pair were heading for the same section of beach near Southampton which they had been using before.

The Widow was immediately on the phone to Skippy, an Australian officer from another team, who was handling the close surveillance. He had already been briefed on the job and had made a reconnaissance of the beach. Now all he had to do was turn up and move into position.

Close surveillance officers are specialists. Using techniques first developed by special forces, they go into a target location under cover of darkness and dig themselves a 'hide' where they can stay for days or sometimes weeks. It can also mean becoming adept with milk bottles and clingfilm for toilet purposes. There aren't a lot of volunteers.

The advanced tactics of close surveillance were quite new to some of the older hands on the Division and things didn't always go smoothly. A friend of mine had joined a team working on a target at an isolated farmhouse. They badly needed to cover the farmhouse yard to get car registration details and, if possible, photographs of the people meeting there. But there seemed no way to get close enough.

My friend thought he could make use of a drainage ditch which ran between the road and the hedgerow opposite the entrance to the farmyard. His army officer background meant that he hadn't been easily accepted by his new team. Here was his chance to impress them – or so he thought. He told them his plan. They told him to go for it.

The ditch was about half a mile long and it took him almost an hour, covered in camouflage netting and bits of foliage, to crawl through the muck and rusty old metal in the bottom of the ditch. Finally he wriggled into a clump of brambles and radioed that he was in position.

He had only been there for ten minutes or so when he heard a voice: 'Pssst, pssst.' He looked up to see one of the team crouching at the edge of the road with a steaming mug in his hand.

'All right then?' said the officer. 'It's a bit nippy out here so we thought you might appreciate a cup of tea.'

It's hard to imagine the expression on my friend's face, but the other officer must have realised what he was thinking because he looked over his shoulder at the entrance to the yard.

'Oh, don't worry about that, mate. There's no one in. They're not expected back for another hour or so. Do you fancy a biscuit?'

Control radioed that Skippy was on his way and would be with us in an hour or so. The Kilos followed the trailer on its way to the coast. The Widow and I were at the rear of the tail, Patrick and Carl had eyeball. Suddenly Carl's voice came over the radio: 'All mobiles hold back, hold back.'

The Widow pulled us into a side road, rapidly span the car round and then pulled in. We waited.

For a while there was silence, then Carl reported that Lard Boy was out in his father's Range Rover. He was parked up on a rise from where he could watch the main road towards the coast. He had another thuggish-looking guy with him.

We waited while Lard Boy watched. His presence was good news. It suggested that this was the real thing rather than a dummy run. The lump was still transmitting and Patrick was confident that the boat was heading in the direction of the beach.

Eventually Lard Boy was satisfied and moved off. There was no sign of him heading towards the beach, but he might re-appear at any time, effectively coming up behind us as we covered the network of small roads down there. We couldn't get too close

140

but we had to know what was going on at the beach. The Widow sent Patrick in on foot.

The rest of us moved to positions so that we could get to the beach as quickly as possible when we were called in. One of the mobiles peeled off to make a call to Marine Division to see if a Customs cutter was available. It wasn't. They also phoned to ask about the availability of the Sussex Police helicopter based at Shoreham Airport. They said they'd come if they could, but, as usual, they were on the police budget and police jobs would come first. Finally the Widow phoned Don to discuss bringing in armed police. We weren't expecting trouble, but it was best to be prepared. The police firearms units were very good at what they did, but they would want to take over the whole area and after several difficult operations, we never felt at ease with them. We only called on them when we were absolutely sure the other side had guns. Otherwise we relied on speed, surprise and sheer weight of numbers.

The Widow put the phone down.

'Well, looks like we won't be getting any outside help on this one,' she said grimly. It didn't really matter; referred teams are supposed to be prepared to go in without backup. It just ratcheted up the pressure another notch.

'We could call for more troops from the Division,' I suggested.

She shook her head. 'If we can't do this with ten we couldn't do it with twenty. The textbook says that this should be a straightforward round-up. They land the drugs, we hit them on the beach before they can react. End of story.'

We both grinned in the dim light from the dashboard. By now even I knew that no job ran that smoothly. There was always some unexpected twist. I wondered what it would be this time.

A mobile spotted Lard Boy's vehicle heading towards the beach. Kilo 8, Patrick's backup while he was out on foot, had pulled off the road on to the drive of one of the houses near the junction. We needed to warned him that Lard Boy was on his way, but he was out of the vehicle speaking to the house owners to let them know who he was. We couldn't afford the local robbery squad turning up a second time. We desperately waited for him to return to his vehicle. The radio crackled into life. 'Yeah, this is Kilo 8. The owners are kosher with this.'

'Kilo 8 from Kilo 3, warning, we have Lard Boy seven one your position.'

'Understood. Wait one.'

There was a pause of a few seconds then: 'Kilo 8, Lard Boy six six.'

That meant that he could actually see the Range Rover. There was another pause. We were keeping the transmissions really short in case Lard Boy or someone we hadn't yet seen was using a scanner to look for radio traffic.

'He's going dead slow through the junction. Now he's stopped. Something's spooked him.'

The Widow was slowly chewing one of her immaculately manicured fingernails and staring at the radio. 'Kilo 8, that's Lard Boy foxtrot.' That meant Lard Boy had got out of his car and was having a look round.

There was another long silence, then: 'Oh fuck. He's coming right towards the house.'

The Widow wasted no time. 'Kilo 8, get out of the mobile now. Get right out of there.'

We discovered later that Carl had got out of the car just as Lard Boy started coming up the drive. He had ducked round the back of the house only to find the couple who lived there staring out of the kitchen window. He had signalled frantically and they had let him in through the back door.

We never did know why Lard Boy stopped to check. It may have been that he recognised the vehicle or something about it, or he may have thought he saw Carl in the car. In any case, he took a look up the drive, saw the car was empty and wandered back to his own vehicle. The first we knew that he had moved on was when Patrick reported him driving into the small car park near the beach.

'Tide's out,' said Patrick, 'I don't think they'd allowed for that. They're trying to get the trailer and their vehicle on to the beach.'

There then followed a comedy of errors as the smugglers tried to get their car on to the beach, but it got stuck. They spent some time rescuing that. Then Lard Boy had to use the Range Rover to get the trailer on to the beach and into a position from where they could launch the rhib. This was good. The more Lard Boy got involved, the better we liked it. If we could nick him, we could get a warrant to search Davies' house and then there was no telling what other evidence we might dig up.

Finally Williams and Shannon set off out to sea and disappeared in the darkness. Lard Boy towed the trailer to the car park. He then seemed in two minds as to what he should do about it. Williams' car hardly mattered as that was a battered old wreck. The trailer was a different matter. Clearly Lard Boy was worried about it being pinched, which, considering what he was up to, was pretty funny. Finally he left it in a parking space alongside the yobs' car.

'Shouldn't we stay with Lard Boy?' I asked. 'They could be doing a run back to some other point and abandoning the rhib. This may just be the launch point.'

The Widow shook her head.

'I don't think so. Why bother coming to a secluded little spot like this just to launch the boat? You saw how much trouble they went to. It would have been easier just to launch it back in Newhaven or somewhere. Besides, these boys haven't shown that much imagination yet and you've seen how jumpy the kid is. Follow him now and we risk a show-out, then the whole job is down the pan. The best thing we can do is wait, Harry.'

So we sat and waited. This was the worst bit. Hour after hour sitting in the dark and the silence. Two more Kilo mobiles moved in closer to strengthen the perimeter. Then Skippy turned up by the Widow's side of the car, a large rucksack over his back.

'All right then, Princess? Where do you want me?'

There was an awkward pause. In over a year on the Division I'd never heard anyone call the Widow 'Princess'. I ducked down to get a look at this man with a death wish. He was an officer on a two-year exchange posting from Australian Customs. Listening to that Aussie accent and seeing his shock of bleached blond hair as he leant against the car, you realised that, corny though it was, there was no way the Division could have named him anything except Skippy. I waited for the Widow to explode.

'All right, Skip,' she answered in a world-weary voice. She proceeded to tell him what was happening and how much time we had.

He made his way down on to the beach. He would have to be close. Even with night-vision equipment it would be important that he saw exactly what was happening, not just to tip us off, but because eventually this case was going to court and if we didn't see exactly who did what we could lose the whole job. This meant that Skippy had to dig himself into a hole on the beach. Patrick then helped him cover the hole with a tarpaulin and covered that with sand. Finally Skippy radioed that he was in position and ready.

'This is Skippy, nine nine.'

More waiting. It was now well past midnight.

Had we got it wrong? Was the landing going to be somewhere else and were months of surveillance work about to go out of the window? It was too late to worry now. The Widow and I took turns kipping while the others watched the road for any sign of the return of Lard Boy. The other Kilos were doing the same.

In the early hours of the morning the pattering of rain on the roof of the car woke me up. The Widow was peering out at it.

'This isn't going to make them very happy,' I said.

'Well, I just hope we don't have to get out of the cars to chase them,' she replied. 'These are new shoes.'

At 3 a.m. Lard Boy returned. We weren't near enough to read the licence plate, but there couldn't have been too many Range Rovers out at that hour. I gave the rest of the team and Skippy the 'heads up'. 'From Kilo 3, stand by, X-Ray 1 past our position, seven one the beach.'

Shortly after that, Skippy reported that they were just sitting in the car park, but with their headlights still on. Probably acting as some kind of beacon for the returning rhib. The problem was that Skippy couldn't use his night-vision equipment to see if Lard Boy was alone. He didn't have much time to worry about that as the rhib appeared at high speed out of the darkness.

'Here we go! That's the rhib complete the beach. I've got one out and heading for the car park.'

'All mobiles stand by,' said the Widow. We were now at the most delicate point. Call the knock too early and the shore team could claim that they weren't involved, call it too late and they could do a runner with the drugs. We had to catch them somewhere in between and that meant allowing for the drive on to the beach.

The team rolled their cars forward slowly down the lane with the lights off. At the first sign of trouble we would pull back.

'I now have X-Ray 1 mobile at the rhib,' said Skippy, his voice quite calm despite the rising tension. 'That's X-Ray 1 at the rhib, rear door open.'

The Widow was still considering her options as we drove. 'Kilo 8, Kilo 3.'

'Kilo 8.' It was Carl.

'When we knock this, cut the Range Rover off. If he makes a run for it, ram him. We can't let him get off the beach.'

The Widow halted the car. There seemed to be an interminable wait, which gave me a chance to think about how sick I felt at that moment. Perhaps Peter Bennett had felt this way before he lost his life attempting that arrest. Skippy gave the final call: 'And we have boxes from the rhib into X-Ray 1.'

'Knock! Knock! Knock!' called the Widow and hit the accelerator. We must have been on a patch of gravel or mud because the back end kicked out on us for a moment. She swore, span the wheel

145

and the tyres gripped. We hurtled off down the lane, the Widow flicking the lights on to full beam.

Although I'd seen the beach in daylight it made little difference. All I could see was the beam of the headlights, the rest was just blackness. The lights of another car were coming in fast from the right. Ahead, the shore party scattered. Lard Boy leapt into the Range Rover which immediately began to pull away. Carl's Sierra slammed into it, head-on before it had a chance to get going. I thought I heard the crump of the impact above the roar of our engine. The Window's attention was fixed on one of the yobs who was running off along the shore. The Citroën bounced hard as we roared over the uneven surface of the beach.

'Fucking hell!' I shouted.

'Are you criticising my driving?' called the Widow as we took off into the air again.

'Not at all' I gasped. 'I've always wanted to fly!'

Then, as we crossed one brow and were just about to catch him, the Citroën hit the ground with a bang and stopped dead. We were both thrown forward, the wind knocked out of us.

The bang had been so loud that it was clear we weren't going any further in this car. I didn't have time to worry about that as I clambered out and started off across the beach after the fleeing figure. Patrick appeared beside me, running hard. But whoever was ahead of us was fast – bloody fast. He was pulling away from us. I thought we were going to lose him in the darkness. Then suddenly a figure like a giant bat emerged out of the night and dived into the runner, sending the two of them crashing to the ground. Both Patrick and I stopped dead for a moment.

'Sodding hell!' gasped Patrick, 'It's the caped crusader!'

When we caught up, we found Skippy sitting on top of Shannon fastening the handcuffs. His Batman impression had been due to the huge camouflage cape he was still wearing. Luckily for us, Shannon had run almost directly past Skippy's hole. All he had to do was jump out and grab him.

146

Back at the rhib, resistance hadn't lasted very long. Lard Boy and a man I didn't recognise were in handcuffs. Williams had got away in the confusion, but there wasn't too much to worry about. There was a large depression further back from the beach. It wasn't too big – about fifty metres by one hundred – but it was a tangle of vegetation. We knew he was somewhere in there, we just couldn't see where. Several officers were placed at points around the depression in case he made a run for it, but the beach was fairly clear in all directions. He wouldn't get very far.

Patrick was trying to talk him out, but Williams said he had a knife and challenged us to come in and get him.

'Ring the local Old Bill. Ask them to send round their dog unit. That'll shift him,' said the Widow.

There were two large boxes in the rhib and six more in the Range Rover. Someone had already taken the top off of one of them. 'Soaps' of cannabis resin were visible inside. The three suspects who were under arrest were loaded into vehicles to be taken to local police stations. The cannabis was stashed into another vehicle to be taken to the Queen's Warehouse in Southampton.

The Widow rang Don to tell him the good news. Don had been drumming up support for the house searches. Troops from the other Branch 1 teams and any other team which owed us a favour were being gathered together. There were addresses in Edenbridge, Crowborough and Southampton to search, and that of the man who had been in the car with Lard Boy once we identified him. But most of the remaining Kilos were heading for Davies' house. It was going to be a big team and the Widow wanted to be there to arrest Davies personally. I went with her.

A convoy of Kilo vehicles roared into the yard at the front of Davies' house. We also had a police car with us as required by law for a search during the hours of darkness. There were a lot of lights on upstairs in the house, so either they were up really early or they had been tipped off that we were coming. There were metal security shutters over the ground-floor windows and several security cameras were fixed to the walls at strategic points. One of them was moving, so they clearly knew that we were there.

One part of the search team went to the front door and someone shouted, 'Customs and Excise! Open up!' through the letter-box. When there was no answer they started hammering away at the steel reinforced door with the 'magic key', the small portable battering ram.

I went around the back with another officer in case anyone made a break for it that way. As I stood in the chilly dawn light, I looked around at the half-dozen cars I had admired from a distance before. There seemed fewer than there had been. I wondered if this was something to do with Davies' financial crisis that Danny had spoken about. I looked down at a car tyre by my foot. There were big teeth marks in it. Then I had a nasty thought.

The dogs!

Carnaby had warned us about Davies' dogs and I had seen them several times running loose in the yard. In all the excitement we had forgotten about them. There was a porch at the back of the house and through it I could see that the rear door of the house was ajar. I dashed forward and as I did so I was sure I could hear paws thudding towards me. I pulled the door of the porch shut just as the first of the dogs crashed into it, barking furiously. The officer standing next to me looked at me in shock. That had been close.

Our first thought was that Davies had tried to set the dogs on us deliberately. It later turned out that the door was always left open. Just inside was a utility room where the dogs slept. They were allowed to prowl the yard and any burglar who thought the open door was a soft option was in for a nasty, but probably very brief, shock.

Meanwhile the team at the front had finally broken in and met Davies and his wife on the stairs. Davies was arrested in his pyjamas. His wife was sent into the kitchen to quieten the dogs down.

On the way to Customs offices at Southampton I sat in the back of the car with Davies in handcuffs. He said nothing, just peered out of the window. He had dressed for comfort: in an open-necked shirt, a big loose pullover and slacks. He was well tanned but he had a surprising amount of grey hair which I hadn't really noticed from a distance. Perhaps it was the stress. Up close he reminded me a little of my father. Similar age, similar build. If I hadn't know who he was I wouldn't have given him a second glance.

Once booked in he was asked if he wanted to see the Duty Solicitor, the free legal adviser who is available on twenty-four-hour call for detainees. But of course Davies had his own lawyer, an expensive one, who would have to be roused from his bed and travel all the way down to Southampton. The Widow agreed with the lawyer to suspend the interview until he arrived, but warned him that if he took longer than two hours she would start without him.

In those days most Customs custody suites did not have cells to hold suspects in between interviews. So someone had to sit in an interview room with Davies while he sipped coffee and smoked fags. It was the sort of job that always falls to the junior officer and this time that was me.

Two hours is a long time to wait when you've just been arrested and sooner or later almost every suspect wants to talk. It's partly nerves, partly a desire to know more about the people who have made the arrest, and there is always the hope of learning something about the case. Suspects know there is no chance of what they say being used against them because there are no witnesses, and even if the conversation was secretly taped they could claim to have been entrapped, so it's a sort of free ride for them.

Despite his long experience I could see that Frank was burning with curiosity and the delay before the interview was irritating him almost as much as it was irritating us. At first he stayed silent, just looking at me occasionally. He was clearly as mad as hell. I wondered whether he was thinking about the money he had lost or how his son had fouled things up. Outside in the corridor we could both hear voices as people and property from the arrests arrived. It sounded like a lot of activity, but we couldn't actually hear what was being said. It must have been driving Davies crazy.

It was Granville who finally broke the ice. He brought Davies another cup of coffee, and then stood staring at him. Finally Davies couldn't stand it any more.

'What are you staring at?'

Granville shrugged and smiled. 'I was just thinking it was neat, you two sitting here.'

Davies shot me a look. 'What do you mean?'

'This is the guy who's been chasing you all this time, now you're in the same room.'

'Hey!' I shot Granville a warning look.

This was well out of order and could cause all kinds of trouble if Davies repeated it to his lawyer. Perhaps Granville was just trying to wind Davies up before the interview started in the hope that he would talk. He looked at me, then shrugged and left.

As the door closed, Davies said, 'What was he talking about?'

'Nothing. I've just read a few files.'

'Oh, I see,' he said meaningfully, 'you've got files about me, have you? I shall be asking my lawyer to have a look at those.'

I decided it was best not to say anything more.

We continued to sit there, but now Davies began to ask occasional questions. When could he make a phone call? When would he appear before a magistrate?

Then he suddenly changed tack completely. He sat back and said, 'You're a mug, do you know that?'

'What?'

'You heard.'

I still thought it was best not to say anything. Those are the rules. But I just couldn't resist it. After a minute or so I said, 'At least I'm not the one under arrest.'

'Not for fucking long.'

A few minutes later he added, 'My son's only a bit younger than you, got his own Porsche, got his business, got an apartment in London, what have you got?'

We hadn't known about the apartment. I stored away the information.

Davies rambled on a bit more. The fact that I was staying mostly silent seemed to irk him. He didn't admit anything, but it was clear that we both knew what he was talking about. At one stage he said, 'You know why you're a mug, don't you?'

'No, go on. Why don't you tell me, Mr Davies?'

'Because you don't understand business.'

I gave him a quizzical look.

'Suppose you actually managed to stop half the drugs getting into the country. What do you think happens to the other half?'

'I haven't a clue.'

'It doubles in price. In fact, you'd probably find the price would go up ten times. You'll never win. It's the simple law of supply and demand.'

'You seem to know a lot about drugs.'

He shook his head.

'Nah, but I do know a lot about business.'

I had often wondered what Davies would be like in the flesh. Now that I had finally met him I discovered that he certainly wasn't a criminal mastermind. Although he had evaded capture in several different investigations, he wasn't particularly bright. Nor was he 'evil'. My overwhelming impression was that he just didn't care – about the destructive power of drugs, about anyone or anything. I suppose that's what enabled him to live the way he did.

Finally his lawyer arrived – some public-school type with an expensively lined suit, immaculate diction and a double-barrelled name. The interviews were going to be handled by the Widow and Don, and since I was no longer required for babysitting, the Widow sent me back to Davies' house in the hope that my knowledge of his organisation might help turn up some useful evidence.

By the time I arrived, there were still a few rooms left to search, which gives some idea of how big it was. Every room was beautifully furnished, as if it was straight out of *Homes and Gardens* magazine. Deep carpets, leather, mahogany, antiques. There was a huge television screen set into the wall of the living room and a Bang and Olufsen music system which looked complicated enough to launch a space probe. I thought about my cramped little terraced house and the tatty hand-me-down furniture we had. Clearly I was working for the wrong side.

I finally chose a cellar downstairs from the main hall. No one had touched it yet. It was full of junk; all sorts of odds and ends, but it's often in these forgotten areas that you find some of the best stuff. I'd been hard at work for some time when I moved a shelf of books aside and found a small safe set into the concrete of the cellar floor. Bingo.

I called Mrs Davies and the officer in charge of the search. We asked her for the combination. She claimed she didn't know it.

'Look, Mrs Davies,' I said, 'you might just as well tell us or we can let you call your husband to ask for it. If you don't, we just call out a locksmith and he'll drill it and it will be opened anyway. Why not save the mess and the damage? We'll be out of your house a lot quicker.'

Finally she went and got a piece of paper with the combination written on it and opened the safe. Several officers gathered in the cellar hoping that it would reveal crucial evidence, but the contents seemed disappointing: passports (genuine), family papers, some jewellery and a dozen videotapes. I looked through the papers then put the videotapes into an evidence bag. Mrs Davies was standing just behind me. She put her hand on my arm and whispered, 'Please don't take those.'

'Mrs Davies, I have to.'

'There's nothing on them, only private things.'

She was clearly distressed. I wanted to believe her, but then I thought, this is the wife of a major criminal, I would have to be a complete fool to trust her. Besides, these tapes were in a locked safe. That was pretty suspicious, whatever they were.

'How about if you look at them on a machine here?' she asked. 'Then you wouldn't have to take them.'

152

'I'd have to review the whole tape. That would take hours. They have to go.' I was also aware of the old trick of reversing a tape in the cassette to disguise what was on it. I felt sure she was covering for something.

Finally she gave up and went away.

The smugglers arrested at the beach had all given 'no comment' interviews. That was no surprise and as they'd been caught red-handed it didn't really matter. Davies had been quite different. Once his expensive lawyer had finished with him, he had started the interview with a long tirade alleging that he had been viciously assaulted by Customs, that his wife had been assaulted as well and that he would be launching a legal action for massive damages. Having let him get that off his chest, Don and the Widow started to go through the evidence. At first he refused to answer, but he soon realised that there wasn't very much against him, so he started to give an explanation. As far as contact with Williams and Shannon was concerned, he simply said that they were friends of his son. He denied giving them any money. He admitted visiting them at the beach, but claimed that he was simply delivering a message from his son. After holding him for the rest of the day in the hope that something would turn up from the house searches, he was finally released the following evening. We had always known the case against him was weak, but we had hoped for some kind of break.

The house searches had proved disappointing. After two days of sifting through mounds of paperwork, the most we could do was tie Shannon and Williams to the planning of the trip. Lard Boy had given a flat in London as his home address rather than Frank's place. The flat turned out to be practically empty.

By the end of the second day, I had been so immersed in paperwork that I had more or less forgotten the videotapes. There were so many documents relating to companies and off-shore bank accounts owned by Davies that it was going to take months of work by the Financial Investigation Branch to sort it all out. He must have been worried about that because his lawyers were already trying to get them back.

The men on the Kilos were already pretty certain what was on the tapes anyway.

'It's porn,' they agreed as I set up a screen to review the tapes that afternoon. Several of them produced cans of lager and pulled their chairs closer. The noise attracted several of the Juliets from next door. I ran the first tape.

It was porn – but not what we expected.

At first it just showed a bedroom, but soon Davies and his wife appeared. They were then joined by another man we'd not seen before.

'Bloody hell, he's got a monster todger,' said someone at the back of the room.

'Perfectly normal if you ask me,' smirked Carnaby and was instantly showered with jeers and empty lager cans. There were whistles and cries of encouragement from some officers at the action on screen. Davies had caused everyone problems for years. This was a kind of revenge.

But the sex got rougher and rougher. It was pretty clear that Mrs Davies was either a consummate actress or a less than willing participant. I remembered her face in the house and had a terrible feeling that I knew which was true. Gradually the officers drifted away. They had all probably seen worse during their time reviewing smuggled material at ports and airports, but this was nasty in a different way because we knew the woman involved. Eventually, I dimmed the screen and turned down the sound so I could just hear it. The tape still needed to be reviewed in case anything incriminating was said or something else was recorded somewhere. But there was no need to watch it any more.

Afterwards I sat and talked with the Widow about what we ought to do. The other tapes were similar. This woman might need help. But the Widow was adamant. It wasn't a problem for us.

The look on Mrs Davies' face at the house still haunted me. I

154

decided that I wouldn't return the tapes with the rest of the property. Instead, I would find a way to return them to her personally, so that I could let her know that we had seen what was in the tapes and that we could put her in touch with people who might help if she needed it.

That was my intention. I'd like to say I carried it out.

But the following day I was sent away on a job assisting another team. When I got back there were lots of other things to worry about in the office, at home Nicky and I were having furious rows about the amount of time I was spending at work, and by the time I remembered my good intentions, it was too late – Davies' lawyers had won their case and all the property had been returned.

Meanwhile, Operation *Krossfire* wound its way to court. Unless someone got at the jury we knew we had Shannon and Williams. But soon it was clear that Lard Boy was going to get away with it. The case against him was always slim as he had never actually been seen in the boat. Now Williams and Shannon, who had refused to say anything before, readily gave statements that Lard Boy had known nothing about it and that he hadn't known that there were drugs in the boat when they had asked him to bring the Range Rover to the beach. Clearly a message from Frank had let them know it would be healthier for them if they got his son off the hook. Even Lard Boy's associate, who we found out was some hired muscle provided by Charlie Johnson, Frank's enforcer, gave a statement saying that Lard Boy didn't know what was happening and claiming to have driven the Range Rover on to the beach himself – even though Skippy had seen Lard Boy do it.

But that wasn't the end of it. Although we thought we had got very little out of Operation *Krossfire* except for taking out another medium-size consignment, we had blown a hole in Davies' orga-nisation which would shortly bring it crashing down.

The tapes were about to have consequences.

155

7

Operation *Krystal*

After Lard Boy escaped prosecution, we were despondent. We had waited so long for an opportunity to break into Davies' organisation and now the chance had slipped away again. We had the likely prospect of successfully prosecuting a couple of his mules, but with remission they would probably be back on the streets in less than two years and Davies would no doubt give them enough cash for it to have been worth their while. It was the old, old story – it was straightforward enough to nail a consignment or two, but an organisation like Davies' could survive almost anything except a direct hit on the man himself – an opportunity he would almost certainly never give us.

My organisation chart now covered more than ten sheets of paper, all carefully taped together, and there were so many inter-connections and crossings-out that it was almost impossible to make sense of it. But one small part of it was going to be worth all the trouble.

It was the middle of the night when my pager went off. I staggered downstairs in the cold and sat shivering in the hall while I phoned Control. They gave me a number down in Dover docks and said that one of the Tangos wanted to talk to me. Who the hell did I know in the Tangos?

It turned out that I knew Terry Boyle. I'd met him on the BITs course a few months earlier. He'd been a pharmaceuticals salesman before he joined Customs, cold-calling doctors' surgeries and chemists trying to sell them his company's latest drugs. Having spent six weeks with him, I reckoned he could have sold just about anything. He dressed like an East End barrow boy made good and talked like one. He wore a lot of gold jewellery, including a half-sovereign ring. Someone from undercover training should have snapped him up. He could have walked into almost any of the London syndicates and not have stood out at all.

'All right, Chummers,' he shouted down the phone. All the engine noise and clatter behind him made it sound as though he was in a breaker's yard. 'How would you like a quarter of a tonne of hash then?'

'Don't fuck me about, Terry, it's three in the fucking morning.'

'Straight up, Chumley. We've got about two hundred and fifty kilos sitting down here and the guv'nor says you can take it 'cos we've got something else cooking. He says Don's got two hours to get a team down here or he'll give it to the locals. He would have already given it to them, but it seems this one's down to you on CEDRIC.'

I didn't have a clue what he was talking about, but then I had so many flags on CEDRIC now that it felt as if anything that came through the docks was mine. I rang Don who decided to send only a couple of cars down.

So for about the hundredth time since I had joined the Kilos, I drove down to Dover, picking up an EO called Vinny on the way, M2, A2, down Jubilee Way, the route was so familiar I drove it half asleep and could time the journey almost to the minute. Vinny snored in the passenger seat. As I drove over the flyover and into the docks, I remembered how the floodlights and activity of the port had once seemed so exciting. Now I hardly noticed it.

I met Terry at the examination sheds. There seemed to be lorries everywhere: in the sheds, queuing up waiting to get in, gridlocked trying to get out. Engines were roaring, horns were blaring and drivers were swearing at one another.

'How long has it been like this?' I asked

'All fucking night,' Terry laughed. 'Come with me, we've got your baby in one of the bays down the end. The driver's in an interview room upstairs.'

He took me round the back of a double trailer – effectively two containers linked by a coupling and pulled by one enormous rig. Examination staff were standing guard on the pallets they'd removed.

'Bloody good concealment. It's down to Caldwell here that it was found. We've had some pretty good information that a load of smack is coming through in a consignment of textiles. To protect the source of the information, we've made it look as though the dock is running an import exercise, stopping anything that comes in with a textiles consignment code, turning 'em over for appearances, like. Of course we're here all day and all night and our bloody stuff never turns up, but this does. Fucking typical.'

I peered into the depths of the rear container. All I could see was electrical equipment.

'Doesn't look much like textiles to me, Tel.'

'Yeah, it's a groupage load. Various small consignments all shrink-wrapped in plastic on different pallets for stops all over the country. According to the driver's papers he's picked up in about three different countries and he's got delivery addresses all over the place. Anyway, Caldwell pulls a couple of pallets. Cuts 'em open. Computers. But the paperwork's wrong anyway, and while they're checking it out, one of the drugs dogs is brought past. It goes straight for the computers. So we unpack them, open them up and,' he held a soap of cannabis resin, 'bingo, as they say. Paki black, quality-stamped and everything.'

'We've haven't opened 'em all. There's about a dozen screws in each computer so it would take some time. But on a rough count it's got to be at least two hundred K.'

He pressed the soap into my hands and slapped me on the shoulder:

158

'And it's all yours, old son. I'm off to bed down in a nice local brothel, then we're going to be doing all this again tomorrow! Don't say I never give you nothing.' He winked and was gone through the mêlée of truck drivers and examination staff.

The Widow and Carl had arrived in the middle of the conversation, in time to hear the important bit.

'Right,' said the Widow, 'let's go and chat to the driver, see if he'll play ball. Vinny, you and Carl help the locals to get as much of the stuff as you can out of those computers and into the Queen's Warehouse. Leave me about four pallets untouched just in case he decides to go along with it and we manage a controlled delivery.'

'He does well on his travels anyway,' said Carl, pointing to five number plates attached to the front of the tractor unit. They were all girls' names, such as Michelle and Lulu. Above them were the metal silhouettes of two reclining naked women such as you see on the radiator grilles of half the trucks that come through Dover.

'Bloody hell,' said Vinny, 'he must be a monster shagger!'

The interview room was a cold, cheerless room up a flight of metal steps behind one of the examination bays. We looked through the glass panel in the door. The driver was sitting in there chain-smoking Gitanes. He was over six feet tall, with a huge bald head, the arms and shoulders of a weightlifter and a massive beer gut as well. Judging by the number of dog-ends in the foil ashtray on the table, he'd been sitting there for a while.

'We've got to move fast,' said the Widow. 'A lot of time has already been wasted. It's probably too late for a controlled delivery, but we have to try.'

We walked in and the uniformed officer nodded to us. The driver continued playing with the dog-ends.

'How's he been?' asked the Widow.

'Hard to say,' the officer shrugged. 'He doesn't speak much English. Likes a mug of tea though. He understood that all right.'

'Where's the on-call interpreter?' asked the Widow.

'She's sick. The reserve went to a dinner dance last night and apparently hasn't come home yet. We've got hold of one of the others from the standby list, but she won't be here for an hour or so.'

'Oh Jesus,' sighed the Widow. She thought for a minute, then turned to me. 'Do you speak any French?'

'Not really. I did an O-level, but that was years ago.'

'Well, it'll have to do. With his poor English and your poor French we might get something out of him and every minute counts.'

We sat down and went through all the usual rigmarole of setting up a tape-recorded interview. Fortunately we had a sheet with his rights written down in loads of different languages. Finally the machine was running. 'Monsieur Ducrane, do you understand that you are under arrest?'

He just shrugged.

'Go for it, Chumley,' the widow said.

'Eh . . . *comprenez vous ça vous êtes* . . . um . . . under arrest?' I ventured. Out of the corner of my eye I saw the Widow hold her head in her hands.

'Ah,' said the giant, 'yes, arrest, I understand.'

'Hooray,' muttered the Widow.

'Do you understand that you are under arrest for drugs in your lorry?' Although I said this in English, I accompanied it with the kind of frantic hand gestures which the English are so accomplished at when talking to foreigners.

'Yes.'

That was better. The Widow went for the big one. 'Are you prepared to speak to us now, without a lawyer?'

We were back to blank incomprehension again. The Widow glanced at me.

'Um . . . *voulez-vous parler* . . . um . . . *avec nous*,' I pointed frantically to the two of us, '*sans* . . . um . . .' I couldn't remember the French for lawyer, I had a feeling it was something like the English word brief '. . . um . . . *sans* . . . *le bref?*'

A look of absolute horror came over his face.

'What the fuck did you say to him, Chumley?' asked the Widow.

'God knows. I may have asked him if he wants to speak to us without underpants.'

The Widow banged her head against the table. The driver just stared at us in confusion.

And so the pantomime continued, but, given the state of my French and his English, we got nowhere. Fortunately both the interpreter and a Duty Solicitor arrived about half an hour later. We'd given up hope by then, but it was still worth a try.

'He didn't understand our French,' the Widow explained to the interpreter.

'I'm not surprised,' she replied. 'He's speaking Flemish.'

'We asked him if he was prepared to be interviewed before you arrived,' I explained to the solicitor, 'but the language difficulties were too great.'

There was a stony silence. The lawyer looked at me suspiciously.

'Incidentally, if he mentions being asked to remove his pants, that was just a misunderstanding.'

The lawyer now looked very suspicious indeed.

'Anyway, it's all on tape,' I said hopelessly.

For once it really was 'darkest before the dawn'. Once he had spoken to his lawyer, the driver was happy to be interviewed. He agreed to take part in a controlled delivery and it turned out that his first call, in East London, was not until the following day. There was still time to make it on time.

'We'll need someone in the cab with him,' said the Widow as we planned the operation a few hours later. Only the week before a controlled delivery on a heroin job had gone horribly wrong. A Dutch youth in a camper van who had been caught with two kilos of cocaine had agreed to undertake a controlled delivery. On the A2 just outside Dover, with the surveillance team watching in horror, he had swung his minibus into the path of an oncoming juggernaut and had been killed outright.

'I'll do it,' I offered. I'd been waiting for a chance to do something useful. How hard could it be, sitting in a cab while a Belgian weightlifter drove up to London?

'I don't know,' said Carnaby, who had been sent down to help out. 'He's a big bugger and a bit too keen to co-operate for my liking. I don't trust him. If he decides to make a break for it in that rig we'll never stop him.'

The Widow thought for a moment.

'Okay,' she said to me, 'go for it.'

It was agreed that I should only carry a radio handset in the cab, rather than carrying a concealed radio in the usual way. It was just possible that I might have to get out of the lorry once we got to the warehouse and that a suspicious reception committee might frisk me if they had been expecting Ducrane to arrive alone. Although he seemed friendly enough, we had to consider the possibility that he might be in on it.

Ducrane had been taken off to the cells at the local police station so that he could get a few hours' kip. In the meantime, we continued with the planning. We wanted to have the warehouse where the computers were going staked out before our arrival, but most of the rest of the team were committed to another job. We scraped together a scratch team of Deltas, Juliets and a couple of Kilos. It meant we would only have three cars for the tail, with the Widow driving alone, but it would have to do.

We went over the route we were likely to take, looking for possible 'choke points' – areas with no alternative routes where the opposition might sit and watch for surveillance on their vehicle. We had contacted German police asking them to check out the yard where the loading had taken place. If it was a small, back-street operation, then it made it much more likely that Ducrane knew what was in the load. But the German police called back within a few hours to say that it was a large commercial yard which handled a huge volume of business and they had nothing on Ducrane.

At noon the following day I was waiting in the lorry park, kitted out in a donkey jacket and woollen hat which I hoped made me look suitably Flemish, but probably made me look more like the man from C&A. The monster lorry was there, but its monster driver wasn't. There was some hold-up with his paperwork at the police station. His lawyer was insisting that a police inspector saw him or something. It was going to take another half an hour.

The team sat around and waited again, listening to the radio, reading the paper or just staring into space. The Tangos turned up and gave us a lot of ribbing about the fact that they'd given us a job on a plate and eight hours later nothing seemed to have happened.

Finally, Carnaby arrived in a car with Ducrane and Ozzy in the back. As they climbed out Carnaby said, 'If you see his lawyer on the way out of town, run the bastard down, won't you? He was only trying to talk him out of it.'

Ducrane looked at us all in a slightly bemused fashion. The Widow threw him the keys for the lorry and signalled to him to start the engine up. Ducrane grinned and walked around his rig checking it out. Then, he hauled his massive bulk up into the cab.

I turned to the Widow. 'Well, I'll be off then.'

She smiled at me. This didn't happen very often. She smoothed the lapels of my donkey jacket and said in a caring voice, 'Now, you've made sure you've got a clean handkerchief, haven't you?'

'Yes, Mum.'

She raised an eyebrow. 'If you ever call me that again, I will rip your bollocks off.'

'Fair enough.'

I climbed into the cab and admired the view over the docks.

'Okay?' I asked the driver.

He puffed out his cheeks and rocked his head from side to side. I pointed to myself and said, 'Harry.'

He just grunted.

'*Allons-y,*' I said and waved him ahead.

It was fascinating to sit there and watch Ducrane manoeuvre the massive rig out of the tight confines of the lorry park and through the dock gates. I wondered what its combined weight was as we laboured over the Jubilee Way flyover at about twenty miles an hour.

I spent some time flicking through the contents of the truck's console. There were lots and lots of comics. For some reason comics are always popular with truckers from the Continent and their cabs are often stuffed with them. You might find plenty of certain magazines in a British driver's cab, but never a comic. These were all cowboy and detective comics like Tintin. It didn't really tie in with the evil drug-smuggler image I had of Ducrane.

He reached over and switched the tape machine on. It blared out some mindless Europop which sounded like the 'Birdie Song'. I was buggered if I was going to endure that all the way to London. I reached over and turned it off.

'*Non,*' I said, displaying my genius for foreign languages again. I waved the radio handset at him and put my fingers in my ears.

'Ahhh,' he said, put his thumb up and grinned.

Who needs to speak Flemish, I thought. Even so, I still didn't trust him. For involvement in an importation of this size he could be looking at five to ten years. It was in his interests to make a break for it and in a rig this size there wasn't much that could be done to stop him. I also thought that he might tip off his mates at the other end. We might not be able to have a conversation, but I thought I ought to do something to break down the barriers. I remembered the number plates at the front of the unit. I pointed down at the front of the cab. 'Michelle, Lulu, Monique, *très bon*, eh?' I said mimicking a fisting motion which suggested that something other than poetry was involved.

He looked at me and then laughed.

'*Non!*' he boomed with a smile. He reached into a pocket on the dashboard and produced a small book of photographs. He flicked though it with one hand until he found the one he wanted. He passed it over. It was a picture of five young blonde-headed girls, all apparently aged under ten.

He reached over the central console with both hands, bracing the steering wheel with his knee: '*Ma fille, Marie,*' he said indicating himself with his hand, and then he lowered his hand to the photograph. '*Les filles de Marie,*' he pointed at each girl in the photograph. '*Marie, Lulu . . .*'

'Oh, granddaughters!' Shit. He barely looked old enough to have granddaughters. 'Um . . . *Elles sont très beaux. Bravo.*'

He stuck a fruit gum in his mouth and offered the packet to me. I flicked through the other photographs. No doubt about it, they were his family all right. We'd all jumped to the wrong conclusion. Maybe he wasn't so bad after all. I chewed my fruit gum and looked out at the empty road. A red Mini practically on the horizon ahead of us was our only company. I called the Widow on the handset. She replied that the tail was with us. I decided that undercover work with drug smugglers wasn't so bad after all.

Then, Ducrane suddenly burst into tears. He held his head in both hands and sobbed his heart out in great keening wails. I climbed up on the seat so that I could reach over the enormous central console which separated us. He still had the steering wheel braced against his knees.

I shook his shoulder:

'Hey! come on! It's going to be all right!'

But he just kept sobbing. And now he wasn't even driving with his knees and we were veering towards the hard shoulder. I grabbed the steering wheel with one hand, it barely moved and felt as though it weighed a ton. I was still shaking his shoulder with my other hand.

'Hey, we're going to crash! *La rue! La rue!*' What the hell was Flemish for 'crash'?

By now he was hysterical, almost screaming and hunched up in his seat. But his feet were still on the pedals and we were accelerating. We had been cruising at a steady fifty. Now we were doing over sixty.

'Kilo 17 to any mobile!' I shouted into the radio handset.

'Go ahead, Kilo 17.'

'It's the driver, he's totally lost it, he's crying his eyes out and he's lost control of the rig! I could do with some help up here!'

I steered with one hand as best I could, still shouting at Ducrane to snap out of it in English and token French. The Mini ahead of us, which had once been so far away, was now getting awfully close. The radio crackled into life. It was Carl. 'Hang on, Chumley, we're coming alongside.'

'No, don't do that,' I shouted, 'I can't control this fucker!' What the hell was he planning to do, leap into the cab cowboy style?

I could control the cab fairly well, but any movement seemed to be magnified by the trailer and it was getting worse. It felt as though we could tip over at any moment. The Widow's voice came over the radio. 'Come on, Harry! Do something. Snap him out of it.'

'I'm fucking trying,' I shouted into the handset and then chucked it aside. The team were bugger-all use and I needed both hands. The Mini was now only a few hundred metres ahead.

I'd never had to deal with anyone who was hysterical before. I began hitting Ducrane on the back with my fist, desperate to get any sort of reaction. But the muscles in his shoulders were so massive it was like a gnat attacking an elephant.

'Hey, snap out of it,' I shouted in his ear as loud as I could. The wailing just went on and on.

The rig was on a long downhill stretch of the motorway and the needle on the speedometer was near eighty. We were right up behind the Mini. I could see that there was only one person in it and they seemed blissfully unaware of us. I looked around desperately for the horn, but I didn't have a clue where it was. There was only one thing to do: try to steer round them.

I tried to make the turn as smooth as possible, but it was almost impossible to move. That was when I nearly lost it. There seemed no way we were going to avoid a crash. I wanted just to duck my head and wait for the inevitable crunch.

Then Ducrane put one hand on the wheel again, even though he

166

was still sobbing. I wrenched his fingers off the wheel and pulled at it again. The nose of the tractor unit pulled out gradually into the outside lane and we had missed the back of the Mini by inches. The driver of the Mini furiously hit the horn, but I breathed a sigh of relief. We were going to miss them.

Then I saw the trailer swinging out in the wing mirror. It was going to sideswipe the back of the Mini as we went past. I tried pushing the wheel back the other way, but it was too late. We were going to hit.

Then, as suddenly as he had become hysterical, Ducrane suddenly lifted himself up saying, 'Okay, it's okay.' He glanced at the wing mirror, gave a heave on the steering wheel and the trailer swung into line behind us. We were still breathtakingly close to the Mini and still whacking along at seventy to eighty, and the turbulence of us passing almost swept the Mini off the road: I saw it wobbling in the wing mirror as we pulled away. The driver wound down the window to wave a fist at us as we pulled away into the distance. They'd never know how close they'd come.

'Sorry, sorry,' mumbled Ducrane, wiping his eyes on the back of his sleeve. 'It's okay.'

I slumped back into my seat, shaking. I radioed to the convoy that Ducrane was all right and sat staring at the road ahead. The Widow asked if he was fit to continue. How the hell did I know? He reached over and switched on the 'Birdie Song' again. This time I didn't stop him. As long as it kept him sane, he could play it as much as he liked.

As we got into heavier traffic nearer London, I followed the agreed plan and signalled to Ducrane to pull into a service station for a short stop. We thought that it would be easier to spot any counter-surveillance there. One vehicle seemed to follow us in, an innocuous little red Datsun saloon. We pulled into the lorry park and stopped. I told Ducrane not to get out.

The driver of the red Datsun had passed us, heading for the car park. But the driver soon re-appeared on foot at the end of the lorry park. He stood there smoking, barely concealing the fact that he was watching us. I warned the Widow over my handset.

'Kilo 3, received. We've got him covered.'

We sat there for about ten minutes while I waited for the Widow's next move. Ducrane signalled that he needed the toilet. The Widow had no objection.

Ducrane and I climbed down from the cab and walked towards the central buildings. If Ducrane was going to attack me or make a run for it, now was his best chance. I had no covert radio with me and had left the handset in the cab. Hopefully some of the Kilos would be out on foot covering me. In case things turned really nasty, I had a heavy, long-bodied Maglite torch in my pocket. It was about the size and weight of a police baton, although as I followed Ducrane's massive bulk into the services, I wasn't sure that it would make much impression on him.

It was desperately tempting to look around for the driver of the Datsun. But I knew that the first eye contact was likely to tip him off, so I kept my head well down. I watched Ducrane's face and hands closely in case he tried to make a covert signal to someone. But he didn't appear to try anything.

When we got back to the cab, the Datsun driver had disappeared, but the Widow called to say that it was time to move on and that they had the Datsun driver where they could see him. We headed on into London.

Everything was going nicely to plan when suddenly Ducrane came off a roundabout at the wrong exit. We had carefully planned this route the night before so that the surveillance team could use parallel routes and I was directing him from a copy of the map on the dashboard. I had clearly pointed to the exit we were supposed to take.

'Hey! Hey! Stop! *Arrêtez vous!*'

I banged on the central console. He didn't want to stop, but slowed down and looked at me quizzically.

'Stop! You must go the other way,' I made frantic hand signals to let him know what I meant. He gabbled away but all I understood was that he was disagreeing with me and insisting we go this other way.

If the drug runners had anyone in a following car, they would be getting more and more suspicious. This was not good. We had to go somewhere or the controlled delivery was off. The cars behind us were beginning to sound their horns. I was going to have to trust him.

'Okay, *allons*.'

He nodded and put the rig into gear and we lumbered on our way. We deviated further and further from the route the Kilos had agreed the previous night.

At one point Ducrane turned and gave me a really evil look. My grip tightened on the torch in my pocket. This looked like it.

'*Café*?' he asked and offered his Thermos across the central console. Then he grinned as if he knew he had me worried. Not only had he recovered from his apparent breakdown, he was starting to get cocky.

The route eventually wound back towards the target premises. With hindsight, I think he was taking a route which he knew avoided low bridges and difficult corners. We'd allowed for that on our route too, but there was no way of letting him know that.

We finally turned into the road at the end of which was the small industrial estate with the new units.

'Kilo 17 to any unit.'

'Yeah, Kilo 17, Juliet 2,' said a female voice, 'like we could miss you. Couldn't you find a bigger lorry? Be aware that we have Zulu 3 in the area, complete a nearby indigo.'

Indigo was the codeword for a café and Zulu 3 was Charlie Johnson, Davies' head of security.

That was the first time that I began to suspect that Danny and the rest of the Intelligence Team weren't playing it straight with us. The fact that the consignment we had picked up was headed for Davies was quite a coincidence. The fact that they had spotted Johnson was one coincidence too many. How had they managed to spot him? Were they looking for him? If so, why? It was only a suspicion, but I was determined to have a word with Danny and Don when this was over.

'Yeah, we also have one minder, complete the corner of Hampden Street, behind you on your four four.'

We pulled up outside a small group of modern industrial units. The one we were looking for had a large steel roller door pulled down over the entrance.

Don's voice came over the radio. It wasn't often that you got an SIO out from the warmth and comfort of his office. This must be important. He was telling the Widow to nick Johnson at the café as soon as the job was knocked.

'Any foxtrots at the back of the unit?' Don asked. Foxtrot was the codeword for an officer on foot.

'Delta 5, yes, yes.'

'Delta 5, Kilo 1, any way in back there when the knock is called?'

'Delta 5, we've got one single door, probably a fire door. Looks pretty thick, wouldn't like to have to break in through it.'

'Kilo 1, received. All call signs, whatever happens, if that steel door starts to come down after they have unloaded, then we knock it. I don't want this turning into some kind of siege while they sit inside and destroy the evidence. Kilo 17, take him in when you're ready. Don't let him out of your sight.'

'Roger that, Kilo 1.'

I switched off the handset. It would be staying in the cab. Ducrane finished manoeuvring the rig up to the loading bay. He turned the engine off and gave a deep sigh. I signalled to him to get out of the cab and handed him the clipboard with the paperwork on.

Together we walked up to the doors. There was still no sign of life. My first thought was that the job was off – either Ducrane's arrest at the port had been noticed or the tail had been spotted on the way up. But if that was so, why was Charlie Johnson in the area?

If the job was still on then the lack of life at the unit could signify a 'rip'. A rip is when the smuggle is organised as usual, but the load is stolen either on the road or at the destination. It is usually done with large consignments of cigarettes or alcohol. Sometimes the driver is in on it and plays along, sometimes not. But rips often turned nasty.

I glanced at the yard, but couldn't see anyone else around. If it was a rip, this would be the perfect place to do it.

We walked up the steps on to a platform. There was an intercom by a side door into the unit. Ducrane hit the call button with his thumb. I hung back about ten yards, still looking around the yard.

By now I was convinced there would be an attack from the other side of the yard, so it was a bit of a shock when the door opened behind me to reveal a skinny guy in his thirties, dishevelled and unshaven. He'd obviously been expecting us because he simply took the clipboard, looked at the papers and said:, 'Yeah, okay, I'll open up. Can either of you guys handle a fork-lift?'

Ducrane didn't even understand what was said. The guy looked at me and I just shrugged and grunted in what I hoped was a suitably Flemish way. The unshaven guy sighed, then went inside to open the roller door.

I stood out of the way as Ducrane opened up the rear of the trailer and the unshaven guy unloaded the pallets. When it was all done, he and Ducrane sorted the paperwork.

At that moment there was a stampede of feet from behind us. My first thought was that it couldn't be the Kilos because this was way too early for a knock. But a dozen officers streamed into the unit, two of them throwing the unshaven man up against the wall.

'Get him out of here, Chumley,' shouted Carnaby pointing at Ducrane.

Ten minutes later Ducrane was in protective custody and the rig was being driven by a Customs officer to a secure car park. As he was led away, Ducrane looked afraid. I explained to him that it was all okay. He smiled and nodded and gave me the thumbs-up sign. Then he was gone.

At the unit a full-scale search was underway. On benches around the walls of the unit, the whole smuggling operation could be seen. The computers were first unpacked and disassembled so that the cannabis soaps could be removed. Then the computers were reassembled and repacked. A pile of plastic holdalls had been found, which were probably to be used for carrying the drugs away. There were empty pallets and a machine for wrapping the pallets in plastic. Worryingly, there was also an opened box of plastic gloves. It looked as though whoever was unpacking the drugs had been careful not to leave forensic evidence. Sure enough, the local police SOCO was never able to get any meaningful prints from the unpacked computers in the unit.

It was clear from the paperwork that the computers containing the drugs were supposedly being shipped to England for repair. Once empty, the computers were simply to be repacked and shipped back to the Continent for the whole cycle to being again. It was a neat little operation.

The little red Datsun had disappeared after the motorway services and the driver was never traced. There had not been enough vehicles in the tail to follow him and stay with the lorry. But we did have the satisfaction of nicking Johnson thanks to a neat bit of work by Kilo 1. Johnson had a criminal record for extreme violence and a reputation for a hair-trigger temper. We had enough officers to go in and make the arrest, but checks with the local police had shown that the café he was in was considered dodgy by the local police. The problem was how to apprehend Johnson without turning it into a major incident.

Apparently, Don simply went into the café, found Johnson and sat down at the table opposite him. He placed his warrant card on the table and said quietly, 'Hello, Charlie, I'm from Customs and Excise and you're under arrest for suspicion of being involved in the importation of controlled drugs. I've got six officers outside, but we can do this quietly instead if you want. I'll give you time to finish your tea and then we'll just walk outside.'

If you or I had tried that, Johnson would probably have hammered us into the ground and run out the back. But he simply looked at Don, thought for a moment, downed his mug of tea and came out of the café as meekly as a lamb to be handcuffed by the waiting officers.

Still, there were a lot of questions to be answered back at Customs House. I couldn't understand why the knock had been called so early. We had the address under control. All we had to do was wait for the real smugglers to turn up. Charlie Johnson was just across the road. Surely he would have gone to the unit and we could have nicked him there? As it was, we had nothing to link him to the unit. What had gone wrong?

I went to see Danny.

A quick call to Terry had confirmed my suspicion that the Tangos had been asked to stop that particular lorry by our intelligence team. I asked Danny what he was hiding.

'Straight up, Harry, we weren't planning to hide anything. The honest truth is that it looks like we've got a new source on Davies.'

I couldn't believe it.

'We've got an informant on Davies?'

'Looks like it. And someone with pretty good access too. But the information came by a strange route – it was phoned into the home address of a police sergeant at Milton Keynes with a request that the information be given straight to Customs. Is that strange or what? At first it sounded so odd that we were suspicious. Davies was pretty pissed off after he and his son were nicked for that rhib job and we thought this might be some kind of time-wasting exercise or possibly some kind of trap. The information also came through at very short notice, which could have been another ruse to make sure we didn't have time to check it too closely. In fact, we were lucky that the Tangos were down there working that exercise.'

So that was why Don had been on the scene of the knock. It was typical of him that when there was a threat to the team he had come out on the ground to supervise things personally. It also helped to explain why he had arrested Johnson himself rather than ordering someone else to do it. Johnson was Davies' enforcer. If a revenge attack on Customs had been planned, then Johnson would have been the man he sent. Johnson could have been carrying a gun, a knife, anything.

'We've looked at the shipping records and there have been seven previous deliveries to that unit. It seems that the call really was genuine and we've actually disrupted a nice little operation belonging to Davies.'

'So now that we've got a source inside the organisation, can we give it to a dedicated target team who will really take Davies apart?'

'Don's discussing it with the Branch 1 Assistant Chief now, but it doesn't look likely. The Bs and Cs have got a lot of work on over the next few months including a planned interception of a freighter at sea which is going to involve the navy. Furthermore, we don't know when this source is going to get in touch again – maybe never. Don't quote me on this, but I think the Kilos are still going to be the first stop for anything Davies-related.'

And that was how it turned out.

As with most referred work, it was quite difficult to make the charges stick on the computer job. The man at the unit claimed that he had only been hired for the day to take the delivery by 'a man he met in a pub'. Once again a pretty unbelievable story, but since we could find no way to link him to the unit, including fingerprints, the jury found him not guilty. The evidence against Johnson was even thinner. He simply claimed that it was a coincidence that he was fifty miles away from his usual neighbourhood and just happened to be at the café waiting to see a girl he had met in a club. Davies made sure that a woman came forward to support his claim. Johnson was released without charge.

Once again, we had got the drugs but hadn't been able to get at Davies. But I felt good for two reasons:

First, I felt sure that the mysterious informant would re-appear. I can't explain why, but we had struck three times in just over a year at the Davies organisation, and even though we couldn't get at him, I was sure we were stirring things up. Whenever I looked at the number of Davies' contacts, I felt that there must be a lot of tensions and rivalries there. Something had to give.

Second, this was the first time I really felt part of the team. Several members of the team told me that I had done well to keep Ducrane's lorry on the road after he broke down in tears. But the real shocker was Carl.

Officially, we still weren't talking to each other. But that day, after searching Johnson's house, Carl suddenly called to me as he leant on the roof of his car, 'You did a good job today, Harry.' He didn't smile, but the look on his face showed that he was being serious. I couldn't think of anything to say in reply and just nodded to him.

Although I was making progress at work, things were falling apart at home. Nicky and I had our worst fight yet. A few weeks earlier we had been invited to a party by one of our old friends from university. It was at a large private house in London and lots of Nicky's friends from other City firms were going to be there. Things didn't start well as I was two hours late – an officer from another team who was supposed to take over from me in an OP had 'forgotten' that it was his night on duty. That didn't really matter, because when I arrived it was clear that this party was going to continue well into the early hours of the morning and probably past dawn.

As I stood at the bar waiting for a drink I had my first hint of trouble. The over-friendly public-school twit standing next to me was unusually cheerful, and as his eyes rolled in his head from time to time, it was clear that he was on something. That wasn't a big deal, but as I wandered around the house and gardens trying to find Nicky it was clear to me that quite a few of the people there were in the same state. It was nothing worse than you saw at any party at university, but after a year on the Division I found that the sight of

them really irritated me. These were the people who were supporting bastards like Davies. I wasn't like Carl. I wasn't going to
thump anyone over it, but I was damned if I was going to sit around
and watch it. When I came across a couple in the bathroom snorting
about a hundred pounds' worth of powder up their nostrils, I finally
snapped.

I found Nicky standing on the lawn with some of her friends and
told her that we were leaving. Not unnaturally she wanted to know
why, and when I told her she suggested that I just have another
drink and ignore it. It was 'only a few losers'.

'Well, you can stay, but I'm going,' I snapped.

'Fine. Go,' she said.

'But,' I hissed, 'you had better tell some of your friends that it's
time to make a quick exit because the Old Bill will be arriving
shortly, understand?'

Of course I didn't call anyone. Things weren't so bad between us
that I wanted to cause her that kind of embarrassment. I was just too
tired and overwrought to be tolerant.

But the whole thing simmered between us and a few days later
broke out into a full-scale row again. She argued, quite rightly, that
I shouldn't feel responsible for the morals of every trader in the City.
I said that as long as I was in the job I wasn't going to stand aside
when I saw it happen. Otherwise what was the point of doing the
job?

We went round and round the houses and finally just left it. But
it was clear that we were going to argue about this again. The two
worlds we were working in were too different. Underneath it all,
what we were really arguing about was that there wasn't room for
two full-time careers in one marriage. I kept hoping that this was
just a difficult patch and that we would pull through. But I was
about to find out just how serious our problems had become.

8

The A2 Chase

'I think we should talk about living apart for a while.'

It was only two weeks since Nicky and I had fallen out over the party and things hadn't improved between us. As the words sank in, I remembered what Ozzy had said about how his divorce started. I think Nicky was taken aback by my shocked expression because her face softened and she said, 'We need to sort this out, Harry. Not next week. Right now.'

We both called in sick and took the children to a friend for the day. And then we talked. We both knew what the basic problem was because we had yelled about it so often. We just couldn't make two high-intensity careers fit. But as the day wound on we agreed we still loved each other and that what we had to do was find a compromise – now, before it was too late.

So we declared a truce. In future Nicky would let me know the times she absolutely had to have my help, such as picking up the children or going with her to some social function. I would make sure that I got out of whatever commitment I had at the Division so that I could be there. In return she would try to cover for me being at work as often as possible, by not taking trips abroad or by leaving work early to collect the children.

We had no idea if this would work, but at least we were trying.

I had thought the job was hard work before I qualified as a

surveillance driver. It was only after I passed the driving course that I realised just how much stress the job can really produce. It wasn't just the pressure of driving at high speed, it was the tension of trying to do so many things at the same time: drive through heavy traffic, watch out for pedestrians, follow the navigator's instructions, look out for counter-surveillance, try to think about collecting evidence. And all this has to be done while making sure that the vehicle always remains hidden from the target. Although sudden or illegal man-oeuvres might be necessary, they must never take place in sight of the target, so you always have to have a mental image in your head of where you are in relation to the target and the rest of the team. This sort of driving has to be done in all weathers, and on an active surveillance shifts can last ten hours or more. The constant stress began to give me medical problems. Soon I was on painkillers for stomach cramps. The tablets affected my sleep so that when I was back on duty I felt even more tired than when I was finished.

Eventually it all caught up with me. I was on loan to another team when there was a knock at a service station just off the M25. One of the targets made a run for it down a slip road. I gave chase in a car. Just as we were closing on the suspect, a female officer who was also chasing him leapt over a low hedge at the side of the road and landed right in front of the car. There was nowhere to go, it was a single carriageway with a high kerb on either side. All I could do was slam the brakes on and pray. As the tyres squealed and we seemed to take forever to stop, there was a bump and she disappeared under the front of the car.

Any driver who has been in a similar situation will know the mounting horror I felt as I clambered out of the car. To my relief, the officer was practically unhurt. The front bumper had just clipped her foot and knocked her down, but the car hadn't actually run over her.

The commander of the knock said that the incident was no one's fault, just one of those things which could happen in the confusion of any knock. But it brought home to me the difference in the work

I was doing now: if a navigator makes a mistake, it can usually be corrected, but if the driver makes a mistake, it is potentially fatal. In future I always made sure that I double-checked any dangerous manoeuvre. It didn't help my speed but it helped me to sleep at nights.

Still, whilst the work had in some ways become more stressful, in others it had become easier. I realised just how much I was beginning to understand the way the team thought when we went on one of our regular bouts of arrest and restraint training. This wasn't (as you might think) for our protection when making an arrest, but rather to make sure that we didn't injure the criminal we were arresting and thus expose the Division to an expensive law-suit. There are few sights quite as funny as an ID team of considerably varying waistlines and levels of fitness, dressed in old T-shirts and tracksuit bottoms, lined up for arrest and restraint training. It was like exercising with the Addams Family. An ex-army PT instructor would take us through a series of arm and wrist locks which we would all forget five minutes later.

The Widow had a particularly low opinion of the value of this sort of training. She even refused to change clothes. The most she would agree to do was kick off her shoes so as not to damage the mats. Occasionally she would leave the room for a 'medicinal' cigarette. It was as she returned from one of these forays that the exasperated instructor asked, 'Do you think you know all this then, sweetheart?'

We all winced at the word 'sweetheart'. The Widow looked around at us all.

'I think I know enough to make an arrest,' she said grimly.

I knew straight away what she was thinking and started to edge forward. The instructor stepped forward until he was only a foot away from her.

'Fine. Let's see you arrest me then.'

The Widow's eyes narrowed for a moment and then she said, 'Get him.'

We piled on to him from every direction. It was all good-natured. Soon a muffled voice from underneath thirteen bulky ID officers shouted, 'You bastards!'

The Widow walked over to where his face was sticking out from the bottom of the pile. She leant over him and said, 'You do not have to say anything unless you wish to do so. Anything you do say may be written down and given in evidence . . .'

Meanwhile, back in the office, the new intelligence source which Danny was counting on had been silent for several months. Davies himself seemed to be lying low. His phones and bank accounts showed hardly any activity at all. Lard Boy appeared to have been banished to the family villa in Spain. We were too busy to spend much time on an inactive subject, so Davies' name began to slip down the list of team priorities. I was at home covering for Nicky when the case suddenly burst into life again. It meant that I missed one of the most exciting knocks of the whole year:

Late one Friday, the phone rang at Customs House. There was a groan right through the room. It always happened on a Friday afternoon just before we were due to leave.

The Widow picked up the phone and sat listening intently, occasionally muttering 'Uh-huh' into the receiver and tapping her teeth with the end of her pencil. She made a few notes.

All heads sank as she said, 'Okay, we'll take it. Tell Dover to give us a "heads up" if they move.'

Automatically people began grabbing kitbags, pulling radio batteries out of the chargers and arguing over who was going to have which car. The Widow's piercing whistle brought all this to a halt.

'Right. There are two Austrian lorries parked up at Dover having just come off the three o'clock ferry from Calais. The drivers appear to be taking their compulsory rest stop. Apparently, one of the drugs dogs' handlers was exercising her dog . . .'

This time there was a really loud groan around the room. The team had no faith in the dogs which they considered fine for TV appearances but little else. They were okay for picking off the occasional mule or badly wrapped concealment, but most of the drugs we encountered were securely wrapped, hidden in compartments, often behind a layer of concrete or mastic and sometimes mixed with coffee or some other strong aromatic to hide the scent.

'Yeah, I know, I know, but she swears the dog is right about this one and the Collector has asked that we take it.'

More boos and a few paper darts. There was a cry of 'Why can't the Unit take it?'

'The dog doesn't trust them,' said Ozzy to widespread laughter.

'The Unit are out on another call. It's probably nothing and we don't know how long these targets are going to be stationary so I'll need seven volunteers and we'll need to get down there fast.'

After an hour or so of high-speed driving, the team were well on the way to Dover when they got the call that the lorries had moved off. The Widow had to make a quick estimate of where on the motorway the Kilos and the lorries would intercept at their current speeds, then the team had to switch to the opposite carriageway and spread out to wait at several different vantage-points.

The Austrian lorries were soon spotted by the southernmost car moving slowly and steadily in convoy. One by one the Kilos' vehicles fell into a well-rehearsed pattern around them. But just as they were settling in for a long haul up to the M25, the lorries suddenly pulled off the road into a deserted car park. There had once been a roadside café here, but it had long since closed down and was boarded up. This caught the team out totally. They couldn't really go in without showing out. They had to scatter and pull off the road anywhere they could. Rick leapt out on foot and ran into the undergrowth around the car park to keep observation on the lorries. He hid in some bushes on a slight rise and gave a whispered running commentary. The lorries had parked in the middle of the car park. The drivers were just sitting in their cabs as if waiting for something. One was talking on a mobile phone or radio.

After about twenty minutes, a blue transit van drove into the car park. Patrick and Ozzy, who were in a car further down the motorway, had already spotted it as a potential target. The transit van drove slowly around the car park, staying well away from the lorries, and then parked near the entrance. A figure climbed out of the driver's side.

'Jesus,' Rick called softly over his radio, 'you'll never guess who's got out of the transit. It's that big bastard from Chumley's job. Zulu 3.'

It was indeed Charlie Johnson. He spent some time walking around the car park smoking a cigarette and taking care to have no contact at all with the lorries. At one point he stood staring straight up the bank to where Rick was poorly concealed behind the row of bushes.

Johnson returned to his van and Rick soon reported that he was making a call on his mobile. The Widow told all vehicles to stay put.

Ten minutes passed very slowly. Then Patrick called that another transit van, white this time, containing two men, had just driven at speed past his position. Sure enough, Rick was soon reporting that the white van had driven straight up to the Austrian lorries and pulled up at the rear.

The Widow ordered all four cars to move up closer to the entrance. She told Granville to block the entrance when they went in.

Rick watched as the Austrians opened up one of the lorries and the two men from the white transit climbed into it. He noted that they had left the engine of the van running. Shortly afterwards he could see that they were bringing boxes out of the lorry and throwing them into the back of the white transit. The Widow waited until about a dozen boxes had been transferred and then she called, 'Knock! Knock! Knock!'

Three Kilo cars and the Juliets roared into the car park past a shocked-looking Johnson. Rick stood up, shouted, 'Stay where you are! Customs and Excise!' and started to sprint down the hill. In retrospect it might have been better to run rather than shout, because Johnson immediately turned, saw Rick coming and raced back towards his van. (Considering the relative sizes of little Rick and Charlie Johnson and Johnson's record for violence, perhaps it was better that Rick did shout.)

Johnson got into the blue transit and slammed and locked the door a moment before Rick crashed into it. He roared off towards the entrance.

The two other cars had made straight for the lorries. One of the lorry drivers simply threw up his hands and surrendered. The other turned and ran for it. Patrick and Ozzy pulled their car to a halt at the back of one of the lorries to arrest the standing driver and secure the rest of the drugs.

Meanwhile, one of the two men who had been unloading the boxes threw down the box he was holding, shouted a warning to his accomplice and leapt into the front seat of the white transit. He pulled away just as the other leapt out of the back of the lorry. The white transit accelerated away, its rear doors open and loose boxes falling out of the back, the second smuggler scrambled inside and pulled the doors shut as it raced for the exit with two ID cars close behind.

While this was happening, Johnson drove at full speed straight for Granville's car, which was blocking the car park entrance. But Granville didn't move. At the last moment, Johnson swerved to go around the front of Granville's roadblock, but as an experienced ex-copper Granville had been waiting for that. He had the car in gear and simply moved forward to block him off again.

If Johnson had hesitated, Granville would have stopped him, but Johnson was an old hand too. He accelerated hard and slammed his van straight into the front wing of Granville's car. There was a grinding of metal and the Volvo was forced aside. Granville immediately tried to ram Johnson again as he sped past and caught the rear of the van a glancing blow.

For a moment it looked as if the van would tip over completely, but then it righted itself and Johnson was around the bend and tearing

183

north along the M2 towards London. The other transit then hit Granville and he lost control of the vehicle, swerved down a bank and into a concrete post. Two ID vehicles tore past in hot pursuit.

Back in the car park, Rick turned and saw one of the Austrian drivers running away up the bank. He sprinted after him, but the adrenalin surge of the initial charge had worn off and years of booze and fags took their toll. The Austrian was soon at the top of the rise. Rick had already decided he wasn't going to catch him when the Austrian suddenly glanced back and threw up his hands, saying, 'Okay, okay!'

Rick threw himself into a last-gasp rugby tackle which brought the Austrian down. Straining for breath, he sat on top of his prisoner while he handcuffed him.

'What the fuck was all that about? Why did you stop running?'

'I saw your gun. I did not want to be shot.'

At first Rick didn't have a clue what the Austrian was talking about. But as they walked back towards the lorries where Granville already had the second driver under arrest, the truth slowly began to dawn. All officers are supposed to note their observations in their notebooks. So while he was hiding in the bushes, Rick had been writing down what he could see. As soon as the knock was called, he had stuffed his notebook into a pocket, but the large stainless-steel pen was still in his hand. The Austrian had seen the light glance off the metal barrel in Rick's fist and had assumed that he was armed, just as Customs officers are on the Continent.

Granville had already checked out one of the lorries. 'Looks like there's at least another dozen boxes in there, more than we can carry in one car. So we've got at least fifty kilos of drugs, two prisoners and one car is wrecked. Any ideas?'

Rick looked at the lorries and then at the two drivers.

'Fancy riding in a lorry down to Dover?' he grinned.

Meanwhile on the M2, a full-scale chase had developed. Only two ID cars were now left in the hunt, the Widow and the Juliets, but they were faster than the two transits. However, the vans were working together to block them. All four vehicles swerved back and forth around the other traffic in the rapidly darkening evening to the accompaniment of angry car horns and flashing headlights. The job was rapidly sliding out of control. The two ID drivers didn't doubt that they could get past the vans – they had the speed and they had the manoeuvrability – but then there would be another problem: two of them might have the weight to stop one of the vans, but they probably couldn't stop both. Which one should they pick? As the senior officer in the chase, it would be the Widow's decision.

'Which one do you want to take?' asked the Juliets' officer.

'We'll go for the white one, it's got the drugs in. Now listen carefully, we can't afford to fuck this up. I'm going past, but you hold back. We'll try and stay like that for a few more miles, there's still a chance that one of them will make a mistake and crash. Then we can bag both of them.'

The Widow accelerated on to the hard shoulder and then, using a civilian car which had pulled into the slow lane as cover, she moved ahead of the transits and maintained a pace which kept her just in front of them. The trouble was that they were travelling at speeds of about a hundred miles an hour and she had to keep her attention on what was happening both ahead and behind, while telling Control what was happening and calling for police assistance.

'How far are you from the suspects?' asked Control calmly just as one of the transits rammed the back of the Widow's Sierra. At those speeds it was almost enough to send her out of control and off the road.

'If they get any closer than this you can fucking well speak to them,' she shouted.

Meanwhile the Juliet's radio man was desperately trying to raise any other ID vehicle.

'Any ID vehicle receiving on Channel Zero, this is a Branch 1 team in pursuit of two vehicles fleeing a knock currently two miles from blue three zero northbound on the M2. Over.'

Luckily his calls were picked up by a car belonging to the

Yankees which was only a few miles up the carriageway. He pulled over and waited until he could see the erratically veering headlights in his rear-view mirror.

'I can pull out in front and we can try some sort of rolling roadblock,' he suggested.

'No way,' replied the Widow. 'These guys have got the weight to just ram us out of the way. Pull in behind until I can think of something else.'

'You know next time you guys should try and arrest them before they run,' the Yankee joked.

Within a few minutes police assistance arrived, but not in the manner expected. A motorway patrol car was cruising in the inside lane when the chase tore past. It immediately joined in but clearly didn't realise what was going on as it signalled to the Yankees' car to pull over and stop.

Two things didn't help. First, police and Customs radios are not compatible. Whenever we worked with a police team on a joint operation we had to swap a few radio sets just so that we could talk to each other. So there was no way for the ID team to let the patrol car know what was happening.

Second, at that time no metal identification badges had been issued to Division officers despite repeated requests from the rank and file. The only ID we had was a small laminated card with a photograph. The driver for the Yankees slowed down alongside the police car, and held out his identification card with one hand while driving with the other. Of course, in the darkness and speed of the chase the patrol car couldn't see what he was waving or hear what he was saying. Thinking that the Yankee's' manoeuvre meant that he was slowing down, the patrol car tried to move ahead to cut him off. With a curse the Yankee put his foot down. As he did so a second patrol car pulled out and joined in the chase, blue lights flashing.

'Control, this is Kilo 3, we now have Martians in the convoy and they have no idea who we are. There is going to be a fucking accident and you need to inform area traffic control NOW!'

Martians was the code word for police. By now the transits were throwing things out, including their mobile phones, partly in the hope of dissuading the chasing cars and partly to dispose of any possible evidence.

Finally the message got through to the traffic cars who eased off the Yankee vehicle. One of the patrol cars pulled back alongside the Yankee and the officer in the passenger seat shrugged as if to say, 'How did we know?' The Yankee grinned back and gave him a mock salute. A few minutes later a third traffic car joined in the chase and shortly after that a van carrying the police dog unit.

The Widow was trying everything she could think of to slow the transits down, including sudden braking, using traffic to produce bottlenecks, or allowing the transits to move alongside and then swerving towards them as though she was about to ram them. She knew she couldn't actually do this because of the amount of civilian traffic, but ID officers aren't trained in mobile stops and she was making it up as she went along. The police patrol cars were trained of course, but they were holding back as they didn't know who was Customs and who wasn't.

Finally one of the patrol cars roared around the inside of the pursuing group and pulled alongside the Yankee's car. Honking the horn, they signalled to him to lower his windows and then held up one of their radios to show that they were going to throw it across. In a piece of precision high-speed driving, they came close together and the radio was thrown to land safely on the passenger seat. Now at least the two teams could talk to each other. The Yankee turned the radio volume up to full.

'Hello, Customs and Excise,' squawked the radio, 'what shall we call you?'

'Yankee 10.'

'Okay, Yankee 10, do you have any idea what this is about?'

'As far as I know, one of those two transits ahead of us is carrying cannabis which has just been smuggled into the country. These guys escaped when this team were trying to arrest them.'

'Okay, listen, Yankee 10, we have to put a stop to this before someone gets hurt. The Kent Police helicopter has been scrambled and should be with us any minute. We have arranged for more units to intercept at Blackheath, we need you to pull your people out of there so that we can do our stuff.'

'Wait one.'

Yankee 10 relayed all this to the Widow who by now was quite glad to get out of the hot seat.

'Kilo 3 to all mobiles. Pull back to a safe distance, but stay close. This is still an ID arrest when these bastards are stopped. These guys are just helping us out.'

By now the chase had almost reached Blackheath and the searchlight from the police helicopter was trained on the lead transit containing Johnson. He must have sensed that his time was almost up. As they came up on to the Common he could see the blue lights of the intercepting vehicles in the road ahead. He decided to take action.

He swerved violently off the road. There was a ditch around the Common designed to stop travellers using the place as a campsite, but the transit was going so fast that it cleared this. One of the following police vehicles was able to do the same. The police dog unit almost made it, but then its front wheels skidded on the turf and the van was thrown sideways. It went over on two wheels and landed upside down in the ditch. Somewhere in the van a radio was left on transmit for some time after the accident and all that could be heard above the other transmissions was the dog going mad and the profanities of his handler.

'Juliet mobile and Yankee 10, stay with the white transit. I'll take the blue,' ordered the Widow.

The other two cars stayed just behind the police car still tailing the white transit. The Widow kept her eyes on the blue van, but she stayed on the road and went the long way round, not wanting to lose the car in the jump on to the Common and wanting some distance in case Johnson pulled another manoeuvre. She watched as he pulled the transit van back on to the road on the other side of the Common and raced on again, followed by the traffic car.

The Widow saw her chance as she roared around the Common against the traffic lights. She swung on to the road Johnson had taken and drove head-on towards him. No one knows whether she would actually have rammed Johnson, although the other police driver involved later said he was seriously impressed. Johnson didn't hang around to find out. As soon as he saw the vehicle coming towards him, he swung the van into a side road. The Widow followed with the police car close behind.

Johnson must have known the area. He had only gone a few hundred yards down the side road, when he turned into an alleyway. It was a tight fit. He was travelling at such speed that he skidded and crashed off both walls. The van screeched to a halt, wedged diagonally across the alleyway. There wasn't even room to open the doors. Johnson smashed the windscreen and clambered out over the bonnet, disappearing into the darkness of the alleyway.

As the Widow braked to a halt behind the van she saw that there was no way past, even on foot. The two traffic officers arrived seconds later and the Widow shouted, 'Quick, give me a lift up on to the roof.'

She scrambled over the van and set off down the alleyway, pulling a Maglite from her belt. There were gardens either side of the alleyway. Johnson could have dodged into any one of them or he might be sprinting away into the darkness. The Widow couldn't hear him. The other two officers arrived behind her, one of them radioing for support as he did so. Together they set off to find where Johnson was hiding.

Meanwhile, the white transit containing the drugs had sped on across Blackheath. There was confusion at the roadblock and the van was able to swerve through a gap between the police vehicles and head on towards the Old Kent Road. The ID vehicles followed close behind. There were no other police vehicles left and it was up to the two of them to stop the van now.

In desperation, Yankee 10 moved up and tried nudging the transit off the road. He bounced off and nearly lost control of his own car. He eased back and decided not to try that again.

Fortunately, this last effort seemed to make the criminals realise that they had to do something. To this day no one is sure exactly what they were trying; the pair of them weren't very forthcoming about it after their arrest. Entering an empty stretch of road, the transit suddenly slowed down, the doors opened and both passengers leapt out into the road, tumbling over and over. The passenger didn't get up at first and Yankee 10 nearly ran over his body. Yankee 10 screeched to a halt, jumped out and raced over to him just as he was clambering unsteadily to his feet. He was so shaken that he gave up without a fight.

The driver had landed more neatly and soon jumped to his feet. But he had sprained his ankle badly and his dash to freedom became a halting stumble. The Juliets climbed from their car and yelled at him to stop. Defiantly the driver lumbered on.

'Oh Jesus,' said one of the Juliets, looking ahead.

The transit van containing the remaining boxes of drugs had careered off down the road. It followed a straight course before ploughing at about ten miles an hour straight through the front window of an Indian restaurant. Fortunately, the restaurant was closed. There was a crash of glass and the burglar alarm screeched into life.

For a moment, Customs officers and criminals alike stood in the road, transfixed by the sight. The Juliets' driver told me later that his first thought as he saw it happen was, 'Am I going to get the blame for this?'

The driver of the white transit continued limping away down the road. One of the Juliets' drivers climbed back into his car and roared up the street, then pulled the car to a screeching halt in front of him. The driver climbed out and the look on his face must have made it clear that the transit driver wasn't going any further. With a final exclamation of 'Fuck!' he simply placed his hands on the roof of the car and waited to be handcuffed.

The police helicopter had stayed with the white transit when Johnson had sped across the Common. If it had stayed with the cars chasing Johnson, things might have been different. As it was, there was no sign of him even though Customs and police spent hours searching the area. He was later reported to have made it to the Continent.

That was the big disappointment of the night, but the result wasn't too bad considering that an under-strength team went out on a job which they expected to lead nowhere. They had recovered the drugs – 250 kilos of cannabis resin – they had arrested four out of the five smugglers involved, and they knew the identity of the fifth. It would only be a matter of time before he was picked up. Furthermore, following a long car chase and catching them red-handed, it should be a fairly simple matter to put them all behind bars.

At least, that's how it seemed. But as usual the justice system came rushing to the criminals' aid just when it looked as though they were finished.

The first problem arose when the Austrian drivers applied for bail. As usual, in their interviews after arrest they simply followed the advice of the solicitors and said nothing to any of our questions while they waited to see what evidence we had against them. Once they had heard what the case was (i.e. that they hadn't been under surveillance abroad and that we didn't have an inside source on the job), they were able to lay their plans for escape.

From the fact that these men had pulled their lorries into the secluded car park and co-operated with the transit van drivers, it would seem fairly obvious to any sensible person that they were in on the smuggling operation. But at the hearing lawyers for the lorry drivers claimed that they had thought they were unloading a legitimate cargo, that they had offered no resistance when arrested and had previously clean records (i.e. they hadn't been caught

191

before). Their lawyers said that the drivers would surrender their passports and agree to report regularly to a police station and offered a surety. Granville had been appointed case officer and he attended the hearing to represent Customs and Excise. The application for bail represented the kind of bullshit you always hear at these affairs – we didn't do it, we weren't there, blah, blah, blah. Most magistrates' benches would have rejected these arguments because of the amount of drugs concerned and the obvious involvement of the drivers. You can imagine Granville's horror when the magistrates granted the drivers bail and they walked from the court to all intents and purposes free.

Within a week they had skipped back to the Continent and were never seen again.

We saw it coming and some people might argue that we should have put the drivers under surveillance. But the simple truth is that we just didn't have the manpower. We were always working on several cases at the same time, there was always need for work on other jobs. Even if we were in a fairly quiet period, we had to lend troops to other hard-pressed teams. It's the usual problem in law enforcement: there just aren't enough officers to go round.

Even if we had followed the drivers, how long would it have lasted? A week? A month? There was no telling when they were going to make their move. And you can imagine the field day the defence lawyers would have had if the surveillance officers had shown out. There would have been accusations of intimidation and undermining the decision of the court. It would have been a disaster.

But that was just the beginning of our troubles. The driver of the white transit claimed that he was just a driver and had no idea what was in the boxes. He had driven off in panic, not knowing that the arriving cars were Customs officers. The question of why he would throw out all the paperwork in the van as well as his mobile phone wasn't considered. He too was given bail.

By the time the case actually came to trial it was clear that we were in trouble. The problem was that the boxes had not been opened and so the defendants were going to be able to run the defence that they thought the contents were tobacco or something similar. The disappearance of Johnson meant that everything could be blamed on him as the mastermind. The drivers could also be blamed as they weren't in the dock either.

But the real problem was the disappearance of the mobile phones. The transits must have been called at some stage to let them know where to meet the lorries. At least three mobiles were thrown from the two vehicles during the chase. They would have been vital evidence. But during the chase there was no time to stop and collect them in case the drugs were lost. Extensive searches were made the following morning, but it was hard to be specific about exactly where on the chase they had been thrown and there was a lot of grass verge to cover. Even the local council workers whose job it is to clear the verges of rubbish were questioned in case they had found them. Perhaps they had, but the phones were never produced.

Granville did his best to construct a case, tracing where the vans had come from, looking at the history of previous trips by the Austrian drivers and so forth. But then, at the trial, a final error blew the case to pieces, something that no case officer could have allowed for.

Where there is no official observation log, officers are supposed to make notes at the time or as soon as possible afterwards, noting the time this was done. The two men from the white transit were in the dock. Of course, we didn't yet know what their defence was going to be – they had kept silent in the interviews, they would spring their defence on us at the last moment when there was no chance to check it out – but we expected it to be the usual 'We didn't know it was drugs' line.

We were surprised that the defence was cross-examining the police and Customs drivers from the chase. Going over the details seemed to us to make the two in the dock look more and more guilty. If they were just innocent guys who were unloading some stuff for a bit of pocket money, then why did they run, and most importantly, why did they keep running and cause considerable danger to the public when they saw the blue lights of the police cars?

The defence team was fishing through the paperwork. The paperwork associated with an arrest is so complicated these days that there is always a chance of finding an error.

But this time the defence had found a legitimate problem.

The Juliets' radioman was questioned about his note of the incident. Had he said this? Had he said that? Then defence counsel asked him why the note wasn't timed. For some reason, he panicked. He said it wasn't timed because the note was written at the time of the chase. The defence counsel was on to this like a shot. He pointed out the conditions of the chase, the darkness, the speed and the manoeuvres. Then he had the notebook passed around the jury. It was in immaculate handwriting, clearly not something written in the darkness of a speeding car. The notebook had to be withdrawn.

Defence then began to question whether other parts of the Customs record were made up, and the case collapsed shortly afterwards.

Why had the officer panicked and said that he wrote the note at the time? I don't know. I don't think he deliberately lied. Sometimes when you are standing in the dock trying to remember details of a job by then months old, with everyone staring at you, it is easy to panic and say the first thing that comes into your head. But that is no excuse. It was a cock-up and, unlike the defence, we have to be more or less perfect. The defence only has to show one reasonable doubt to win.

I often used to think about the Brink's Mat bullion case: civil procedures were used against many of the criminals involved and the people associated with them. In civil cases, the balance of proof merely has to be in favour of the prosecution (i.e. if the prosecution prove 51 per cent of their case, they win). It was hardly surprising that with their inbuilt advantage removed, the criminals gave up and almost all the money lost in the robbery was later recovered.

Still, although the case had fallen apart, at least Davies had been hit again. He had lost another drugs consignment, but more importantly he had been deprived of Charlie Johnson, his right-hand man and enforcer. Davies would find someone else to fill that role and Johnson would continue to be useful to him on the Continent, but still it was another blow landed.

Danny later confirmed to me that the information had been another anonymous tip from the Davies source. The drugs dog story had merely been a cover which Danny created to protect the source. When the case had come to court, legal means had been used to protect the identity of the original information. The most important thing was that someone in the organisation was still trying to bring Davies down. The source was either being highly selective or only had access to information on rare occasions, but we were anxious to see where he or she would strike next.

9

Beer

Somewhere deep inside Customs House there is a bar called Waxers. The bar is named after the Customs officers' ancient privilege of being allowed to break the wax seals on imported spirits in order to sample the contents (a privilege which I am sure Customs officers in times gone by never abused . . .). The walls of Waxers are lined with shields and pennants from many different law enforcement, intelligence and military organisations around the world and it is a considerable honour for someone outside the Division to be invited to drink there. With work as stressful as it is in the Division, it was hardly surprising that many of the older hands were serious drinkers, and Don was no exception. He could certainly drink anyone on the team under the table and whenever he felt that morale was low or the air needed clearing because some members of the team had fallen out, he would appear in the team room at the end of the day with a full bottle of Scotch and announce, 'Right lads, we're drinking.' It was an offer he made impossible to refuse and by the time we had recovered from the hangover and remembered where we were, it was usually time for work again.

Some puritans may be horrified that such habits were tolerated in an organisation entrusted with enforcing the law, and certainly the senior Customs management often hinted that they would like to see Waxers closed down permanently. As an outsider I might have agreed. The high levels of alcohol consumption are a danger sign of the considerable stress an ID officer suffers. But from within, it soon becomes clear that the traditions of the Division and the freedom officers have to bend the rules are also a matter of trust – they create an *esprit de corps* which gives the Division its particular character. ID officers aren't risking their lives for the money they are paid and they work very long, anti-social hours, often in difficult conditions. Without the intense sense of teamwork and the camaraderie of belonging to a quirky, practically unique organisation, they probably wouldn't do it at all.

Danny, our intelligence officer, was an old hand who, like Don, had been in the Division for almost twenty years. I had been working with him against Davies for over a year now. I could see that he was a highly capable officer who seemed be on good terms with almost everyone in the Division, so at first I was puzzled that he was stuck behind a desk rather than out on operational duties. But after the first few visits to his smoky den on the ground floor of Customs House, I began to notice that there would always be a whisky glass on his desk and very often there would be whisky in it. My suspicions were confirmed whenever he came out to socialise with the team – here was a man who could drink for England. (He could have smoked for England too.) Yet his dedication to his work was total. With several broken marriages behind him and his children grown up, he lived for the Division, and no matter how late I left the office he always seemed to be working later still, chasing up even the slightest of leads.

It was one afternoon about a month after the chase along the M2 that Danny sat down on the edge of my desk in the middle of about six months' worth of court paperwork. The Solicitor's Office was screaming for most of it by yesterday and I wasn't in the best of moods.

'What am I doing?' said Danny cheerfully, pointing at his face.

I shrugged. 'Who knows? Maturing disgracefully?'

He shook his head. 'I'm grinning, and do you know why I'm grinning?'

I threw down my pen. 'Oh, for fuck's sake, Danny!'

'Okay, okay. But I have got some really good news for you. Come down to my office and we'll talk about it. But for you my son, it is fucking Christmas!'

In his office Danny revealed that the Davies source had come up trumps again. The division between intelligence and operations isn't always as clear-cut in the ID as it would be in the world of espionage. This is because, unlike espionage, an investigation by the Division usually culminates in a trial, and all matters, including intelligence leads, will be examined in open court. So there is no reason to keep a case officer in the dark and there may even be some operational advantages. But Danny didn't tell me every time there was a contact by the source, only when it was likely to lead to a further step in the investigation. Also, to keep the existence of the source secret, we tried, whenever possible, to disguise the origin of the tip-offs from the rest of the team. Until Davies was beaten, the fewer people who knew about it the better.

Danny had been spending a lot of time trying to track down the mainstay of Davies' smuggling operation. The source was providing us with some good stuff and it had led to us taking out a few consignments, but from the money flowing through Davies' accounts it was clear that the organisation chugged on. There had to be something else – a more dependable operation which supplied his regular money.

Danny revealed that the Davies source had been in contact three times recently. But the information had been incomplete or vague as though the source didn't understand what we needed. Using what we got plus a lot of work from Customs officials in the Isle of Man, Danny had finally managed to connect Davies to a company which imported bottled beer. Better still, this company was importing large consignments every few months. Danny laid out the import statistics on the desk between us.

'But where does all that beer go, Harry? Thousands of litres of imported Dutch and Belgian beer?' he asked.

'He's got pretty good club contacts. He provides door security. If he's moving gear, why not move beer as well?'

'Nah! He hasn't got that sort of distribution. This is big stuff, there's large companies which could undercut anything he was bringing in. More than that, look how far back the records go. The company's been into this for a long time and his connection with it goes back even further. It was one of the first he got involved in when he got out of the car-ringing business. I reckon this is it, Harry. I reckon this is the one that will break the bastard!'

'Have you had any consignments pulled yet?'

'First one is due in at Harwich tonight. We're giving it a routine tug, nothing too heavy. The company is due one so it shouldn't set the alarm bells ringing. Ask Don if he can stand your boys ready for a call tonight – if there's gear in the container then we'll give it a live run.'

But no call came from the docks all evening. Finally, about two in the morning, my phone rang at home. Rubbing the sleep out of my eyes, I picked up the receiver.

'Sorry, Harry, nothing this time. They opened almost every packing-case in the container, I think the crew leader got a bit pissed off at me, but it was all beer. I reckon we just got unlucky and this was one of the genuine ones they run to give the operation some cover.'

'Okay, Danny. Catch you next time,' I yawned.

But that had woken me up and I couldn't get back to sleep. It was pouring with rain outside, I could hear it drumming against the double glazing. It would have been a long, cold, uncomfortable night if we'd had to go out to Harwich. But my overwhelming feeling was one of disappointment that Davies' luck seemed to have saved him again. And then it struck me. I wasn't as worried about staying in my nice warm bed as I had been for much of the past year. I wanted to be out there, getting after him. Nicky wouldn't have approved. As I looked over at her, I wondered if I was going to become part of the Division's extensive divorce statistics. It was best not to think about it. I rolled over and tried to get back to sleep.

The next consignment came in two weeks later. Once again we stood the team ready for a job, once again the rummage crew found nothing. They even ran the drugs dog over it. Nothing.

Danny was bitterly disappointed. It looked as though all his work was going to waste. You couldn't keep pulling the containers for inspection. If Davies had someone monitoring the docks, and almost every respectable smuggling operation did, then they would soon spot the attention and the whole operation would close down. Danny gambled on one last search.

Once again the container was identified by a rummage crew and opened up. Once again they lifted box after box of bottles out of the container in the floodlights of the dockside. A long, cold, tiring job. They checked the boxes, they even checked the skin of the container and measured its internal and external dimensions as they looked for concealments. Once again they found nothing. Probably swearing that this was the last of Danny's tips that he'd ever follow, the team leader ordered his people to start putting it all back. It was when they were halfway through this that one tired rummage officer dropped a crate, smashing several of the bottles inside. He picked up the box to throw it into the container. As he did so the bottom dropped out, scattering broken beer bottles everywhere.

And amongst all the broken glass were small packages of cannabis resin.

In an ideal world this would have been checked before, but it hadn't been. Once they knew what they were looking for, the rummage team quickly ascertained that almost half the bottles in the consignment contained the drugs. Hidden by large labels and dark green glass, the slim bars of resin were wrapped in plastic to protect them from the alcohol.

As soon as the discovery was made, Danny rang Don. The original plan had been to take the drugs boxes out of the consignment, put in dummy boxes and follow the container when it was picked up. But we couldn't remove half the boxes without the difference being noticed. We considered emptying the boxes and filling them with sand to make up the weight, but that would have taken too long, and if Davies did have someone at the docks it would certainly be noticed. We were going to have to run this load 'live'. Don woke one of the Deputy Chiefs to get authorisation, but it was made clear that we must take absolutely no chances which might mean losing the drugs.

The rummage team closed up the container and had it placed back in its stack by the high loader as though they had once again found absolutely nothing.

We weren't expecting the load to be picked up until at least the following morning, but you could never be sure, so the Kilos drove up to Harwich that night. Port staff would be able to give us plenty of warning about the pick-up, so we spent the first half-hour or so driving around and familiarising ourselves with the area. It had been agreed that Granville would be the case officer, so he went into the port and made contact with the senior Customs officers there. Then it was a matter of finding a hotel within reasonable distance so that off-duty officers would have somewhere to rest.

Someone had done some calculations on the back of a cigarette packet and concluded that the consignment was huge, possibly as much as three-quarters of a tonne. That, together with the fact that a major target like Davies was concerned, made the management at Customs House nervous. They were worried that the contents of the container might be removed while it was in storage out of sight of the surveillance team. So it was decided that electronic alarm devices would be placed inside several of the boxes, alerting us if a box was opened.

It would have been ideal if we could have bugged the container as well, but that wasn't possible without much more time to prepare. A device inside wouldn't have been able to transmit because of the container's metal skin. Something on the outside was almost certain to be spotted or dislodged. But the device in the box should work because by then the container would have been opened and the signal could escape. Well, that was the theory. Like all electronic devices we didn't trust it one bit. We'd take it with us, but we wouldn't be happy unless one of us could actually see the container.

On the second night a dedicated Customs unit went in to place the devices. This carefully selected team specialises in breaking into premises and evading alarm systems. They were the ones who placed microphones, miniature cameras and tracking devices.

No ID team can spend forever waiting for a target. Other live cases required action and there was always the likelihood of another 'fire brigade' case from Dover. Don calculated that we could give this surveillance only four days. After that, we would still take the case, but any lorry which arrived to pick up the container would have to be delayed by the port officials while we got a team together and drove up from London. That risked raising the suspicions of the gang and blowing the job.

This time luck was with us. A driver arrived to pick up the container halfway through the fourth day. Those officers not already on watch rushed from the hotel and drove like maniacs to get into position.

The container was easy enough to follow, but its low speed meant a lot of looping and back-tracking to keep the surveillance vehicles from becoming visible. We were especially alert because we knew that Davies had an interest in this one and experience had shown us how he liked to take counter-surveillance measures such as putting out a watcher.

As soon as the lorry left the port and got on to the motorway things looked promising – the driver headed south, back towards Davies territory. It made the choice of a port well off his patch all the more logical. Eventually the long took the A13 and turned into the massive Hays storage facility near Dagenham.

We plotted up on the entrance and waited. This was a dangerous moment. Lorries were coming in and out of the facility all the time and apart from colour, one container looks much like another. The identification numbers on a container are small and hard to read. It wasn't long before the tractor unit which had taken our container into the facility came out again – empty. The question was: had our container been transferred to another lorry or had it been put into long-term storage?

We couldn't just approach the staff at the facility in case the gang had a contact there who was watching out for Customs. The Widow rang Don to see if we had a confidential contact at Hays who could check on the container for us. We couldn't park too close to the gates without showing out, which made identifying container numbers as they left the facility impossible. We sent individual cars after a couple of lorries which might have been carrying ours until they were able to get a good enough view of the registration number on the container.

'Stand by, stand by.'

It was Jez's voice. His vehicle was plotted up in a nearby housing estate.

'Yeah, we have a suspicious X-Ray going slowly through the estate. Possible Zulu 7 plus two IC1 males. Last seen seven one red four three.'

Zulu 7 was a man called Curtis. Since Johnson had fled to the Continent, Danny had identified him as Davies' new head of security.

'That's towards you, Kilo 9. See if you can get a look at him,' said the Widow.

'Wait one.'

Kilo 9 confirmed that Curtis was cruising slowly with two pals. This was good news. It showed that the gang was still interested in the consignment. The Widow took the handset from me.

'All Kilo mobiles. Off the roads NOW! Watch your radio transmissions.'

We knew that Davies had at least one contact who specialised in driving through an area and scanning the airwaves for police and Customs radio signals. Just because we hadn't seen him yet didn't mean he wasn't there. Davies always told his people to be extremely cautious and if Curtis saw one car, the job would be off. But we still had to keep an eye on the gates in case our container moved.

No one saw Curtis again until, ten minutes later, he was spotted leaving the area at speed along the A13 eastbound. Had he seen anything? There was no way of knowing, but clearly this stop at a storage facility was a blind designed to flush out any surveillance team. We could only settle down and wait.

During the next three hours there were several false alarms as suspicious cars were spotted and then ruled out. Finally Don called the Widow to say that he had spoken to a contact at the facility. Our container was still there. They had no collection date, but they should be able to give us at least thirty minutes' warning before it was moved. The Widow decided that her next task was to find somewhere to use as a base. The beauty of being in London was that off-duty crews could sleep at home, but it was bad practice to leave the duty crews on the street in their cars. It made them easier to spot and meant they were more likely to be tired if something did happen.

There was an ambulance station only two minutes' drive away. The Widow went in and spoke to the senior officer while I sat in the car and monitored the radio. She came out and gave the thumbs-up signal.

We set up a rota for the duty team – twelve hours on, twelve hours off. This illustrated one big advantage which a Customs team has over a police team. We don't have overtime. On the Division, a one-time payment added to basic salary is supposed to cover all out-of-hours working. On the other hand, police overtime is very expensive and strictly rationed. In the late 1990s, a joint police and Customs team was working in Liverpool against Curtis Warren, the leading cocaine smuggler in the north – Operation *Crayfish*. Naturally this kind of high-level target operation entailed tremendously long hours and after a while it looked as if the police were going to be forced to pull out simply because their overtime bill was so high. In the end, the police officers on the operation agreed to work unpaid overtime just to keep the operation alive (which is a tribute to their dedication). Similarly, even though it would have meant more money, I've never met an ID officer who wanted to change to the police overtime system because they know this would drastically cut operational time and no one wants to see drug smugglers escape (although there were plenty of times when we looked longingly at the kind of money police surveillance teams were taking home).

That evening the Widow took a call from Don. She sat back and looked thoughtful.

'Intel have had a tip that there's going to be an attempt to rip this load off. Apparently Davies can't afford to abandon the load, but the gang are worried about picking it up because they're afraid it's being watched. Anyone got any ideas?'

Our first thought was that a rip was highly unlikely: moving three-quarters of a tonne of cannabis from a secure facility is not like a bent airport worker grabbing a suitcase full of smack off a conveyor belt. But the intelligence on Davies had been accurate so far, so we had to consider the possibility.

If the gang were going to rip the container then their only hope was to overpower the security guards at the gate before they could raise the alarm and then bring in a lorry and unload the container into it. There was no chance of a snatch during the day as there were just too many people about. But the yard was only guarded by a couple of watchmen at night.

If we were going to spot a raid, our first problem was that we did not have a view of either the container or the main gates. We would need to find an OP. Our second problem was that the gang would almost certainly be armed for the raid. We would have to try to get armed police as backup and that would cause other problems. If we couldn't get armed police there in time, we would still have to try and stop them. Despite memories of Peter Bennett, I don't believe that any of us would have hesitated.

For a while we considered recommending to Don that we should just knock the job there and then. But all we would have done was seize the drugs. We still couldn't link the job evidentially to Davies which was what we wanted. There was a lot to play for if we were prepared to take the risk.

We decided to go ahead with the operation.

Half the team set off into the night to scout for a possible OP. There were some high-rise blocks overlooking the target area, but they were a very long way away and we would need pretty powerful scopes to keep watch at night. It was Carnaby who finally found what we were looking for – a partially built housing estate. There was a pair of semi-detached houses at the end of one of the roads. One of them was unoccupied and from the upstairs windows we would have an excellent view of the main gate and right into the yard.

Carl tracked down the company putting the houses up and it was agreed that we could use the empty building. Carnaby and Patrick went round the next day to set up CCTV cameras and image intensifiers. The view was excellent. That was the good news. The bad news was that the other half of the premises was occupied, by a woman living alone. We thought about telling her what was happening, but you can never be sure how people will react and every person who knows about an operation is one more chance of a leak. We decided to try to get away with it.

Don started making phone calls to determine if armed police support would be available. It quickly became clear that this was a problem. Like us, the armed response team could not just hang around in the hope that the job would happen, they needed a definite date and time. In the end it was agreed that we would inform them as soon as the attack happened. Unloading the container might give them time to respond. We would just have to hope that they weren't out on another job at the time.

So we began the new stage of the operation. Whereas the ambulance station had been warm and comfortable, the empty house was a nightmare. The weather was freezing and even with layers of clothes and a Thermos of hot coffee it was impossible to keep the chill from your fingers and toes.

As usual we ran shifts in pairs. The officers split time on the binoculars and cameras. While one of us was watching, the other would be trying to keep warm whilst listening to a Walkman or, if he was really lucky, dozing. You didn't really sleep because of the tension of knowing that something could happen at any moment and when you awoke you were freezing, usually with a cramp in your back or neck or both. There wasn't much else you could do. Talking had to be kept to a minimum as the walls were thin and every sound from next door seemed to carry through. Our neighbour's television was so clear that you could sit by the wall and hear every word. Light had to be kept to a minimum as well, just the occasional use of a shielded torch with a red filter, so reading a book or magazine was out.

It was unbelievably cold and boring, even for OP work. Don tried to rotate the standby team as often as possible, but after a week we were still waiting for something to happen. Danny insisted that the job was still on, so we had no choice but to continue.

Back in the office, the grumbling became louder. Morale on the team began to slide. We tried to top each other with stories of our most boring and uncomfortable OP duty ever.

It was during one of these group moans in the office that Granville, who had previously served on a team investigating large-scale VAT frauds, decided to cheer us all up: 'Actually,' he said, 'it's not always bad, is it guys? I mean, on my last team we were looking at this multinational company dealing in bonds. We had an OP looking right down into their offices. There was this gorgeous blonde secretary. Massive knockers, legs up to her armpits. She always wore these short skirts and really high heels. God, it was the only thing that made life worth living in that OP.

'Anyway, one day, she goes into the boardroom with one of the directors. She bends over the boardroom table, hitches up her skirt, and the next thing you know they are at it like rabbits. Thank God for telephoto lenses. We must have used about eight rolls of film. In fact,' he began to dig around in one of his desk drawers, 'I've got some of the photographs right here.'

There was a stampede across the office as red-blooded males fought to get a better view.

'Yes, here we are.' He produced a bundle of snaps. 'This is one of the office block where we had the OP, this is one of Terry – he was the case officer, this is me in the OP . . .' He looked up with an evil grin on his face.

The bastard. He knew he had us. There was not one 'interesting' photograph of the blonde in the whole pile.

Some time later Don walked into the office with some paperwork. Everyone had their heads down, but there was a loud banging sound and muffled cries coming from one of the equipment lockers.

'What's going on?' he asked.

The Widow looked up: 'Some of the lads thought Granville should check out the camera equipment.'

'What, in a locked cupboard?'

The Widow just shrugged.

I was scheduled for one of these night shifts with a rather grumpy Ozzy who had been drafted in at short notice and clearly felt that he had been shafted. He hated the cold and had come equipped with about three coats, a huge furry Cossack-style hat and ski boots. He looked like a badly dressed yeti as we crunched across an unseasonable fall of snow towards the house that night.

The lights were off in the neighbouring house, indicating that our neighbour had gone to bed. The door ahead of us opened silently. Carnaby and Jimmy had been warned over the radio that we were on our way.

'Wotcher,' murmured Jimmy in his familiar soft Irish burr as he handed over the keys. 'You're welcome to it tonight, it's fucking freezing up there. If you find anything rolling around on the floor then it's probably one of my balls.'

He grinned and then disappeared across the snow. I slipped through the doorway and started to creep quietly up the uncarpeted stairs. Behind me an elephant in hob-nailed boots clumped about loudly. I stopped and swung round: 'For fuck's sake, Ozzy!' I whispered, indicating the house next door with a nod of my head.

Even in the faint orange light from the streetlamp outside, which was all the light we had, Ozzy's pudgy face gave me a world-weary look which said, 'You're the new boy, you know fuck-all, I've been doing this since you were at school. I'm tired and cold and fed up. Now, shut the fuck up and let's get into the OP so I can get some kip.' It was a very talkative face when he was in a bad mood.

I checked the equipment. Through the huge telescopic lens of the camera I could see right into the security guard's lighted office at the gates. At least he was warm. We had hung a large black blanket a few feet back from the window. This old trick is surprisingly effective. From outside there was no sign that the room was occupied. The camera and scope poked through slits in the blanket.

Halfway through the shift, a car pulled up outside the house. A white car without lights pulled up further down the road. I turned the image intensifier towards it. It was a police car. Within minutes a second car had pulled up. Soon there were three uniformed officers wandering around the lawn outside looking up at the house.

I crept across the room and gently nudged the peacefully snoozing Ozzy.

'Old Bill have arrived,' I whispered.

He barely woke up long enough to whisper, 'Fuck 'em,' before rolling over and going back to sleep.

It wasn't ID policy to let a local station know if we had an operation on their patch. The fewer people who knew the better. I went back to the cameras and peeked through a gap in the blanket. They were shining torches up at the windows but apparently couldn't see anything. I heard one of them trying the front door and a short while later the back. They rang the doorbell next door and I heard the murmur of a conversation although I couldn't make out the words.

I sat tight. Having spoken to the woman next door, the three of them were now having a discussion in the street. Then one of them went to the boot of one of the patrol cars and came back with a 'magic key'.

They were coming in.

I raced as quietly as possible down the stairs. Just as they got to the porch I pulled the door open. It was worth it for the look of shock on their faces. There were two men and a WPC.

'Good evening,' I whispered.

I had a big grin on my face. For reasons I can't explain, the whole thing struck me as ridiculously funny.

'Hello,' the WPC whispered back. She smiled as well. The other two officers were standing well back. 'Can I ask who you are? We've had a complaint about suspicious noises from next door. She thought this property was unoccupied.'

'Customs and Excise,' I whispered, and then added as an afterthought, 'Hasn't anyone at the station told you about this?'

'No,' she said, still looking slightly stunned. Then she turned to the other two who were gradually edging nearer and whispered, 'He's from Customs and Excise.' They all looked at one another. Then the WPC said, 'We'll tell her we've looked into it and it's all okay.'

After they had driven away, I decided that it would probably be as well if I spoke to the woman next door too. I kicked Ozzy more forcefully this time. When I was sure he was fully awake and understood that it really was his shift this time, I went next door and rang the doorbell. This time I made sure I held up my warrant card nice and clearly in front of the spy-hole.

The door opened on a chain and a young woman in a dressing-gown gripped tightly around her peered out.

210

'Hi,' I said in as friendly a manner as possible. 'I'm one of the officers working next door. Sorry we didn't speak to you before, but it's a bit of a hush-hush operation. We're watching one of the other houses on the estate.'

'Oh, thank God,' she said. 'I've been hearing noises for several nights now. I've been out and looked through the windows once or twice, but couldn't see anything. I thought I was going mad.'

'Sorry. We'll try to keep the noise down. We'll let you know when the operation is over, we'll probably be here for a few days yet.'

Back in the OP I lay in the dark, trying to forget the cold and thinking about how my life had changed over the past year. The woman must have thought how odd it was to have a surveillance team next door. But to me this strange night-time world was now just part of the job. Here we were waiting for a load of drugs to be stolen by a gang of smugglers. They might be armed, we wouldn't be. Here we were, some overweight, some practically alcoholic, some divorced, all of us tired, prepared at a moment's notice to go charging in and try to stop them.

What was happening to me? A year ago I wouldn't have said boo to a goose. Now I was a surveillance driver, driving at stupid speeds and breaking traffic law almost every day. A year ago it was all I could do to parallel park. I swore like a navvy and increasingly often drank like one. It was about a million miles from the cosseted life of MI6. As for being a house-husband, I couldn't remember the last time I spent an hour with the children.

I felt passionately loyal to the job and to the team, but when I took the time to think about it I wasn't sure that I actually liked the person I was becoming.

For three weeks we kept the rota going, while tempers became increasingly frayed. Then finally Don's contact at Hays told us that the container was being collected. He was even able to give us a time.

The lorry headed east towards the Essex marshes. We were well off the beaten track for Kilos and the long winding country roads meant that we had to hang well back, watching for the counter-surveillance we were certain would be there. But eventually the lorry turned into a yard. One of the EOs leapt out of a car and hid himself in a hedge from where he could see into the yard. He announced that the driver was out of his cab and had wandered out of sight. He said it seemed to be a fairly small yard with just a couple of huts and a few lorries. All the vehicle wreckage lying around made it look like a breaker's yard. We parked in country lanes and lay-bys and waited.

Carnaby radioed that he had knocked a job here before. 'It's a real gyppo place. When we did a VAT job here a few years ago we had to take about a dozen police in with us just to prevent a riot. Travellers and all sorts use it. It's not a small yard either, it opens out beyond where the lorry is at the moment. I couldn't tell you how big, but it must be several acres. There's dozens more units back there.'

The officer on watch cut in, 'Stand by, stand by, we have movement from X-Ray 9, manoeuvring . . . wait . . . and that's X-Ray 9 moving off further on to the estate and out of my sight.'

'Okay, Kilo 10,' said Granville, 'don't try and go with it. Pull out of there. We'll make other arrangements.' He threw the handset down on the seat of the car. 'Shit. We need to get a view on that container.' He looked down at the box on the dashboard which was monitoring the container alarms. 'I don't trust this fucking thing.'

The Widow had finished speaking on the phone to the local police. 'Well, the bad news is that they confirm what Carnaby had to say. They don't recommend going in there just with plainclothes. The good news is that they're sending us a couple of uniforms to help out.'

Bob stepped forward. 'I can get in there if you like.'

We all looked at each other. None of us fancied going up close in that area, although anyone of us would have risked it if we had been asked. But if someone had to do it, then who better than an ex-member of the SAS? Granville looked at the Widow, who nodded.

'Okay,' said Granville, 'go for it.'

A few minutes later a police Range Rover arrived with three uniformed officers. They recommended a nearby farmyard where we could pull all the vehicles out of sight except for the two needed to cover the road east and west. They asked how many officers we had. When they found out we had twelve, they recommended sending for more – the site was really big. At first we thought they were joking, but after hearing some of their horror stories about the resistance the people there might put up, the Widow phoned Don and soon three more cars full of Deltas and Juliets were on their way.

We stood around in the farmyard and waited. It began to get dark. Granville placed the control box for the photoelectric alarm on the roof of the car as we all stood around. We waited for it to beep at any moment, but it stayed silent. I stood and watched the police in their car playing hangman. It started to rain.

Occasionally Bob would radio his position as he worked his way around the perimeter of the area looking for a sight of our vehicle. Eventually he found it parked in the middle of the estate. The driver was with it and so far there appeared to have been no attempt to open it up.

After an hour or so, the car with a view on the gate reported a white Vauxhall Astra arriving and soon Bob reported that the car had pulled up alongside our lorry. Four men had got out and were talking to the driver. Bob said that he was going to try to get a better view of what was going on.

Granville continued to stare at the box. It was now pitch black in the farmyard. Fifteen minutes went by and there was still no news from Bob, only the hiss of radio static. Granville and the Widow had a chat about when they should start to get worried. Kilo 10 was out on foot and was the nearest officer. He had been relaying Bob's radio messages. He said that the signal had been pretty weak before Bob moved. He didn't want to move to try to re-establish comms in case Bob was making his way back towards him. We didn't want to send any more people into the fields around the site and risk a show-out.

More time passed with no news. Several officers began to look worried. 'Look,' concluded the Widow, 'in the first place, he was in the bloody SAS and he knows how to handle himself. Second, we know that comms are bad. Three, we have the alarms, and even if one of them failed, it's impossible for all three to fail and even if they did, we have the entrance covered. We will see any movement by the Astra or the tractor unit. So we just sit tight. The drugs aren't going anywhere.'

In retrospect, it might seem complacent to have simply assumed that Bob was okay, but he was the sort of man who exuded an air of self-reliance. He hadn't just been in the SAS, he had been an NCO, which takes a special and highly capable type of soldier. So, although we were uneasy, we couldn't imagine anyone getting the jump on him. If they did they were probably in more danger than he was.

The rain was pouring down now, cutting visibility to almost nothing and soaking us all.

We waited another hour. By now the tension was unbearable. One call from Bob would have solved everything, but there was nothing. As soon as he realised his comms were down he should have made his way out to his backup officer. The Widow decided to send another officer in. Carnaby made his way to Kilo 10's position and from there crept closer to the yard. There was no sign of Bob, no sign of the Astra and no sign of the lorry. The trouble was that the yard was so large and the layout so confused that Carnaby could not be sure where the lorry had been. One of the policemen listening in to the radio transmissions shrugged sympathetically:

'It's a fucking jungle in there. They keep putting units up and taking them down. Even I couldn't tell you how many units there are in there.'

Eventually the Widow had to admit defeat. The order was given and ten cars raced through the main gate and into the complex.

We searched the units that were still open and spoke to anyone who was still in the area. Most of them were hostile, those who weren't simply claimed that they hadn't seen anything and didn't know anything. Eventually Ozzy found an old man who said that he had seen the lorry parked outside three industrial units. All three were locked tight. The trouble was that we didn't know if he was just trying to waste our time – and in any case, how the hell had something as big as the lorry with the freight container left without being seen? There was only the one entrance. It was impossible that the lorry could have driven out over the boggy farmland.

As we continued the search, I found Carnaby staring down into a huge concrete-lined pit. At the bottom light could be seen reflecting off black, oily water. Large jagged scraps of metal poked up through the surface. There was still no news of Bob.

I stared down into the water. It would take hours to find a body in that. We glanced at each other. 'You don't think . . .'

Carnaby shrugged.

'Let's fucking well hope not. Come on.'

Time was ticking away fast. Wherever that lorry and the drugs had gone they were only getting further and further away. It felt as though Davies had pulled a fast one on us. No one seemed to know what to do. Amused onlookers gathered to watch the free entertainment and jeer.

'Right,' said Carl, 'I'm going west on the main road. I'm fucking well tired of standing around here.' He climbed back into his car and sped away, his horn blaring to scatter the gawpers. A pair of the Juliets' cars also drove off, one heading east in case the lorry was making for the coast.

The rest of us stood in the pouring rain outside the three suspect

215

units, trying to decide what to do. It was as if the entire lorry, the drugs and Bob had been beamed up by aliens. Granville was staring at the control box for the now useless alarms. Suddenly he shouted, 'Fuck!' and threw it down into the mud. He went to the boot of the car, pulled out a sledgehammer and splashed through the mud to one of the units. Snarling with rage, he started attacking the padlocks. After three massive blows, the padlock flew off and he wrenched the doors open. The burglar alarm went off, its howling siren and a flashing blue light making the scene seem even more alien.

The unit was empty. Granville moved to the next unit and started hitting the padlock but it refused to give way. The rest of us watched helplessly, feeling that this was a pointless expression of rage. The uniformed policemen shook their heads and tried to disperse the crowd. To his credit, Ozzy went to the boot of his car, produced one of the 'magic keys' and also started to attack the padlock. That shook the rest of us into some sort of life. We started in on the other units and lock-ups, pushing owners who tried to stop us out of the way. If they weren't going to help then they could fucking well suffer. Somewhere around here there had to be a clue to what had happened.

Finally the padlock at Granville's unit gave way and he threw open the doors.

'Kilo 11 to all units, we've found it. Looks like all of it,' sounded in our earpieces.

We rushed over. Granville found a switch on the wall and flooded the unit with light. The boxes were stacked in large piles all over the floor. Some of them had been opened on a line of trestle tables and the packages of cannabis extracted. There were even buckets full of waste beer where the bottles had been emptied. We did a rapid count. If it wasn't all of them, it was bloody close.

Meanwhile Carl and a couple of other cars were driving like maniacs in search of the Astra and the lorry. They didn't know that the drugs had been recovered because they were out of radio transmission range. In the driving rain and the darkness, in an area they didn't know, it must have seemed a hopeless task, but even when they got to a point beyond which they thought the lorry could have reached, Carl kept going.

They were almost back to the motorway when Carl spied the high tail-lights of what he thought must be our HGV with the container at the front of a queue of a dozen vehicles held up at a red traffic light. As he pushed his car into the other lane of traffic, flashing his lights and sounding his horn to warn oncoming cars, the lights changed and the lorry started to pull away.

Carl skidded his car sideways to a halt in the middle of the junction. The HGV driver sounded his horn as Carl leapt from his car and rushed towards the cab. The Juliets' vehicle was only a moment behind and skidded across the junction to reinforce the roadblock.

But the HGV driver wasn't going to stop. Even as Carl leapt on to the running board and hammered on the side window of the cab, the driver locked the door and tried to manoeuvre the HGV around Carl's car. One of the Juliets had leapt on to the running board on the other side and wrenched the door open before the driver could lock it. The driver produced a cosh, but the Juliets' officer trapped his hand against the dashboard. By then another officer had also clambered in through the door. There was a brief tussle in the cab and then the driver gave in.

All around them in the pouring rain, drivers who had no idea what was going on sounded their horns. The logjam of vehicles took so long to clear up that it featured on the evening television news.

Back at the yard, we were still standing looking at the boxes when Bob walked into the unit. We stared at him in shock. He said hello and acted as if nothing unusual had occurred, mumbling something about trying to make his way round to the other side of the yard, getting lost and having to walk miles to get safely back into position. We couldn't really believe that, but perhaps it was just weird enough to be true. It didn't really matter because we were so glad that he was safe and jubilant that the drugs had been found. That really only left one mystery: why the alarms in the boxes hadn't been received. Clearly one of the alarms had been found by the smugglers because it was lying in pieces on one of the tables. Granville banged on the metallic sides of the unit:

'This would do it.' he said, 'If they backed the lorry right up to these doors to unload, then there's probably enough metal in this structure to disrupt the signal. We should have thought of it.'

But Granville's anger had turned a potential disaster into a success. All the drugs were recovered. With photographs which Bob had taken and by tracing the Astra, we were able to arrest three of the four men who had unloaded the container. The story of what had actually happened that evening began to emerge.

These men were the usual crew who unloaded the boxes from the containers. This time they had unloaded the container as usual and the driver had gone on his way. Normally the container would have come straight to the unit from Harwich, but because he was aware of the searches there, Davies had used the Hays storage facility as a halfway house so that he could check for surveillance.

Once they had the boxes in the safety of the unit, the men had begun to separate the drugs from the bottles. Davies had warned them to look out for anything unusual, and so when they found the alarm device, they dropped everything, locked the unit and ran. In fact they had left the yard almost at the same moment that the Customs vehicles had driven in. They had been missed in the dark and the confusion.

Despite these arrests we were still some way from showing that Davies was behind the company which imported the beer. Danny set to work on proving that connection. But on the other side of the Channel, the case had more of an impact. Belgian police raided the premises where the bottles were filled with the packages of resin. Their investigation showed that the scam had been running for several years and was used to distribute drugs to countries other than Britain. Several successful arrests were made.

Davies' main source of cannabis had been disrupted. Information was soon coming in to Danny that the Davies organisation was in trouble. Davies himself went berserk. He knew that Customs must have been tipped off and he was determined to find out who was responsible. According to a police informant, he even smuggled Johnson back into the country to help try to find the leak, and there were reports of the two of them interrogating likely suspects. They took several suspects to 'the workshop', a joinery firm in the Sussex countryside which Davies used as a legitimate company for laundering drugs money. We only heard rumours about what happened, but at least one of the people taken there was held down over a work bench and stabbed in both legs with a bowie knife just for being 'lippy'.

Despite the violence, Davies never found the leak in his organisation. But for us it was to be a different story.

Danny and I were about to have a face-to-face meeting with the informant.

10

The Drivers

Danny and I were a little nervous as we drove down to a police station deep in the Kent countryside. We were going to meet a young police sergeant who was supposed to take us to meet the Davies informant.

The prospect of the meeting posed a number of questions. Davies was known to be a brutal man when crossed, who took the security of his operation seriously. Why, after almost a year of passing material anonymously, should the informant suddenly risk everything by asking for a face-to-face meeting? And why go through the police to get to Customs? We wondered if it was some kind of complicated trap.

The meeting had been proposed by the informant two weeks earlier, while the Kilos were still working on Operation *Kanister*, the container of imported beer at Hays storage. The informant had been insistent about meeting representatives from the team working against Davies – which was odd – but eventually it was agreed that as case officer I should go together with Danny. The sergeant, who had been the first point of contact, would represent the police.

The first surprise of the morning was the sergeant himself. We had expected some grizzled veteran who might have good contacts among street-level dealers, but the officer who greeted us at the reception desk hardly looked old enough to be out of school. It turned out that he was a university graduate on the accelerated promotion scheme and was based in Milton Keynes. He didn't seem the type who would have contacts within the Davies organisation. 'The man we are going to meet this afternoon is my uncle,' he said. 'Well, we call him uncle, but he's really just an old friend of my father. For reasons of security, I have agreed with my Chief Inspector that I won't give you his full name or any other details about him. During the meeting we will call him Mick.

'He doesn't actually have contact with Davies, but he is passing information from someone who does. I don't actually know a lot about this Davies character, he's not on my patch. I haven't asked too many questions down here. He's a member of a local Masonic Lodge and . . . well, you know . . . sometimes there is contact between criminals and police at those things. Not that I'm suggesting there's a risk of a leak here,' he hastened to add.

'No, of course not,' murmured Danny.

We drove into town and parked near an up-market tea room. The informant was already waiting for us. 'Uncle Mick' was as surprising as his nephew. Expensively dressed, in a smart suit and highly polished shoes, he looked like a pillar of the local Conservative Party rather than an informant on one of the largest drug smugglers in the south-east.

As soon as Mick started to speak, I began to see where the connection with Davies might be. His accent was definitely East End rather than Southern Counties. Somewhere along the line he had made or married plenty of money.

'Thank you for finally meeting us,' I said.

He gave me a hard look through a cloud of cigarette smoke as he took a deep puff. 'I didn't want to, but our previous arrangement wasn't working too well, was it?'

'Wasn't it?'

'Jesus Christ! What do you people want? Over the past few months, we've given you enough stuff to bury Frank. He seems to walk away every time.'

'I think you may be mistaken about how useful some of your

information has been,' said Danny. 'Don't get me wrong, sir, we're extremely grateful, but some of it has been, well, vague. I need specifics. Dates, times, routes. Otherwise I have to spend weeks digging through paperwork trying to make sense of it all.'

'I pass what my friend tells me, but it's not easy. Frank only talks business with certain people.'

'Will we ever get to meet this friend of yours?'

'Perhaps, but not yet. Frank has a vicious temper. If he knew, he would . . . Well, anyway, that's why my friend is passing this information through me and that's why you need to get your fingers out. Why can't you just bloody well arrest him?'

'We need something which definitely ties him in to the importation. Can your friend provide that?'

Uncle Mick shrugged. 'Dunno. She's trying.'

As soon as Mick said the word 'she' the police sergeant and I looked at each other. Mick didn't even seem aware of what he had said. Danny hid his surprise better than we did and quickly moved the conversation on to tell Mick what sort of information he really needed.

'We know that he imports a lot through road haulage using the cross-Channel ferries. We need to get at those smuggling runs. We need to know who is involved in the organisation, who is hiring the drivers and where the drugs are being packaged on the Continent. Could your friend help with any of that?'

'I'll try,' said Mick, 'but the most important thing is that you get Frank. If we get this information to you, will you promise to do that?'

Danny turned to me. Thanks a lot, you bastard, I thought.

'We'll do our best. What we really need to know is any time when Frank will actually be found with the drugs.'

'In that case it sounds like you can do bugger-all,' said Mick bitterly, lighting another cigarette from the stub of the old one. 'Frank isn't mug enough to be caught near the drugs.'

Mick was insistent that if he provided more information we must arrest Frank. We kept telling him that we couldn't arrest him without the right information. He didn't seem to understand that we couldn't just pick him up. After half an hour he left saying 'Maybe you'll hear from me, but maybe you won't.' As the police sergeant followed Mick out he whispered to me, 'Don't worry, he'll be fine.'

I hoped so.

On the drive back to the office Danny and I wondered if we had blown it, whether we should have promised an arrest just to get one more piece of intelligence out of him. We also tried guessing who the source might be. The fact that it was a woman narrowed this down, especially in a largely male organisation like Frank's. It could be the disgruntled wife or mistress of one of the gang. But we didn't really have a clue.

In spite of his parting words, however, 'Uncle Mick' came through. With the information he passed on Danny was able to isolate a contract haulage firm in Silvertown, East London, as the one Frank was currently using to organise his drivers. The consignments seemed to be legitimate, which meant that the drugs were probably added to the load after it was collected. The lorries changed too often for there to be concealments within the vehicle, which had been Van Hohn's favourite method.

The system was almost perfect. It was flexible – Davies could have drugs added to the load any time he needed – and the company was also a reputable and regular fixture on the ferry lists so that it didn't attract undue attention from Customs. 'Uncle Mick' hadn't given us any dates when the drugs might be imported, but by monitoring the ferry bookings, Danny was able to select two lorries which were likely targets.

We took a small team down to Dover. The two lorries were due in on consecutive nights. The same team would arrest and interview both drivers. We based ourselves at the St John's Road offices of the Dover Investigation Unit and waited to hear from the uniformed staff at inward controls whether drugs had been found.

We soon got the call that boxes of cannabis had been found on the first lorry. As we drove the short distance from St John's Road to the docks to take over the case, I was more nervous than usual. Don had decided that I would be case officer for this job. It would be the first time that I had directed an investigation from arrest through to prosecution.

The tractor unit, with a canvas-sided thirty-foot trailer, was already in the examination bay. It was being stripped down by uniformed Customs officers when we arrived. As in Operation *Krystal*, it was a groupage load – several different kinds of product all carried together on wooden pallets. Some twenty cardboard boxes of cannabis were hidden about halfway along the load under some large rolls of plastic. There hadn't been any great attempt to hide it.

Customs and Excise doesn't have its own forensic officers, so we had to use the Scene of Crime Officer (SOCO) from whichever police station was nearest. This often meant a long wait as the police naturally gave their own jobs priority. The police also charged Customs for the use of the officer – ridiculous, since we were all on the same side, but no doubt satisfying to some petty-minded bureaucrat in Whitehall. Tonight we were in luck and the SOCO from Dover Police Station was already clambering around the load taking photographs of and trying to lift fingerprints from the wrappings of the cannabis soaps. He wasn't hopeful of success. The cardboard was unlikely to show fingerprints and any prints he lifted from the wrappings around the drugs would almost certainly be those of some anonymous packer in Turkey.

The driver, a stocky man in his forties, was being held in a nearby interview room. I told two officers to take him away to begin the custody process. This was long and complicated because of all the various rules which had been introduced under the Police and Criminal Evidence Act (PACE). First we had to take suspects to the nearest police station. Then we had to find a Customs office with a suitable interview room to tape the interviews, but we had to remember to return the suspect to the police station periodically to have his detention reviewed. By the time you added in the meal breaks and rest periods which the suspect was allowed, together with the inevitable long wait for a lawyer to turn up and have a lengthy consultation, it sometimes seemed as though you were lucky to have time for any questions at all.

I stayed at the docks to complete all the paperwork. Agencies had to be informed of the seizure and legal forms had to be completed for the seizure of both the drugs and the vehicle. All of this had to be separately logged on CEDRIC. Even with Carnaby helping me, this took over an hour. I also had to ensure that the half-tonne of cannabis was safely transported to the Queen's Warehouse nearby.

All the delays meant there was now no hope of progressing the job by getting the driver to co-operate. As I studied him through the spy-hole in the door of the interview room I doubted that he would have done so anyway. His name was Bartlett and according to his record on CEDRIC, he was a minor figure in the London drugs world, an occasional courier and hard man. With his shaven head, tattoos and beer gut, he looked like the sort of thug you could find in any pub or transport café. He was perfect for Davies because he was the sort of low-level goon who didn't know enough about the organisation to cause any damage if he was caught.

Carnaby and Jimmy took him through the interview while Patrick went through his personal belongings and the paperwork from the cab. Like a lot of lorry cabs on a drugs run it was a pigsty. These guys aren't professional drivers making a living from haulage. The money is in the drugs. It was going to take a couple of hours just to look through all the notes, scraps of paper and till receipts from months of driving both in the UK and on the Continent.

Bartlett was as cool as you would expect a career criminal to be. He didn't want a solicitor. He was happy to talk, almost too keen to get his story out. With the aid of a map, Carnaby and Jimmy made him outline his route. Somewhere along it he picked up the drugs. If we were going to get a successful conviction, it was up to me to prove where.

I went in with Carnaby for the final interview. I told Bartlett that I was going to be the investigating officer in the case. I explained that we wanted the people behind the smuggling operation, not him. I tried to appeal to his better nature. Everyone has seen it done in the movies, but this was the first time I had to do it for real. 'Look, I know you're going to say no, but just try and think for a moment. We both know that the guys at the top make all the money so that guys like you will take all the heat. When you're inside for this, they'll still be out there living the good life. If you're prepared to help me, I will do everything I can to help you. If you won't, then I promise you that I'll do everything I can to make sure you go down for this. This is not Customs talking, this is me. It's my word. It's personal.'

Bartlett stared at me as if he had heard it all before and sneered. He just didn't have the intelligence even to think about it. He was taken away to Dover Police Station to await a remand hearing at the magistrates' court the following day.

Patrick appeared from his trawl of the cab's contents. 'Jackpot,' he said. He was waving a box of tachograph discs. 'Looks like we've got a full set.'

A tachograph is a small machine that sits in the cab. It contains a small card disc. Each disc records one day's activity. The disc slowly rotates to record the time as a needle moves up and down to record the speed.

'What's so great about that? Surely all we can prove is how fast he was going at a particular time?'

'No, mate. Hidden away in the depths of the Welsh countryside, there are teams of little men with machines and magnifying glasses who can take these discs and show everything that happened on the journey. They can practically tell you what the driver had for breakfast. If Bartlett lied about his route, we should be able to prove it.'

The following night we were able to hit Davies' transport organisation again when another half-tonne of cannabis was found on the second lorry. This time I was part of the interview team and Carnaby was the case officer.

The second driver was a thin, pale man called Steele, a complete contrast to a bruiser like Bartlett. He sat hunched on the other side of the table in the interview room. It was as though he'd been briefed to do the same things as Bartlett. He didn't want a solicitor and he was quite keen to tell us his story. He gave us the route and claimed that the boxes of drugs must have been slipped aboard without his knowledge. Once again I made my little speech about truth and justice and once again he just shook his head.

But after the tape machine was switched off and he was sitting there drinking his cup of tea, he suddenly asked, 'Can you really get me off?'

We were on dodgy ground. I was taking a risk by talking to him. It was all unrecorded. A defence lawyer would have a field day in court if I stood in the witness box and admitted talking to the driver when the tape machine was off. He would be able to allege that I had used all kinds of coercion and promises – it would almost certainly result in the collapse of the case. On the other hand there was no way Steele would have a conversation like this on tape in case Davies got to hear it. It would be like signing his death warrant. I had to take the chance.

'You know that I'm not allowed to make deals, but you tell us what you know and I give you my word I'll move heaven and earth to help you.'

He gulped his tea and thought for a while.

'Look, all I'll say is that you need to look at the manager at the yard. If you think about it he'd have to be involved in something like this.'

'Oh, come on, I could have told you that. You're not telling me anything. I need names, dates, paperwork.'

He thought for a long time.

'I need to speak to my old lady. I might speak to you after court tomorrow.'

I knew that would be too late. It would give the gang a chance to get to him and make sure he kept his mouth shut. But he wouldn't be budged. I would just have to hope. At least we had got this far. If a lawyer had been present we wouldn't even have had that.

Sure enough, when I managed to speak to Steele the following day, he was more scared than ever.

'Look, try and see it from my side,' he said when I made my disgust with him clear, 'I've got a wife and three kids. If I play along, they'll make sure they're all right. But if I talk to you, what happens to them then? There's nothing I can do, is there?'

I tried making promises of protection and even relocation, but it was no good. The fear had got to him and I couldn't blame him. We just make it too easy for criminals to maintain their control of the people they use. Officers have no authority to offer deals of any sort and the protection we can offer to witnesses who do agree to testify is severely limited.

Looking for a way to cause maximum damage to the organisation, Don decided that we would arrest the manager of the haulage firm, a man called Tony Dickens. We didn't have any evidence against him because neither driver had talked, but we had to let Davies know that we were on to him and that there was no way we were falling for the story that this was a matter of two drivers who were trying to make a bit of money on the side. We had already done a search of the yard, but there was always the chance that a search of Dickens' home might turn up something following the arrest. Slim, but a chance.

We phoned Dickens and asked if he could present himself with his lawyer at Customs House. He clearly thought that he was turning up for a standard interview and had nothing to worry about. Don sent me out to the car park to arrest him. At first the words didn't seem to sink in, but there is a little-known part of the arrest process when an arresting officer actually has to 'lay a hand' on the arrested person. Without this, the arrest can actually be ruled illegal. As soon as I put my hand on Dickens' arm to lead him away, he became furious, pulled away and started to look for somewhere to run to. Carnaby and I moved forward to grab him, but his lawyer quickly got between us and told Dickens not to worry. He was still angry in the interview room, assuring us that 'we hadn't heard the last of this'. He refused to answer any questions, but then of course we had never expected him to. The main purpose of this interview was to deliver a message to his boss.

We held him for as long as we reasonably could, and searched his house. The search revealed nothing but the message got through. Within a week Uncle Mick was reporting that Davies was sure that Dickens had made a mistake somewhere and that was why he and the two drivers had been arrested. He had thrown Dickens out of the organisation and was busy trying to set up a new haulage firm. Later we heard that Dickens was taken for a trip to 'the workshop' for further questioning and that he subsequently disappeared. I never heard of him again. The disruption part of the plan certainly seemed to have worked.

Meanwhile, the long hard slog of trying to prosecute the drivers began. The tachographs would have to be sent to Wales where a company specialised in tachograph analysis. With the lack of evidence elsewhere, their analysis would be paramount in prosecuting the drivers. We didn't just have to prove that the two drivers had brought drugs into the country, we had to prove that they had done it 'knowingly'. If we couldn't, they would be found not guilty.

Other Kilos had told me that it paid to tell the technicians about the job in person, so I drove all the way down the M4, wondering if this company was as good as everyone claimed. The lead technician, whose name was Reg, was a slight man in his sixties, with wire-framed spectacles and a kindly smile like a benevolent uncle. I explained the background of the case to him and he began examining the tachographs with a magnifying glass, tutting under his breath occasionally. I couldn't tell if this was a good or a bad sign.

229

'I hear that you can tell me what the driver had for breakfast.'

'Well,' smiled Reg, peering over the top of his glasses, 'maybe not *what* he had, but I should almost certainly be able to tell you *where* he had it.'

'You're joking, surely.'

'No, really. Look, I'll show you. First he has to manoeuvre off the ferry. See these small movements of the needle here? They indicate speeds under twenty miles an hour. But then we have this area of the graph where he is doing a steady sixty. That represents him on the motorway. This lower speed area of the disc here indicates him coming off the motorway. I can find exactly where that was.'

He produced a small metal instrument with a tiny wheel at the end. 'I simply run this micrometer measure along the lines which show him on the motorway,' he said, carefully moving the tiny disc along the spidery lines. 'That gives us a distance of sixty-four kilometres. Now, if we look at the map from the beginning of the motorway to sixty-four kilometres, it takes us to . . .' he opened a pair of dividers and opened them to the appropriate width, using the scale at the bottom of the map . . . this exit here.' It was almost pinpoint accurate.

'Of course, the actual process is a good deal more detailed than that. In three weeks I will give you a road map with his entire route plotted on it.'

Sure enough, a brown envelope duly arrived containing a series of European road maps and a statement from the laboratory. A red line showed Bartlett's course with the time of day noted at significant points. Instead of following the straightforward route into France and back which I had expected, the red line disappeared up into Holland and stopped near Amsterdam before heading back into France. I was gobsmacked. This was practically the entire case proved by just one document.

The good thing about cases involving cross-Channel lorry runs is that someone has to travel into Europe to take statements from

230

people. It is one of the few perks of the job. Don decided that he would travel with me to 'supervise' my first ID trip abroad.

Taking statements across jurisdictions is not straightforward. A Commission Rogatoire has to be sent from the Division's Solicitor's Office to the relevant judicial authority abroad. This is a legal document which, once it has been authorised by the Ministry of Justice in the relevant country, enables a British officer to travel to Europe and obtain the assistance of local police and judiciary in taking statements relating to the case. It can take some time to draw up a Commission as it has to explain in great detail which people the officer wishes to interview and why. The Commission can be delayed again and again as additional details are requested.

One of the best things about these journeys to Europe is meeting European officers. Whether we are meeting police or Customs, the fact that we are all on the same side of the line means that we always receive a warm (and usually very alcoholic) welcome. We make sure we return the favour when they visit us.

I needed to take a statement from the owners of the yard in Belgium where Bartlett had loaded. Don and I drove out to a small Belgian town where the office of the local drugs squad turned out to be in a converted barn on the outskirts.

The squad were, like all drugs teams, a tightly knit crowd, mostly young and mostly male. As soon as we entered the barn, you could sense that atmosphere of intense activity and camaraderie – the clatter of keyboards, the shrill warble of telephones, mementoes of previous jobs hanging on the walls. It was like visiting an ID regional office. The barn had been divided into cubicles by partitions six feet high. It must have been a great place to work – like a clubhouse. But I instantly noticed one difference from our Division – every one of the shirt-sleeved men and women carried an automatic pistol in a holster on their hip.

A gruff-looking member of the team called out something in Flemish and the lieutenant in charge of the unit appeared from one of the cubicles. He spoke a little English, so together with my O-level French we managed to get by.

Over the next five minutes, with much hand-waving and occasional excursions into French, the lieutenant explained that the owners of the yard, the Dutreaux brothers, had been sent a letter from the local justices informing them that some English 'police-men' wanted to see them about some drugs. They should have arrived half an hour ago, but the lieutenant suspected that they were going to be reluctant. So he had sent some of his men to pick them up.

'Are they villains then?' asked Don suspiciously. The word 'villains' caused a bit of trouble.

'Ah! No. They are good boys, no trouble with us. But I think they worry there will be trouble if they speak to you. It does not sound good when the letter says "drugs". I think they are a little bit frightened.'

About twenty minutes later a Renault saloon sped into the car park and slid to a halt in a hail of gravel. The Dutreaux brothers were led into the barn. They were in their thirties, dressed in grubby jeans and checked work-shirts. One of them was taken into a tiny cubicle and we followed. The elder brother sat in a chair with the lieutenant at his shoulder. Don and I squeezed along one wall as another Belgian officer heaved a huge, ancient typewriter on to the table with a bang. Then there was a tedious pause as he carefully arranged and inserted a thick wad of paper and carbons. Finally, after much fiddling with the roller and swearing in Flemish, we were ready.

'Okay, ask your questions,' said the lieutenant.

Don asked Dutreaux to state his name, age and occupation. The lieutenant then repeated this in Flemish and Dutreaux replied slowly while the typist laboriously used two fingers to bang away at five keys and promptly jammed three of them. It was going to be a long interview.

It was also noticeable how different this was from an English interview. In England, contrary to what you see on the television, suspects are barely through the custody process before they have to be offered their first cup of tea and a biscuit. Officers have to be very careful that their interview style is not considered 'oppressive' or the defence may be able to get the whole interview thrown out as evidence. On the Continent the questioning can be surprisingly confrontational. This interview seemed to be going the same way. I glanced at Don uneasily.

Dutreaux became more and more enraged while the lieutenant's voice got louder and louder as he leant over Dutreaux. There was a lot of hand-waving on both sides and at one point the lieutenant slapped his hand on the gun at his belt. Don leant towards me and murmured, 'If that gun leaves that holster, we walk out of here now.'

But the argument ended as soon as it had started and after another excruciating hour with the Belgian officer doggedly wrestling with his typewriter, the interview was over. As usual in criminal cases, it amounted to little more than 'I heard nothing, I saw nothing'. We weren't bothered. We knew that Bartlett had picked up the drugs by driving to Holland after the load was collected from Dutreaux. We were only here because defence would insist on a statement – and to collect Don's duty-free allowance.

The Belgians invited us to lunch in a nearby village before we set off on the next stage of our journey. It seemed as though the entire unit just packed up working on the spot. We drove through the twisting country lanes at high speed, the Belgians hooting their car horns and daring us to race them. We were only too happy to oblige. When we arrived at the restaurant, Don handed me the car keys and simply said, 'You drive afterwards.' He was clearly in the mood to be 'sociable'.

That lunchtime I got to see one of the things Don did really well. He bought extra rounds, filled glasses and proposed endless, some-times nonsensical toasts. The Belgians hardly spoke English and we certainly didn't speak Flemish, but with big smiles and plenty of sound effects, Don held court about jobs he had been on, villains he'd arrested and the general state of the world. The Belgians were fascinated by his performance.

Towards the end of the meal, one of the Belgian police officers leant across to me and said admiringly, 'Your boss. *Fantastique!*'

And he meant it.

If I had made the trip on my own, the visit would have been over and forgotten in a matter of hours. But Don knew that this was an important opportunity to establish a good base for any future requests for assistance we might make. The building of this kind of trust between organisations doesn't appear on any balance sheet and some bean counter somewhere would have disapproved of our three-hour drunken lunch, but by the time farewell gifts and handshakes had been exchanged and we climbed into the car to leave, you could be sure that any team from the Division which came out here in future would be assured of a warm welcome.

Within five minutes of the car pulling away, Don was snoring loudly in the passenger seat as we set off north to collect more statements the following day.

In Holland, the Dutch police were equally courteous and, unlike the Belgians, spoke impeccable English. I was shown the car park where Bartlett had undoubtedly picked up the cannabis. Don had gone off with a different group in order to take a statement from a transport company on another job. The Dutch police officer who was my guide seemed curious.

'Cannabis is a big matter in England then?'

'Well, the amount is big – half a tonne. That's worth a lot of money in England. That would be worth a lot in Holland, wouldn't it?'

'Yes, but it does not cause us the same amount of trouble. A lot of it is caused by the English and others coming for the drugs. With the Dutch people we have much less trouble. It is not such a big thing.'

And, right or wrong, that was typical of all the Dutch officers I spoke to during my career. They were always more than willing to help, but they could not understand why we spent so much time dealing with cannabis when there were more serious drugs to worry about.

Back in England, at the plea and directions hearing, the defence announced which witnesses they would require. This should have been fairly straightforward – Bartlett claimed he had made a simple trip into Belgium and France; his tachograph showed him driving up into Holland. By sticking to the relevant evidence, the entire trial could be over in a couple of days. But none of us was surprised when the defence announced they would require the attendance of every single witness including all the foreign ones and all foreign legal officials. This was a standard defence tactic which also happened to cause maximum cost and difficulty to the prosecution. They would probably not call any of them. Defence lawyers never seem to care. There appears to be no sanction against them for the enormous waste of time and money this tactic entails.

More importantly, if the defence call all the foreign witnesses, there is always the chance that one of them won't show up. Then the defence can ask, 'Why hasn't this person turned up? Perhaps they are part of some dark conspiracy to frame my client.' After all, the defence only have to plant the seeds of one reasonable doubt in the minds of the jury. That is all it takes to acquit, no matter how strong the evidence for the prosecution. It is frightening how many juries fall for this kind of line, but they cannot be blamed: they are only ever in court once and do not see how often this tactic is used.

After the hearing, I had a conference with the Solicitor's Office. They had concluded that Bartlett's lawyers were going to spring some sort of surprise defence on us during the trial. In legal circles, this is known as an 'ambush defence'. The defence suddenly come out with a story which they claim their client has only just told them and which the prosecution will have no chance to investigate. Again, anyone involved in the criminal legal process hears this sort of thing all the time and sees through it instantly. But with juries who are made up of people who have never been in court before and don't realise how often this sort of thing goes on, it can be surprisingly effective. It is repeatedly drummed into juries that there need only be one reasonable doubt, and the emphasis always seems to be on the word 'doubt' rather than on the word 'reasonable'.

So just when I started to think the case was won, I began to realise why others on the team had worries. I began racking my brains for what sort of story I would try to come up with in Bartlett's position. I began to take extra statements, gather extra pieces of documentary evidence, went through the contents of Bartlett's cab again and again. I would write down a possible cover story and then make a list of any evidence which would refute it, so that I could instantly give it to the prosecuting barrister. Bartlett could claim he lent the lorry. He was doing a favour for a sick mate. He was bigamously married in Holland. Anything.

Of course, the other problem was 'jury nobbling'. Bartlett came from a well-connected organisation in London, and Davies would also have an interest in seeing Bartlett cleared. He had the money and the muscle to either bribe or coerce a member of the jury. But, as in Operation *Kansas*, which had given the Widow so much trouble, without hard evidence to show that there would be an attempt to get at the jury, the police could do nothing. They just didn't have the officers, and neither did we.

Bartlett had two older brothers who were thought to be involved in the drugs business. Sure enough, on the first day of the trial at Maidstone Crown Court, Bartlett's brothers were in the public gallery watching the members of the jury. At the end of the first day they hung around the car park across the road from the court. Except in unusual circumstances, jury members are given no special protection. They simply leave the court by their own exit and make their own way home. It is easy for anyone who has been in the courtroom to pick them out and follow them. I had asked for as many members of the team as possible to come down for the trial and we let the Bartlett brothers know that we were watching them watching the jury members. I only hoped it would be enough to scare them off.

The case was largely going to stand or fall on the tachograph analysis. Unsurprisingly, the defence launched their strongest attack against it. Reg was forced to go through his tachograph analysis step by step. It was the usual defence tactic, try to find an error in the paperwork, plant the seeds of doubt in the minds of the jury. But in this case, the tactic was to our advantage. Reg was an excellent witness, and the more detailed his explanations were, the more convincing the evidence became. By the time he emerged from the court, clutching his boards and charts, he was grinning.

As case officer, I was banned from being present in the courtroom itself. This is another common defence tactic. They know that the case officer is the one person who has seen most if not all of the evidence in the case. They try to find errors in the details and then call the case officer to the witness box last to try to ambush him with them. Any case officer can expect a grilling on the minutiae of a case and as the last person in the box after weeks of waiting, this can be pretty stressful.

It is not difficult to place doubt in the minds of a jury. As an example, take something we used to call the 'watch trick'. Have you ever told the truth when accused of something and yet the truth has sounded really weak? That is how the 'watch trick' works.

The defence wait for an event which several officers have witnessed and have all duly noted in their separate duty notebooks. This often happened on foot surveillance. Amongst four or five people it is unusual for all their wrist-watches to tell the same time to the minute. Defence counsel would pick up on this, especially if they had a young or inexperienced officer in the witness box. 'Why,' they would ask, 'is the time in your notebook several minutes different from officers X and Y's? You failed to get your stories straight, didn't you?' Replying, 'But that is the time the event occurred according to my watch' sounds really pathetic and un-convincing. The defence counsel turn and nod knowingly to the jury.

Yet if all the times in the notes were the same, defence could say,

'All the times were exactly the same because you got together and concocted this story didn't you?' There is no way to win that kind of game. If one or two jury members believe police and Customs fit people up, that's effectively the end of the case.

By the end of the first week of the case, I was exhausted. The public doesn't realise that all the witnesses have to be met, chaperoned (even housed in hotels if they have come a long way), and all this work has to be done by the operational officers. In the ID this means the case officer and the team admin officer. There was barely time to follow what was happening in the courtroom.

It was worst for the foreign witnesses, many of whom didn't speak English and who expected to be looked after almost twenty-four hours a day. During days which were often taken up with endless legal arguments requiring no one but the lawyers in court, we all had to sit in the stuffy corridors, in cramped and uncomfortable seating areas, often mixed in with the relatives and supporters of the very criminals against whom these people would shortly be giving evidence. There was no segregation, no special protection. It is hardly surprising that so many witnesses failed to turn up. Of those who did, almost none were called: more wasted time and money.

These tactics bore at least some fruit in the Bartlett case. The elder Dutreaux brother failed to turn up. Defence counsel made a lot of that. He had helped load the lorry. Perhaps he placed the drugs in there? The question of how he was supposed to reclaim the drugs wasn't mentioned. One doubt. That's what they were going for.

Those foreign witnesses who did appear in the witness box were thoroughly disgusted with the way they were treated. Most of them were merely officials, but the forcefulness of defence counsel's questioning made them feel that they had been treated as smugglers themselves. The Kilos used to have a theory that it was a deliberate policy of defence lawyers to give foreign witnesses a rough ride in the hope that it would discourage more of them from appearing at English trials. It certainly seemed to happen a lot.

Finally, it was my turn to appear on the stand. Although I had given evidence before, this was the first time I had appeared as the case officer. The prosecution had so far gone according to plan and the whole thing now depended on me not making a mistake.

I had never felt self-conscious in the dock before but a lot of people find giving evidence difficult. Even the Widow, although she was always composed and authoritative, used to blush every time I saw her give evidence. It is like acting. You stand there with everyone staring at you, aware that someone is going to deliberately try to trip you up. Even hardened officers I've known have hated giving evidence, not because they go into the box with anything to hide, but because of the way the process of giving evidence distorts things. It's a game with rules they don't understand.

As I stood there taking the oath I wondered what the defence would go for. Was there some error in the paperwork I had missed? Some witness I hadn't spoken to? The prosecution counsel went quickly through a few facts. Then it was time for the defence to have their shot at me. I was aware of Bartlett leaning forward over the front of the dock. Defence counsel rose to his feet and with considerable gravitas intoned: 'Now then, officer, have you ever been to Blackpool?'

Immediately, my mind was racing. What had Blackpool got to do with the job? I couldn't think of one person, one piece of paper that had anything to do with Blackpool. Where was he going with this? Of course you only have a moment to think all of this and I was immediately afraid that my hesitation had made me look shifty.

'I think I went on holiday there when I was about three, but not since.'

'Don't you think you ought to have gone?'

'I generally go to Greece for my holidays.'

There was laughter in the court.

'The point is that Mr Saunders, director of the haulage company, lives there. If you were carrying out a thorough investigation as you

239

claim to have done, why wasn't his home searched? Why did you immediately rule him out?'

I almost collapsed with relief. The simple truth was that there weren't enough officers to follow up every lead on the night and that the subsequent investigation had cleared him. If that was the best he had, we were almost home and dry. In fact my time in the box was surprisingly brief. It later turned out that Bartlett's defence was that he was an innocent dupe of his bosses in the haulage firm who had set him up to be an unwitting courier. But this was one of the defences I had prepared for and by the time I had finished answering questions about the company, they only had the ambush defence to fall back on.

As we waited for the defence to open their part of the trial, I met with our counsel to discuss the case. He didn't think that the defence had done enough to stop us yet. They were forced to put Barlett himself on the stand. The ambush defence was coming. The question was: would it be enough to get him off the hook? Prosecution counsel didn't bother to speculate what the story would be. He had seen Barlett and was confident that he could outwit him in the witness box.

Within a few minutes, Bartlett took the stand. His counsel got straight down to the burning question: why had he gone hundreds of miles out of his way to Holland and lied about it? Bartlett claimed that he had a mistress living near Amsterdam. He hadn't said anything to us because he was afraid his wife would find out. Immediately, I was scrabbling through files of paper, looking for records of Bartlett's previous trips to see if there was any way that might undermine his story. Defence questioned him at some length about the 'affair', but Bartlett even managed to bring a tear to his eye as he refused to name her as a 'matter of honour'. Hearing him use those words, Ozzy, who was sitting next to me as the support officer for the day, choked audibly. The judge glanced up with a grim look, but said nothing. Bartlett reckoned that the drugs must have been put on the trailer when it was left in the lay-by in

Belgium while he nipped up to Holland. I made a note for our counsel to mention that the seals and security cables on the trailer had been unbroken. The only way to get the drugs on there in the lay-by would have been by teleportation.

That concluded the case for the defence. They called no other witnesses. I was worried. It was short and simple, plus the jury thought Bartlett was an honest lorry driver with no previous record, since British law does not allow earlier convictions to be mentioned in court. Compared with that, we had all the detail of tachograph analysis, import and export records, Rogatoire procedure and a missing foreign witness. I was afraid that the jury might just find their one reasonable doubt. Our counsel was unimpressed. In his cross-examination, he simply taunted Bartlett in the witness box: 'You're a liar, aren't you, Mr Bartlett?'

'No.'

'But you lied to the officers when you told them you hadn't been to Holland.'

No answer.

'Didn't you, Mr Bartlett?'

'Yes.'

'You lied to them when you said you had kept the trailer with you at all times?'

'Yes.'

'You have even lied to your wife about this affair, haven't you?'

'Yes.'

'In short, you are a liar, aren't you?'

That was the moment when Bartlett looked up and made eye contact. The façade of the poor duped truck driver fell away and the professional hard man stared out. For a moment I thought he might actually leap out of the witness box and try to get to our counsel. But then he brought himself back under control, lowered his eyes and mumbled, 'No.'

I only hoped that the jury had seen that look.

By the time he had finished, our counsel was well pleased. He felt

241

that he had shown Bartlett in his true colours. I was not so sure. To me he had pressed the point so hard that it looked like bullying and the last thing I wanted was for Bartlett to get the jury's sympathy. That was the end of the evidence. It only remained for the closing speeches and the judge's summing up. The jury were sent out to consider their verdict the following day.

'As I see it, the longer they're out, the more likely it is that one of them has bought this sob story about Holland,' said the clerk from the Solicitor's Office. 'Over three hours and the probability is that we've lost it.'

In the corridor outside the court, those who had an interest in the case paced up and down, read their newspapers or just sat and stared out of the window at the stagnant green surface of the River Medway. Most of Bartlett's family seemed to be there – about thirty people in all. At one stage I found myself leaning on the same window ledge as Bartlett's older brother. Although we were on opposite sides of the criminal law, I had spoken to him a couple of times outside the court when returning some of his brother's property. He had seemed okay. No animosity, just a sort of professional courtesy between criminal scum and a champion of justice.

'This is the worst bit, waiting,' I said.

'Yeah. Seem to spend a lot of my life in court just lately.' He told me how the previous week he had been at Liverpool Crown Court for the trial of a cousin being done for fraud. In that bizarre English way, the conversation ended up with me telling him that I thought the defence had done a pretty good job. He in turn thought that we had been too good and that his brother was going to be found guilty.

'Bet you a fiver they acquit,' I said.

'You're on,' he smiled.

At lunchtime, I went to a nearby pub with some members of a heroin target team who were down for a separate trial.

'Well, if you do get a win,' they told me, 'you want to watch out that his family don't come after you. Some of them can take it a bit personal if you put one of theirs away. Last January, one of the Papas got jumped on his way out of court by two guys with baseball bats. He was in hospital for a week.'

'Nah, I've been speaking to the members of the family all the way through the trial. They seem fine.'

The target team officer gave a short, sharp laugh. 'Yeah. That's always how it is – until they lose.'

On the way back, I popped into the court security officer's office. I mentioned that I had a verdict coming up in Court Two and that it might turn a bit nasty.

He smiled knowingly. 'Don't you worry about it,' he said. 'I'll get them to give me a call when the jury comes back. I'll pop up with a couple of the lads.'

The afternoon wore on. One hour, then two. The chap from the Solicitor's Office saw me and shook his head sadly, tapping his watch. I held up crossed fingers.

Then, after four and a half hours, the usher stepped out of the court to say that the jury were coming back. We all swarmed in. Bartlett's family filed into the public gallery, which was actually just a few rows of seats separated from the rest of the court by a hardboard partition three feet high. We were all a bit too close for my liking, so I went and sat in the centre of the court next to the Solicitor's Office clerk and tried to calculate how quickly I could get to the nearest exit.

The foreman of the jury stood up. I felt slightly dizzy. All those months of work, Bartlett's freedom for the next few years, all depended on the next few seconds. Two wrong words and all the work which had taken up much of the last six months of my life would have been wasted. All I could think of was the verdict in *Kansas*. I saw that two of the jury members were smiling in Bartlett's direction. My heart sank. I watched as three burly security officers filed in through the swing doors.

'Guilty,' said the foreman.

There was no howl of outrage from Bartlett or his brothers, no shout of triumph from us. It all seemed too serious for that. And we were all waiting for the interesting part: the maximum sentence for smuggling cannabis is fourteen years – what would he get? For a moment there was silence. Then the judge went through the usual form of words and sentenced Bartlett to seven years.

'That,' murmured the clerk approvingly, 'is a lot of porridge.'

One of the younger members of the Bartlett clan started kicking the hardboard partition, screaming profanities and eventually putting his foot clean through it. The security officer went over to stop him and that's when the ruck started. Bartlett was dragged shouting out of the dock by two prison officers. Several members of Bartlett's family clambered over the partition and first tried to get to the dock and then made straight for us. Fortunately the security staff were straight in. One evil-looking bastard took a huge swing at me which I half-ducked, pushing him over backwards. After that it was a sort of giant scrum with the security staff gradually pushing the family out through the doors while they screamed abuse at the judge, the guards and me. A woman threw a stiletto-heeled shoe which missed me by a couple of inches. Eventually we were able to close and lock the doors, leaving the family kicking at them as they waited for us. The security staff called for police to come and clear the area, but it would take a while.

'I suggest,' said the judge, 'that you all come and wait in my chambers. I'll have some tea sent in.'

We stood in the peace and quiet of his chambers as he told us stories of other trials which had ended in riots and noted that it was an increasingly prevalent phenomenon.

'Aaah,' he said as he was looking out of the window, 'that young man who decided it was a good idea to kick my courtroom appears to have been issued with a parking ticket.'

I looked out of the window and hoped that the traffic warden was a long way away.

'Perhaps there is a God after all,' murmured the judge.

Seven years sounds like a long time. Three years later I was at

Dover on another job. I was looking at a list of people who had been arrested the previous week and there was Bartlett's name! I did some checking and sure enough, it was the same guy, this time smuggling in a load of tobacco. It turned out that with his time on remand taken away and full remission for good behaviour, he'd been released several months before. Perhaps it's time that courts started framing their sentences in the American way, such as three to seven years. At the moment you only hear what the maximum sentence is and it often sounds like justice, but the criminal is usually out in half the time or less.

As a curious footnote, over the next five years both Bartlett's brothers were also convicted for drug smuggling. One was caught in a yacht carrying cocaine by a Customs cutter just off the coast of Norfolk. The other was arrested at a warehouse in Liverpool opening a concealment in a camper van which contained heroin.

Two weeks after Bartlett went down, Steele's case also came up for trial at Maidstone. I was the support officer. In four days he was found guilty and sentenced to seven and a half years.

Bartlett was an established criminal who was deeply involved in drug smuggling and was soon back smuggling again. Steele was a weak character who was tempted and took a chance. It didn't feel right that he should be in longer than Bartlett and I've no doubt that it was a more traumatic experience for him.

It seemed that even if we won, we still couldn't get justice.

11

The Participating Informant

For once I was enjoying a quiet Sunday afternoon at home. The kids were playing in the back garden and after a big roast Sunday dinner (which, like a true ex-house-husband, I had cooked) it was time to sit back with half a hundred weight of Sunday newspapers on my lap and just doze. Of course, that was when the pager went off. I stumbled into the hall, yawning heavily, and sat down with a thump on the seat by the telephone. I called Control.

'Good afternoon, Kilo 17, I hope I'm calling at an inconvenient time.'

It was that cheery bastard on duty again. One day I was really going to have to go down to Control's office and find who he was.

'Okay, what's happening?'

'Dover car terminal have received an anonymous tip on the Customs hotline. They have checked out the ticketing details and they think it's worth a look.'

This didn't sound good. The chances of a genuine tip-off on the hotline were about a hundred to one – usually it was little old ladies who saw what they thought was suspicious activity on the ferry and of course we got our fair share of hoaxers. A real informant who actually knew something was more likely to approach us directly and ask for money.

I rang the docks and spoke to Terry, one of the front-line staff who had by then become something of an old friend. The

246

anonymous tip claimed that a red BMW 7 Series saloon towing an expensive boat would be on the three o'clock ferry out of Calais. It claimed that there were fifty kilos of resin concealed in the boat. Also, and this was very unusual, it gave a name.

'We ran it through the computer, Harry, and it looks good. There's no criminal record on the driver, but the vehicle details check out and get this – it was a cash-paid ticket and he went out yesterday without a boat. Today the boarding details show that he's on his way back with one.'

'Come on, Tel, that's just too bloody obvious even for fifty kilos of resin. Are we sure this isn't some sort of bait so that we miss something else that's coming over on the same ferry?'

'Well, you know what they say, mate, only the stupid ones get caught. We'll keep our eyes open for something else, but I still think this one is worth a go. But remember the new rules: if you want us to search it, you've got to beetle on down here and watch.'

'All right, give me a moment to get clearance from Don and I'll ring you back.'

The last thing I wanted to do was go screaming down to Dover on what was almost certainly a wild goose chase. For a while I toyed with the idea of pretending I had rung Don and telling Dover that we weren't interested. My conscience finally got the better of me. But I still hoped Don would show mercy and tell me to stay at home.

An hour later I was standing behind the reflective glass of an office overlooking one of the vehicle examination bays at Dover. Next to me was a detective sergeant, Chris Hartnoll, who had been seconded to the Kilos for six months from Number Nine Regional Crime Squad. It was a bright idea from someone in the senior management to improve co-operation between police and Customs.

I was watching the driver. Something was very wrong. He was short, and overweight, with greasy, unkempt dark hair. But he was wearing a smart suit which looked expensive. Gold watch. Gold rings. His wallet, which had been taken off him when he was stopped contained all the major credit cards and over five hundred pounds cash in sequentially numbered notes. He was pacing up and down, chain-smoking as a string of Customs officers climbed in and out of the vehicle in order to scatter his belongings all over the concrete. He looked unconcerned, stopping his pacing every so often to point out an expensive piece of luggage or kit and remind the officers that it cost far more than they'd earn in a month. He was goading them, challenging them to find something. And this just meant that every time they emerged they took even less care about where his stuff was thrown.

I was puzzled. This wasn't right. Where was the anger, the denials of guilt, the threats of retaliation once 'your superiors hear about this'? He just wasn't acting the way 99 per cent of other people do when subjected to this kind of invasive treatment. And even more suspiciously, every so often he would stare up at the window. There was no way he could see us, but it seemed to me that he knew we were there.

Terry stamped up the metal staircase to our office and slapped the paperwork on a desk.

'He's definitely not right,' he muttered. 'You should have seen his face as soon as we waved him out of the queue and into the bay. It was like he was pleased.'

'Well then, he's got to be drawing us away from something else on that bloody ferry.'

'Believe me, we're looking. We've got everyone on it and anything that looks even slightly wrong is getting a tug. But I tell you this, he's too cocky even for a decoy. He's winding up the search team something rotten.'

'What's his story on the boat?'

'Says he's picking it up for his uncle. Claims his uncle runs some hire company up in Norfolk and bought this one in Calais. Offered to pay his ticket if he'd pick it up. Our boy thought he'd take the opportunity to pick up some duty-frees at the same time. The

248

company exists, but there's no purchase paperwork that we can find.'

'So what's next?'

'Well, we've taken everything out of the car and the boat. We've given it a good look and found nothing. Even run the drugs dog over it. The next stage would be to pull the fucking thing completely apart. The boys want to do it, they really hate this bastard, but I've got to be honest with you guys, that is an expensive piece of kit and if we don't find anything the bill is going to be really fucking ugly.' He paused. 'And it won't be coming off the Collection's budget, know what I mean.'

It was going to be a big call. Not mine. You had to be an SIO to spend this kind of money. Don would want to know as much as possible. I decided that the time had come to talk to the driver.

He saw us coming down the stairs. The uniformed officers left to take a well-earned tea break.

'Well, well, well, looks like they've finally called in the A team,' said the driver in a heavy Welsh accent.

'Actually, they were the A team,' said Chris, nodding in the direction of the rummage crew, 'we're more like enthusiastic amateurs.'

'So are you going to tell me what you're fucking looking for or what?'

'All I can say is that we have reason to believe that you may have undeclared goods secreted on your . . .'

'Yeah, yeah, yeah,' said the driver, waving a hand. Then he took a long draw on his latest cigarette. 'It's drugs, isn't it?'

'What makes you say that?'

He took another long drag:

'I'll bet someone told you I had fifty kilos of cannabis in that boat, didn't they?'

Whoops. Chris and I exchanged glances.

'Ahhh, that surprised you, didn't it?' he sneered. 'Well, I haven't got any, so you lot might as well piss off.'

'So what do you do for a living?'

'I'm a pilot.'

'Any particular airline?'

'I'm a private pilot. I do my own flying, got my own planes. I run executives jets to the Continent, that sort of thing.'

He went on at some length telling us about his money, his cars, his birds. Eventually we got bored. But the fact that he knew exactly what had been said on the hotline looked very odd. If he wasn't a decoy he must be some kind of masochist who wanted to be strip-searched by burly Customs officers.

'It's all wrong, Don,' I said on the phone a few minutes later. 'He's too cocky about all this. He knows we've been tipped. I reckon whatever did come through on that ferry, we missed it. Having a go at the boat now will just add to his smug sense of satisfaction. Terry says the bill is likely to be several thousand. Believe me, you would not want to give this guy the satisfaction of paying him several thousands of our money. Chris agrees with me.'

I held out the receiver for Chris to say something, but he just shrugged. There was a long silence while Don mulled this over.

'Do it, Harry. If he wants to challenge us, we'll take him on. Wreck the fucking boat if you have to. And if we don't find anything, give him a compensation form. His claim will have to go through me anyway. By the time I've lost it a couple of times he'll be lucky to get one pound, let alone a thousand.'

Terry was in the room waiting. I gave him the nod and he stepped through the door and gave the thumbs-up to the rummage crew. They didn't need telling twice.

Despite being on the Division for almost two years, I'd never actually watched a boat being taken apart before. The shed was filled with the whine of electric drills and angle grinders as every piece of the interior fittings was taken out. They even started peeling off the wooden skin which covered the outside even though there was no room there to conceal anything. Then they worked on the car. Seats, door panels, everything came out. When

250

car and boat lay in about a million pieces across the shed, they stopped. The crew were exhausted and angry. They'd found nothing.

The driver was in heaven. You could see it in his eyes as he strode towards us.

'Are you fucking satisfied now? Are you? ARE YOU? I'll tell you, by the time I've fucking finished with you, you'll be out on your arses! I want your fucking numbers and the number of your fucking boss. I'll have the fucking lot of you.'

'Charming man,' murmured Chris.

But there had been plenty of time to prepare for this. I let the abuse wash over me. It was just background noise. I handed him two closely printed sheets of paper.

'What's this?' he demanded.

'This is a claim form. When your insurers have assessed the damage, fill this in and send it to the address at the top. You should hear from us within three months.'

'Three months? You're fuckin' . . .'

'The other form is a complaints slip. I've put our names and office address on it for you.'

And with that we turned and started to walk off.

The rummage crew were already chucking the contents of the boat back inside its wrecked shell. They weren't being gentle about it either. Like us, they were sure we'd been decoyed and they weren't happy.

'You'll be hearing from me again,' the driver shouted across the shed as we headed towards the car park.

And, as it turned out, he wasn't wrong.

Two weeks later Don stormed into the office.

'Have you seen this? Fifteen thousand pounds for damage to a boat. Is this you?'

'You know it is,' I protested. 'It's that prat down in Dover. You authorised it.'

251

'Not fifteen thousand fucking pounds I didn't!'

'He's trying it on.'

Then Chris put his head around the door from the next office.

'Are you talking about that Welsh bastard down in Dover?'

'Yeah, so what?'

'You'll never guess who I've just put the phone down on! He wants to meet and, get this, he says he has some information which quote unquote "might be of use to us".'

'Bollocks!' said Don.

Chris shrugged. 'You're probably right, but that's what he said.'

'Well, whether he's got something to say or not, set it up,' snarled Don. 'And while you're there tell him there's no fucking way on earth that he's having fifteen thousand quid!'

We arranged to meet at a police station near Bedford. Originally, our Welsh friend wanted to meet at a motorway service station. Ordinarily this would have been okay, but we didn't trust this guy. It could have been that he was so pissed off at having his vehicle ripped apart that he wanted some of his mates and a couple of baseball bats to meet us. It could be that he was trying to set up some kind of sting for a newspaper or television programme. We didn't doubt that he was making his money illegitimately, but he was such an odd character that we wanted everything official and above board – at least for our first meeting.

He turned up right on time. While Chris waited at the station, I had parked in a place from where I could watch our new friend approach, just in case he was being followed by anyone – friendly or unfriendly. We were well out of the way so any following vehicle would have stood out like a sore thumb. He was alone. He parked his car some way from the station and walked the rest. I followed on the other side of the street, but he didn't look back once.

He walked straight up to the desk with me right behind him.

'I'm looking for DS Hartnoll,' he said in the now familiar Welsh accent.

I clapped a hand on his shoulder and he leapt into the air. He was certainly spooked about something.

'Hello there,' I said, 'come on through.'

Nodding to the officer on the desk, I led him through the door which would take us through to the back of the station and the interview room where Chris was waiting.

The driver got straight down to business:

'First of all, I think I owe you guys a sort of apology,' he grinned.

'Oh really?'

'You see, it was me what put in the call about the boat and the drugs.'

That was good and bad news: good because now there was no way he was getting fifteen thousand off us for the damage to the boat. By giving misleading information he'd committed an offence, so that was me off the hook with Don. But bad because there went the drugs connection. So what was he up to?

'So you got us to pull your boat apart,' I said. 'What the fuck for?'

'Calm down,' he said soothingly. 'I wanted to meet you guys. I needed to meet someone from Customs who wasn't just a bag searcher. I wanted to meet real investigators so that I could give you this information. My life won't be worth spit once I tell you about this.'

Out of the corner of my eye I remember seeing Chris pass a hand over his eyes. He must have been thinking the same thing I was. We had some sort of Walter Mitty character who wanted to be a super-spy.

'Couldn't you just approach a uniformed officer and ask to see us?'

I had to admire Chris. His voice and manner were still pleasant even though we'd driven a hundred miles on a wild goose chase.

'No way, man. I couldn't risk it. The people I'm involved with have eyes everywhere – even in the police. I couldn't risk this information going anywhere. I had to go straight to the top. As soon as I saw you guys coming out of that office, I knew you were the real deal.'

Well, that was the last shred of his credibility out of the window. I began to read the notices for suspects on the walls of the interview room and plan my holiday.

'So who are these people you're involved with?' asked Chris.

'Well, I can't give you all the details, a lot of it is on first-name terms, you know, but I got hooked up with this guy called Johnson, Charlie Johnson, Rozzer his mates call him. But I think the guy you'll really be interested in is his boss. I don't know his last name but everyone calls him Frankie.'

Our little Welshman had become interesting again, but I still didn't believe he was genuine: what would Johnson be doing with this loser? How had he got introduced to Frank and how the hell could he not know Frank's last name? It must have been a name he'd heard and he was trying to reel us in on the little bit of information he had.

But Chris patiently went through the whole story. The Welshman claimed that Johnson had just turned up two years ago at the flying club. They'd got talking at the bar and Charlie had asked what the range of his plane was and how many passengers it could take. He'd pretended to be interested in flying lessons, claiming that he didn't want to go with one of the flying schools who would rip him off. He wanted to learn from someone who would teach him straight.

'Of course, it was obvious to me right from the word go he was up to something,' said the Welshman, 'but I decided to play him along. I thought to myself, okay, let's see what your little game is.'

Johnson had told him that he was an arcade manager in Hastings. At least that much was accurate. He claimed that Johnson took a few lessons and they then became drinking buddies. None of this rang true. I couldn't see a professional bruiser like Johnson spending two minutes around this wannabe spy, but then informants often disguise the way they became involved with a criminal group, so it was a matter of waiting to see what else he had to say.

'Anyway, we were having some drinks at this club in South

London and he admits that he's into other stuff as well as the gaming arcades and that. He says that he has a mate who runs stuff into the country, tobacco and stuff. Says would I be interested in earning some money if the right opportunity came my way. I decided to sound him out like, so I said, "Tobacco, eh? And stronger stuff too, I'll bet." And Johnson said that was right.'

'You were very cunning. Did he say how they brought the stuff in usually?' asked Chris.

'No. I did ask, but he just goes all cagey on me. Anyway, I said I might be interested, but that I'd have to meet his mate, you know, see if he was on the level like. I knew that when I came to you with all this, you'd want to know who the big boss was.'

It took two hours before we got the whole story. By the time you had cut out most of the waffle about aircraft and drinking and how useful he could be to us, we were left with the fact that he clearly knew Johnson and claimed to have met Frank. I was convinced he was making 90 per cent of it up. He wanted £10,000 up front to stay in contact and produce more information. We sent him off having agreed to another meeting, but I expected that nothing would come of it.

As we drove back to the office, Chris asked me what I thought of our new informant.

'Simple. Complete time-waster – and I can tell you how I know he's a time-waster: he says he's a pilot, but I know for a fact that Frank relies on a pilot called Myers who has a cottage in Sussex with a helicopter pad out the back. I've been working on him for months. So I don't buy all this stuff about Frank suddenly needing a pilot. I don't doubt this guy has met Johnson – he knows too many of the right details – but Johnson has been out of the country for months. And what was all that stuff with the boat and "You're the only guys I can trust with this information"? Even if he was on the level, he's completely mental.'

'Well, I don't know. There's no such thing as a standard informant. I've run quite a few and they've all been odd in some

255

way. He's clearly mad, but then you would have to be to go up against Davies, wouldn't you? I think he may turn out to be more use than you think.'

I passed the Welshman's details to Danny to check out through his sources. Danny said that it would take time. In the meantime Chris and I checked him out with the Civil Aviation Authority. They knew him all right. He was infamous throughout the airfields of central England. An official described him as 'like an asteroid – you never know when he might suddenly crash down out of the sky'. His plane was an old single-engine Cessna that was so poorly maintained it was a liability.

'Frankly, he's about this far from having his licence suspended again,' said the official.

Over the next few weeks my phone rang almost every other day, with 'Taffy', as we were now calling him, demanding another meeting and going on about the great new information he had. Finally I had to tell him to 'piss off' and threw the phone down on to the hand rest so hard that it bounced.

Two days later, Danny called me and Don down to his office: 'I have some bad news for you: everything your Welsh friend says is true. In fact, more than that. He seems to have convinced both Charlie and Frank that they can trust him. Apparently Frank already has plans to use him on a job in the near future and has been having him round to his house for drinks in the hope of keeping him sweet. According to our informant, Frank actually trusts him.'

Don groaned. Then he said, 'There is no way we are using this psychopath. I don't care how good his access is.'

But Danny was adamant that Frank's organisation was on the brink. Following the loss of his smuggling operations using lorry drivers, he had tried to set up another road haulage firm. But thanks to 'Uncle Mick' we had been able to intercept the very first driver Davies used. Now no one trusted him to bring gear safely across the Channel. Danny was sure that one more good push would bring Davies down. 'Christ, Don, we've got to! You've seen the reports on Davies. We are so close to getting him. If we miss this opportunity we might not get another for months. He'll re-organise and we'll never catch him.'

Normally we would have rejected a character like this without a second thought, but the prospect of finally nailing Davies was too tempting – even for Don. By the end of the meeting, we had decided to run him.

But Don was adamant that everything would have to be clearly recorded and monitored by senior officers every step of the way. Our big fear was that Taffy would back out at the last moment and try to sell his story to the newspapers. This had happened before with Customs informants. Worse still, his bottle might go and he might confess everything to Davies. We had little doubt that Davies would have him badly beaten or perhaps even kill him.

So now I had to eat humble pie. I rang Taffy and said that we had decided to meet with him after all. I told him that shouting at him was simply a test to see how determined he was to see the job through. It was so corny that Chris, who was listening on the other line, grinned and made violent gagging sounds across the office. Taffy didn't care. He agreed to meet us again at a pub in the countryside.

But this case was never going to run smoothly.

When we met him, Taffy's character had changed again. His confidence had evaporated and now he seemed scared. He kept looking around as though he was afraid that he had been followed.

'I think they suspect,' he said. 'I hadn't truly realised how heavy these guys are. I was in Frank's car the other day when this guy cuts him up. We must have chased him about five miles before we ran him off the road. Frank had this iron bar and hit him about a dozen times . . . it was horrible. What the hell would he do to me if he knew I was talking to you?'

This was what we had been afraid of: there was no way that this guy would stick it through an undercover operation.

'Look,' said Chris, 'we don't want you to do anything you feel uncomfortable with. If you want to call it quits, that's fine.'

But Taffy was insistent that he wanted to keep going. Even when he found out that he wasn't going to get any money up front.

'Okay,' said Chris, 'you just keep us in touch. Let us know any little bits and pieces you hear. That's all we want. But remember, don't get involved. You're not to take part in any smuggling operation. Understand? If you do, we'll break contact with you and you'll be arrested.'

With that warning ringing in his ears, Taffy left. But Chris and I could almost predict what he was going to tell us at the next meeting two weeks later:

'I've got them just where we want them,' he said exultantly.

'What do you mean?' asked Chris suspiciously.

'Frank has asked me to do a run for him. He wants me to fly out to see one of his contacts in Holland.'

'I thought we told you not to get involved, just to observe,' I said.

Taffy waved a hand dismissively.

'Don't worry, man. I'm only going to see this Dutch contact. I can let you have all the details after the meeting. That's what you want isn't it – information about the gang?'

Chris and I looked at each other doubtfully, but we both knew that we needed to get intelligence as quickly as possible. There was no telling how long Taffy's connection with Davies would last.

'Well, okay, but remember – you don't get involved in a smuggling run. That is absolutely forbidden,' I said. 'Has he given you the name of this Dutch contact?'

'Yeah. It's some guy called Van Hohn.'

Two seconds later Chris was frantically slapping me on the back as I choked on a mouthful of beer.

'You've got to be fucking joking!' I gasped.

'No,' said Taffy, completely unconcerned. 'I even wrote it down to make sure I wouldn't forget it. Frank says he trusts him completely.'

'Is there a problem?' asked Chris.

'Only that we nicked the bastard over a year ago on another Frank Davies job. He got six years!'

Within an hour, Danny had confirmed what Taffy had said. Van Hohn's lawyers had argued that because he was not violent and because he had a heart condition (which was news to everyone involved in the case and almost certainly untrue), he should be allowed to serve his sentence in an open prison. They argued that since he wouldn't have his passport there would be no chance of him leaving the country. Apparently Van Hohn had regularly been allowed to leave the prison and visit the local town. One day he just didn't bother to come back and was in Holland the next day. What angered me was that no one had bothered to tell us. Danny told us that the Dutch hadn't even been asked to search for him. Don agreed that Taffy should find out where Van Hohn was living so that we could let the Dutch police know.

Davies kept delaying the promised meeting and gradually let Taffy know that he wanted him to do more than simply meet Van Hohn. He wanted Taffy to collect a consignment of drugs from him. Don and the Solicitor's Office were united in insisting that he must not make the run. When it was revealed in court that a Customs informant had collected and imported the drugs, the whole case would be likely to fall apart.

Then our hand was forced by something none of us could have foreseen. Patrick came into the office one morning and slapped the newspaper on my desk.

'Looks like your family curse has worked a treat.'

Patrick was referring to a half-forgotten joke. The team had been ribbing me about the fact that I had failed to stop Davies despite the various successes we had achieved. Following one particularly alcoholic evening I had announced that I was placing Davies and his family under a voodoo curse and stuck a picture of him on the wall of the office with a confiscated sheath knife through the centre of his head. Someone had later placed a picture frame around it with the words: 'The Curse of Chumley'.

The article was about Lard Boy. It said that he had fallen to his death from a hotel balcony in Fuengerola. I took the paper straight down to Danny. He was shocked. He said he'd get straight on to the Spanish police and try to find out what had happened.

Three days later we had the whole story. Apparently Lard Boy had been sent to a deal with some Moroccans. Usually Frank would have sent some heavies to the meeting with him for protection. For whatever reason, Lard Boy had turned up without them. According to the Spanish police an argument had developed and the Moroccans had stabbed Lard Boy in the neck and then pushed him out of the window. They were twelve floors up. According to the police surgeon, he might have lived if he had landed in the swimming pool, but he missed it by about six feet.

The death of a long-standing target like Lard Boy was shocking enough, but there were further consequences. A few days after we heard about the death, the police sergeant from Milton Keynes rang us to say that there would be no more information from his source. At first we were desperate to get the informant back. We visited the sergeant and persuaded him to make one last call to try to convince 'Uncle Mick' that it was worth continuing.

Danny and I listened on an extension. He was adamant that it was all over. But one sentence from the conversation haunted us. 'What do you expect, for God's sake? He was her only son.'

It was then that I remembered the look on Mrs Davies' face when I found the videotapes. I remembered some of the things done to her on those tapes. It was never proved and some people had other theories, but I think I know why our informant had been so good.

The drying-up of our source on Frank meant that Taffy's trip to Holland had to be seen in a different light. Don called a council of war. We eventually decided Taffy could make the run. But there would be one condition. Frank would have to meet him and collect the drugs when he arrived back in England. If Davies was as desperate as Danny had claimed, then he would go for it. If not, we agreed that we would end our contact with Taffy.

So the flight was arranged. Davies told Taffy that he should fly from Shoreham Airport near Brighton. Taffy was also told that a contact would meet him in the terminal at Shoreham to hand over money which he would take to Holland to pay for the drugs. We decided that Kilo officers should stake out the terminal to try to get photographs of the handover of the money. We carefully picked officers whom Taffy hadn't met and who wouldn't be likely to spook him. Meanwhile, Chris and I would wait further down the coast at Manston in Kent. There was little chance of Taffy's landing being accidentally sighted by one of Davies' contacts. There Chris and I would photograph and mark the money with ultra-violet ink in the hope that Dutch police would be able to trace it once it was paid to Van Hohn.

The Dutch police had been kept informed about the operation and they would keep Taffy under surveillance during his meeting. Granville had travelled to Amsterdam as a liaison officer. Hopefully he would return with Van Hohn. Once Taffy had collected the drugs, he would fly back to a landing field in Sussex which at the moment Davies was keeping secret. The one piece of good news was that Davies had agreed when Taffy had insisted that he would only hand over the drugs to him personally. Taffy had confided to Davies that he didn't trust anyone else as he was afraid of 'police spies'. Taffy was particularly amused when he told us that part. We had high hopes of arresting Davies at the airfield.

On the day of Taffy's departure, the Widow and three other officers staked out the passenger terminal at Shoreham. Shoreham is a very small airport and the terminal is a tiny building dating from the 1930s which looks as if it was copied straight out of a Biggles book. The Widow's job was to get pictures of the meeting. She was worried. The camera bag was simply a small shoulder bag which contained a normal 35mm camera. There was a badly disguised aperture at one end of the bag and it was operated by pressing a trigger in the handle. No matter what you put in the bag it always seemed impossible to muffle the sound of the camera shutter. The Widow only hoped that Davies wouldn't sit too close.

Taffy turned up on time with his aircraft ready to go on the tarmac outside. He went and sat in the café where Davies had told him the contact would meet him.

Meanwhile, Chris and I were waiting at Manston which is only a few minutes' flying time away. Unknown to Taffy, we also had one of the pilots of the Sussex Police helicopter with us to get a look at Taffy and his aircraft. The idea was that, provided it wasn't already out on a call for the police, the Shoreham helicopter would shadow Taffy when he flew back to England in case he tried to get away with the drugs and also to provide extra cover at the knock should Davies try to escape.

The weather was terrible – steady drizzle and a howling wind. The police pilot didn't think Taffy's little plane would be able to do it. Meanwhile at Shoreham there was no sign of any contact. After half an hour, Taffy rang Davies to ask what was happening. Davies insisted that someone would be there and he should sit tight.

After an hour the weather was worse and we felt sure that the whole deal was off. It was then that a familiar Range Rover was spotted by one of the surveillance officers pulling into the little airport car park at Shoreham. Frank Davies himself had come to hand over the money.

He was carrying a small tartan holdall. He spotted Taffy in the café and signalled for him to come to another room in the terminal. The Widow had been sitting near Taffy in the café at a table with a good view. She hoped that Taffy would stay put in the busy café and cursed when he meekly stood up and followed Davies out.

She had to follow. They had gone to a balcony area of the terminal where plane spotters generally gather. It was empty at the moment. She was afraid she would be noticed by Davies and that he would be bound to hear the camera bag in that empty room, but she weighed that up against the chance of photographing Davies himself making the handover. She went for it. She stood at one end of the room and lit a cigarette. She disguised the sound of the camera with her 'smoker's cough'. Our luck must have been changing because Davies, the man who was usually so paranoid about security, never even gave her a second glance.

She could see that Davies was agitated. Taffy told us later that Davies had said he had been 'let down' by someone who was supposed to provide the money and that was why there was a delay. Taffy had weakened at this vital moment and said that he thought the weather was now too bad to fly. Davies told him bluntly that he could either fly now or have his legs broken. Davies gave him a telephone number to ring in Holland and said that the Dutch contact would collect him from the airfield there. Then Davies left. The Widow rang us a few minutes later to say that Taffy had gone straight out to his aircraft and taken off.

At Manston we waited. The police pilot knew exactly how long the journey should take, but we scanned the skies and there was still no sign of our plane. We began to wonder if Taffy had played us all for fools and done a runner with the cash. As time wore on we apologised to the pilot for wasting his afternoon.

'Not to worry. It makes a change. Mind you, he'll be flying the Channel in the dark if he doesn't hurry up,' said the pilot. 'Is he rated to fly at night?' We both shrugged. 'I think I'll pop over to the tower and see if I can find anything out,' he said in a worried tone of voice.

Eventually the pilot came jogging back.

'Looks like this could be your boy coming now.'

We ran outside on to the tarmac. Sure enough, barely visible through the murk, a small single-engine plane was swooping low over the far end of the airstrip. He landed, bouncing heavily three times, the police pilot wincing at each hop, and then taxied out of sight behind some sheds.

'Bounces well anyway,' said the pilot with a grin as Chris and I left him and walked in the direction of the sheds, 'maybe he's going to skip over the Channel like a pebble.'

Taffy was late, but ebullient.

'Hey boys, look at this!' he called as we got nearer his plane. He pulled open the sides of the tartan holdall and held it up so that we could see the cash inside, wrapped in polythene.

'All right put it away,' snarled Chris, looking around to check if anyone else had seen it.

'We have fucking got 'em, boys,' Taffy laughed. 'As Frank was giving me the instructions, I was thinking, you stupid fucker, we have got you! We have fucking got you! Yes!' He punched the air.

I didn't like all this excitement. I knew it was coming from Taffy's adrenalin rush at having completed part of the job, but it could just as easily turn to panic. That was always the trouble with Taffy: one moment danger was his middle name, the next he was too scared to leave the room.

'Well, I hope you remember what he told you.'

'No trouble. I fly out to a small airfield near Amsterdam. Make my way to a phone and call this number.' We copied the phone number on to another piece of paper and gave Taffy the copy, keeping the original as evidence. 'A guy called Jan will pick me up, take me to the buy and I fly back the next day. Piece – of – piss!' He poked me in the chest with his finger for emphasis.

'Yeah, all right, calm down,' I said. I definitely didn't like this excitement.

We marked the notes and then resealed the holdall. Taffy showed us on a map where he would be landing in Holland. We made sure that Taffy understood the rest of the plan. He was to let us know the point he was flying back to or if he couldn't do that he was to fly to Manston where we would meet him before he flew on to the landing site. We would have a knock team on standby. We also gave him an emergency number if things went wrong. Taffy said he understood everything, but I don't think he really heard a word.

And with that we let Taffy go. We got back to the terminal building where the police pilot was waiting just as Taffy was preparing for take-off. The rain was pouring down across the airfield and the wind was gusting as hard as ever. Taffy's little single-engine plane lurched into the air and wobbled as it puttered down the runway. It seemed to rise only about twenty feet and then it started to come down again.

'Hello,' murmured the pilot, leaning forward.

One wing tip began to dip and then dip lower. It was inches off the ground.

'Oh, Jesus Christ!' he muttered and we all braced for the impact that must surely follow. But at the last minute, the little engine roared and the plane lifted. With the engine blipping ominously it disappeared out of our sight in the murk as another gust of wind buffeted us across the airport.

'Well, I tell you guys, I flew helicopters in the Royal Navy for ten years on all sorts of dangerous jobs including the Falklands and there is no way you could get me to fly that plane in this shit. He is either one very brave or very stupid little bastard.'

I thought I knew which he was. I hoped I was wrong.

Danny had arranged to have Taffy's progress monitored by military radar. We went and drank coffee while we waited for news. Some time later the pilot came back from the control tower.

'Bad news, I'm afraid. They had him up to the coast and then after a couple of minutes over the Channel they lost him. They said he was bloody low. Too low for this weather. I hope he took a life jacket.'

12

Storms on the Horizon

Chris and I sat in the office that evening sipping whisky and waiting for news of Taffy. There was still no news from Holland, but on the positive side, there was no confirmation that he had gone down in the Channel either.

Then, finally, Granville rang from Holland to confirm that Taffy had landed safely. Granville chuckled as he claimed that the Dutch police had been able to track his progress because of the number of complaints they had received about a low-flying aircraft following the streetlights. Taffy had been collected by a local villain who was known to the Dutch police, but sadly it wasn't Van Hohn. We didn't mind. We were just relieved that Taffy had got there without killing anyone.

The following morning I was back in the office early in case there were any developments. The Dutch police had monitored Taffy's arrival for us, but they weren't going to be able to keep him under constant surveillance. So we had to wait now until Taffy contacted us and that could be at any time.

Don was also there early. He called me into his office. My first thought was that something had gone wrong with the operation, but in fact he had a job offer. I had been nagging him for some time. Although I was nominally an HEO on the Kilos, I was still treated as just a junior officer. Worse still, I was still lumbered with the '17' designation. I didn't feel like an outsider any more and although I didn't really want to leave the Kilos, I wanted a proper position on a team somewhere. Don had promised to see what he could do.

'I suppose the good news is that I've found you a team. It's a front-line heroin unit and right now they've got plenty of vacancies, but you may want to think twice about it. They've got themselves caught between a Turkish syndicate in London on one side and a seriously heavy Liverpool dealer on the other. One case officer and his family have already had to be taken into hiding on the witness protection scheme because of threats against them and last week there was an arson attack on another officer's home. Basically they are in a war, Harry. But it's the sort of job you've said you always wanted – a serious position on a serious team.'

I knew the team he was talking about. It had some pretty rough characters in it. The SIO had a no-nonsense reputation as someone who expected maximum commitment and accepted no excuses.

'Think carefully about this, Harry. If you thought the hours were rough here, you'll have a real shock when you go there. They will expect you to be able to drive solo on surveillance a lot of the time and some of the estates they are working on in Liverpool are no joke. It's an important decision.'

We sat and talked about some of the other possibilities, but they would mean moving out of drugs work into alcohol, tobacco or fraud investigation. The heroin team was the best, and also the worst, offer on the table.

'I'm still not sure you're fully qualified for this sort of move, but they are desperate for people and they will take you straight away if you want to go.'

I needed to know what Nicky was going to make of all this. Our truce was holding – just. I didn't dare make a decision like this without talking to her. I had to play for time.

'Things are pretty busy right now. Can I give you an answer once we get Taffy safely back from Holland?'

'Sure,' said Don, 'but make it quick.'

267

The first thing we heard from Taffy was at about eleven o'clock the following evening, when we were in the pub enjoying the team's Christmas celebration. Chris's pager lit up and gave us a number. We dashed back to the office and called the number shown. Taffy was in a panic. 'It's all gone pear-shaped here, man. The deal didn't go down. There was a meet. They said there wasn't enough money. I couldn't help it, man, the guy took some of the money. Frank will fucking kill me, there's no way I can fucking come back. You've got to call Dutch police to come and pick me up!'

We got him to go through the whole story stage by stage. On the first night, when 'Jan' had found out that Taffy had brought cash with him, he had told Taffy that he was supposed to be paid up front for his part in the scheme. Taffy had told him that he was responsible for the money and no way. So Jan had then pulled a knife, at which point Taffy had given him the entire holdall full of cash.

The meet had then gone down the following evening, but the Dutch suppliers had claimed there was not enough cash and said they wouldn't do the deal. Jan had then started an argument which had been unwise seeing as they were outnumbered by the Dutch crew. There had been a bit of a fight which Taffy had wisely stayed out of. The suppliers had then left, taking the cash and saying the balance had better be paid before they returned. Jan was now out of the flat trying to contact Frank to get it sorted. Taffy was terrified that the suppliers were going to come back, there was going to be no more money and things would turn nasty.

We spent the next ten minutes reassuring him and convincing him to stay. We told him that all the work he had done as a 'valuable undercover operative' would be wasted if he backed out now and that the rewards for success would be all the greater because of the personal danger he had been involved in.

Finally, he agreed to stay put. But that wasn't the end of it. Later that night, Chris had another call from him saying that someone was trying to break into the flat and that Jan was nowhere to be found. We told him to hang on and put a call in to the Dutch police who sent a team round. They made an arrest, but rather than the team they had been led to expect, it was only a druggie trying to score a fix. We only hoped it hadn't ruined the operation.

We had an anxious wait, but by early the following morning Taffy had undergone the by now familiar transformation. He was ringing us from the small airfield outside Amsterdam before taking off and returning to Britain. The deal was on. Jan had returned to say that the misunderstanding had been sorted. On a map he had shown Taffy a field where he should land to pick up the drugs. A vehicle would be waiting for him. He had also been given the location of a field in Sussex where he was expected to land and meet Frank to deliver the drugs. Taffy gave us the map reference.

Taffy talked eagerly about how he was going to 'smash the Davies gang'. We told him to be careful and deliver the drugs as planned. We warned him that we would have a team ready for whoever collected the drugs and that he would be allowed to take off. We would meet him at Manston afterwards.

The office was now a hive of activity as we prepared for the knock. The Widow was to head one team at the collection point. We had pinpointed the field on a map. It was going to be tricky. The knock was way out in the countryside and it would be hard to get a team into position without them showing out. We had to consider the possibility that Frank had already arranged for someone to keep watch in the area, which would fit his normal pattern. Another team would be despatched to Frank's house ready to search there. The police helicopter at Shoreham was on standby. We also phoned the Dutch police to let them know that they could move in and arrest the Dutch contact later that day.

It all seemed too good to be true.

And it was.

A few hours later, the phone rang again. It was Control wanting to know if we had an informant who was smuggling drugs out of Belgium. Our hearts sank.

Apparently the Belgian police had called making enquiries: a man had landed at Brussels airport claiming a police emergency and causing air traffic control chaos. He had demanded to see the police and had reported to them that he was an undercover officer for British Customs, and had promptly directed them to several large holdalls which proved to contain cocaine and cannabis resin. Taffy had panicked yet again.

It seemed as if the whole job was off. The Belgians were bound to want to investigate the whole matter. Even if there was only a delay of a few hours, we doubted that Frank would fall for it. Don began a long telephone call to the Belgian police trying to explain what was going on.

Once the Belgians had confirmed with the Dutch that none of their citizens were involved and that the deal hadn't been done on their soil, they were amazingly co-operative. Don even offered to let them dummy up the holdalls and keep the drugs – we would still be able to conduct the knock. But they were marvellous about it, said they would put Taffy and his drugs on the plane, and wished us good luck.

I swear, as long as I live, I will never say a bad thing about the Belgian police again.

They then put Taffy on the phone and, not unreasonably, Chris asked him what he thought he was up to. Taffy said that he knew that Customs owed him a lot of money for his undercover work (this was wrong) and whilst he trusted me and Chris, he was afraid that the Customs senior management might try to get out of their responsibilities and increase the arrest count by having him picked up as part of the gang. He had decided the previous night that he would pre-empt this risk by surrendering himself to Belgian Customs.

We told Taffy to get back in his aircraft and make straight for the landing ground. He agreed, and didn't seem the least bit chastened by all the trouble he had caused. We didn't dare give him the bollocking he deserved in case he refused to carry on. Don was furious and wandered round the office muttering that if Taffy made it across the Channel alive he would personally strangle him.

Before we scrambled teams from the office there was one more strange event. Danny arrived from his office with a pack of photographs which had been sent by Spanish police. They showed Davies' villa. It had been torched. I asked Danny if he had any idea who was behind it. The Spanish police were apparently looking into it, but had told Danny they didn't have any leads.

With that strange news in our minds, Chris and I went to Manston where we hoped we would be debriefing Taffy, while the rest of the Kilos and half of the Deltas headed for the various knocks. It was annoying that I wouldn't be there to see Davies arrested, but it is a strict rule that informant handlers have to be kept away from the main investigation. I only hoped it would run smoothly.

Taffy was detected by radar flying in over the coast that afternoon. The Shoreham Police helicopter did a superb job of shadowing him towards the meeting place.

The Widow had promised me that she wouldn't let me down. Officers were hidden in hedgerows around the field and vehicles had been secreted in some farm buildings within striking distance. The only worrying development was that her team hadn't been able to detect a watcher. Perhaps there wasn't one this time – Davies' use of Taffy showed that his usual standards were slipping and the torching of the villa in Spain proved that he was under pressure from other criminals. On the other hand, perhaps a watcher had spotted the Widow's team first. Chris and I were left pacing the terminal at Manston waiting for updates. We could only hope.

Then, about half an hour before Taffy was due to arrive at the field, the first sign of a reception team was spotted – a battered old Volvo estate car parked in a lay-by less than half a mile from the landing field. The Widow immediately sent a Kilo vehicle out to see if they could identify the driver.

271

It was Curtis, Davies' current minder. There was another heavily built man with him. But were they here to collect the drugs or just watch over whoever did collect them?

Soon Taffy's plane could be heard approaching low over the trees. He didn't bother to land, but simply circled once and the pushed out two holdalls. They dropped heavily to the ground and the Volvo roared across the fields to collect them. The Kilos watched from the hedgerows as two holdalls were loaded into the back of the car. The car then made its way back across the field. The whole exchange had taken less than a minute.

Customs vehicles cut off the car at the entrance to the field and officers quickly surrounded it. Overhead Taffy's little plane circled as he got a grandstand view.

As soon as the arrest was phoned through, the search team at Frank's house moved into action just as we had done several months before. But Frank hadn't been seen in the area all day and there was no sign of him in the house either. He had slipped through the net once again. All our efforts with Taffy had been for almost nothing.

Back at Manston Taffy cared little for that. He landed with the Shoreham helicopter still shadowing him. He hadn't suspected a thing. He was jubilant and danced around the tarmac. As the news began to filter back to us, we were less so. There was about fifty kilos of cannabis resin and a small quantity of cocaine. Altogether the street value of the drugs was almost half a million pounds, but it was a modest catch compared with a normal haul for the Division.

For the rest of the afternoon we took statements from Taffy and waited for news of Frank. It was expected that he would turn up at any moment, either at his house or at any of his usual haunts. Don and the Widow sent out every officer they could scrounge, but nothing was heard. Ports and airports had been alerted, but he wasn't seen there either.

Then I remembered Myers, the helicopter pilot. I had spent many weeks working on him as part of the investigation into Davies. At one stage we had thought that he was using his helicopter to drop parcels of drugs at night on a golf course in Essex. But that had been over a year ago and it had all come to nothing. Davies and Myers hadn't been in contact for at least six months as far as we could tell. Still, we were desperate and his address was worth a try.

I called the Widow and she arranged to have one of the cars at Frank's house drive past on their way home. Later that evening the news came back. Frank's Range Rover was there and the neighbours were able to say exactly when the helicopter containing two men had taken off. They had complained for years about the helicopter using the field at the back of the house and they were noting down the times of all flights as part of their campaign. Frank had left the country less than thirty minutes after the knock.

We never did find out how he had known. It was likely that he had someone stationed some distance away watching the landing field with binoculars. Perhaps it was Frank himself. We took some comfort from the fact that we had driven him abroad, the photographs which the Widow had taken together with Taffy's statements would ensure that he would be arrested the moment he returned to this country. But he would doubtless head for Spain where there was no extradition treaty. He would probably be able to restart his smuggling activities from there. Plenty of other British criminals had.

With Frank gone it felt like the end of an era. I sat down and talked to Nicky about the new job. She wasn't pleased at the idea, but she knew that I wanted to do it and despite what Don had said she couldn't imagine how it could be worse than the Kilos. She agreed to let me try it. Her part of the agreement was that if she found that the conflict between our jobs became too much again, she would let me know straight away before it became a crisis. We would do something even if it meant me leaving the job.

I was worried. I don't know why, but I didn't believe that she meant what she was saying. There was something in her eyes when she told me to take the job. When I asked her if she was sure about this she said yes, and I had to trust her. But I still couldn't help feeling that something had gone wrong. Only time would tell.

Back in the office my last week was spent tidying up case files and returning equipment. There was the inevitable farewell party. I hadn't nailed the big villain, but that's the way it goes, and I felt that we had scored some pretty good hits against him. I was resigned to the fact that some other officer would have a crack at him again at some point in the future, just as others had before me. But just before I left there was one final twist to the Davies story.

Once again it was Danny who broke the news. I could tell by his face as soon as he entered the room that day that something serious had happened. For a moment I thought that Taffy had sold his story to the papers or something, but then Danny said quietly, 'Frank's dead.'

I'd like to say that all activity stopped in the office at this portentous news, but I think I was the only one who heard it. The office clatter continued around us.

'How?' I asked.

Danny shrugged. 'He was shot last night. Twice. In the head. It was on a pathway leading to his villa. Spanish police have no idea why he went there. The villa has been empty since the fire.' Danny slumped down and sat on the side of my desk. 'Dead,' he repeated, 'just like that.'

The Spanish police never did discover who did it and if truth be told I don't think they tried too hard. They had long since tired of the British expatriate criminals who make up the infamous 'Costa del Crime' and if they were bumping each other off now, so much the better.

Taffy was paid a generous sum for his part in the final operation, which really did take a lot of courage, although the fact that he appeared to be completely bloody mad must have helped. Having pocketed his money, he promptly fled abroad. (It is not permitted to withhold informant payments until after a trial because it smacks of bribery.) The danger just seemed too much for him even though Frank was gone. A few years later I heard that he had turned up in Australia. Van Hohn almost certainly organised the supply for Frank, but there was never enough evidence for the Dutch to arrest him even if they had found him and I have heard that he is still at large today. Even Curtis, who had been arrested red-handed, was acquitted on the judge's directions because we could not show that he had known there were drugs in the holdalls.

I sent the Davies files for storage in the cellars of Customs House. It was hard to believe that the man Carnaby had once described to us as the 'King of the south-coast smugglers' had finally gone. He hadn't been brought down in one brilliant operation, we had just nibbled and nudged at his organisation at every opportunity until it had finally fallen apart. But that is how it really is. You always read about drugs gangs being 'smashed', but they rarely are. The target teams sometimes manage it by putting people under intensive surveillance, but there were only three such teams on the entire Division. For the rest, it is left to the referred teams to stop the organisations in any way they can.

It was Friday evening. I was starting with my new team, the Limas, first thing on Monday. I was to be Lima 3 – a real team number and respectability at last. There had been the party, the engraved souvenir hip flask and a brief farewell speech by Don ('Goodbye, you bastard,' if I remember right). I had been on all the training courses, had taken cases from first intelligence right through to prosecution in court, and I now had all the trappings of an ID officer – including a wife who was barely talking to me. Worse than that, I knew that target work would be far more demanding than anything I had seen so far. But that was a problem for the future.

There was one last thing to do before I left the team. I crossed over to the Team Board and carefully rubbed out the line which read 'Kilo 17'. There had never been one before and there would never be another. I took one last look at the empty line for Kilo 2 and remembered Peter Bennett.

' 'Bye then,' I shouted, slinging the rucksack containing my surveillance kit over my shoulder. I had arrived in a pin-striped suit. I was leaving in typical Division dress: leather jacket, denim shirt, jeans and trainers.

Some people raised a hand or called out something, but our goodbyes had already been said during the day. Anyway, they were getting ready to go out on another knock down at Dover. True to the unwritten rule of the team, it was all happening on a Friday evening. The Widow was listening intently to someone on the phone. As I started to turn away, she looked up at me and winked.